MY *Beer* YEAR

MY *Beer* YEAR

ADVENTURES WITH HOP FARMERS, CRAFT BREWERS,
CHEFS, BEER SOMMELIERS & FANATICAL DRINKERS
AS A BEER MASTER IN TRAINING

LUCY BURNINGHAM

ROOST BOOKS
BOULDER
2016

Roost Books
An imprint of Shambhala Publications, Inc.
4720 Walnut Street
Boulder, Colorado 80301
roostbooks.com

9 8 7 6 5 4 3 2 1
First Edition

Printed in the United States of America

♾ This edition is printed on acid-free paper that meets the
American National Standards Institute Z39.48 Standard.
♻ This book was printed on 30% post-consumer recycled paper.
For more information please visit www.shambhala.com.

Distributed in the United States by Penguin Random House LLC
and in Canada by Random House of Canada Ltd

Designed by Daniel Urban-Brown

LIBRARY OF CONGRESS CATALOGING-IN-PUBLICATION DATA

Names: Burningham, Lucy, author.
Title: My beer year: adventures with hop farmers, craft brewers, chefs, beer sommeliers,
and fanatical drinkers as a beer master in training / Lucy Burningham.
Description: First edition. | Boulder : Roost Books, an imprint of Shambhala Publications,
Inc., [2016] | Includes index.
Identifiers: LCCN 2016010941 | ISBN 9781611802719 (pbk.: acid-free paper)
Subjects: LCSH: Brewers—Biography. | Beer industry—Biography. | Beer. |
Burningham, Lucy—Travel.
Classification: LCC TP573.5.A1 B87 2016 | DDC 338.4/766342—dc23
LC record available at https://lccn.loc.gov/2016010941

FOR TONY

CONTENTS

MY BEER YEAR

PROLOGUE

===

*You can, you should, and if you're brave
enough to start, you will.*
—STEPHEN KING

ONE SPRING DAY, I stood in my kitchen and poured a bottle of India Pale Ale into a pint glass with the habitualness of someone making coffee or chopping an onion. Since I'd moved to Portland, Oregon, drinking craft beer had become a common ritual for me, but something about this ale seemed out of the ordinary. It demanded my full attention, starting with its vibrant orange hue and intermittent bubbles that pressed to the surface in neat lines like a festive Cava. As I finished pouring, a compact layer of creamy foam materialized on top. The beer smelled like a tangerine peel in the dead of winter, and the white head reminded me of citrus pith. I took a sip, and a spike of bitterness eased into warm earth and crushed blossoms. Something complicated was happening, a song between the beer and my senses.

Years later, I would think of that beer and regret that I didn't know much about it. I was the prince at the ball, and the beer snuck away before midnight. I didn't know its name, where it was brewed, or its alcohol content by volume. I didn't know what varieties of hops created the floral aromas or during which phase of brewing they were added. I didn't know where those hops were grown or who had bred them. I didn't know what was in the grain bill or how the brewer had kept the yeast healthy. I didn't know if I'd met the brewer or set foot in the brewery where the beer was made. I didn't know whether the beer had won any medals or, instead, had slipped into the canon of unspectacular ales that no one cared about except for me. I didn't know if it had traveled in a refrigerated truck during a heat wave or a container ship during an ice storm. I didn't know whether the beer was inspired by tears or love, the profound or the mundane. Mostly, I didn't know why I liked it so much.

Even though beer is one of the world's most ubiquitous beverages, at the time I had just begun to find it fascinating. Archeologists believe humans have been making beer since about 7000 B.C.E., a few thousand years after our ancestors started farming grains. In the modern world, the liquid sloshes inside ceramic pitchers on dinner tables in France and weights aluminum cans in Japanese vending machines. It's made over fires outside of South African houses. Beer is a staple, a social lubricant, a safe alternative to questionable water, and an object of worship. It lives in barrels, travels through tubes, burps and foams in kitchens, and explodes in heated rooms.

In 2005 I moved to Portland, Oregon, with my then-boyfriend, Tony. Right away, we took up a new hobby: sampling the multitude of beers brewed in our new town. How could we resist? Most Portlanders talked about beer with the passion and intensity of crazed sports fans, the kinds who sleep in jerseys and battle with de-pression after their team loses the championship. These beer fans rattled off stats, from International Bitterness Units to original gravities. They knew brewers' nicknames and resumes. They spent weekends visiting obscure breweries they guessed would become the next big thing. They spread rumors about infections and defections. They were possessed by something I couldn't understand that transcended flavor and taste. Together, the beer and the people formed a unique symbiotic relationship, which forced me to entertain what seemed like a radical thought at the time: beer is an expression of place.

Being interested in beer was a slightly improbable turn of events for someone from Salt Lake City, Utah. I hardly knew about the drink growing up. Until I was a teenager, my parents didn't drink alcohol, so I never saw a single beer in our fridge. I had my first beer in high school, something skunky in a bottle, which I drank while watching a Bob Marley video in a basement rec room. Even before I was of legal drinking age, I resented how the beer sold in Utah grocery stores and gas stations was "watered down" (the law mandates 4 percent or less alcohol by volume). You could buy "real" beer with higher alcohol contents through state-run liquor stores, places that felt threatening to those of us with fake IDs. Besides, the liquor-store beer was expensive and stored at room temperature; you really had to plan ahead to have a cold one. One sound will always remind me of Utah beer: When Tony and I started dating, we developed an unspoken ban on drinking craft beer at home, an extravagance we chose not to afford. Instead we'd buy eighteen-packs of Busch from the grocery store. Tony would dump the cans into the refrigerator crisper drawer that never held vegetables, a percussive moment that was frequently followed by the *pssst* of a can being opened. In Utah, kegs were illegal, so I never went to keggers, nor saw anyone do a keg stand. Instead, I heard stories of people being pulled over and ticketed for having kegs in their car on the way back from Wyoming.

The summer I was nineteen years old, I worked as a busser in a restaurant in a canyon in Salt Lake City. The restaurant's only beer on tap was a locally brewed raspberry wheat ale that tasted like artificial candy. I secretly sipped the beer between bus-tub hauls of egg-smeared plates and empty coffee mugs, and I would smell a strange iteration of fruit seeping from my pores after a long shift.

I had my first dark beer on a brisk fall night in Missoula, Montana, inside my friend Garrett's apartment a few blocks from the train tracks. Not only did the label of the Samuel Smith Oatmeal Stout look sophisticated, like our conversations about literature (we were English majors, after all), but in our glasses the beer—black, opaque, and enigmatic—looked sophisticated too. With one silky sip, I felt like I'd been initiated into a secret club. This was only a few weeks after my mom had come to visit and, at a place that served pizza with exotic toppings like mango and prosciutto, she'd ordered a beer named Moose Drool solely because of the name. When the beer touched her lips, she had closed her eyes and smiled serenely. It was the first time I saw someone derive such pure pleasure from a pint.

One summer during the late nineties, I left Missoula to live in San Francisco, where I worked as an intern and receptionist for the city's regional magazine. I was assigned to work on the food section, which felt unlucky: I thought of myself as a hard news journalist, and reporting on food seemed fluffy by comparison. But soon I was eating dim sum and raw oysters for the first time, and the job didn't seem so bad. At one point, the two food editors invited me to join them for dinner at Zuni Cafe, which they were reviewing for an upcoming issue. When it came time to order an aperitif that would precede the café's famous roast chicken, I politely ordered a beer. "I would not have asked for a beer right now," said one of the editors disapprovingly, as she pinched the stem of a glass of white wine. *But you are not me,* I thought.

In Portland, I couldn't ignore my fascination with beer. Because I was working as a freelance writer, I pitched stories about things that interested me, from truffles to bicycle touring, and soon I was writing more and more stories about beer. In 2014 I realized I'd been writing about beer for seven years. I'd visited hop farms and breweries, and I'd been to a party where people shared thousands of dollars' worth of rare beer. Once, I ended up in the basement of a Brooklyn beer bar, where a taxidermied squirrel had its arms wrapped around a Belgian ale—a koozie unlike any other. Along the way, Tony and I had gotten married, bought a house, and had our son, Oscar. I found myself in my late thirties longing for a different relationship with beer. I wanted more. I wanted to move from someone who observed beer as an outsider to someone who knew beer from the inside. I considered myself a generalist, so this desire felt foreign. I'd never wanted to go deep into any subject, but there was something different about beer. Beer made me want to play scientist, to understand the lifecycle of yeast. I wanted to be able to identify hop varieties by scent alone and to become a historian who could recite tales of German immigrants in the United States.

One day, a friend asked me if I planned to become a Certified Cicerone, which I understood to be a beer sommelier, someone who could speak with authority about brewing techniques and beer history while properly pouring beer into the right glassware. Her question got me thinking. What if becoming a Certified Cicerone could help me undergo the kind of beer metamorphosis I craved? Studying could help me learn about beer with depth and focus, and committing to taking the certification test would give me a deadline, a pressing reason to make beer the centerpiece of my life for a set amount of time.

In many ways, the Cicerone Certification Program was like a wobbling toddler, still learning how to walk; on the timeline of American craft beer, the program was new. Beer educator and author Ray Daniels launched the Cicerone program in 2008 in response to a problem he'd noticed during the early 2000s: a flood of bad beer.

"There was good beer available, but the people serving it were utterly ignorant about beer, how to care for it and present it," he told me over the phone. A certification program that inspired proper training, Ray reasoned, would ultimately lead to a cavalry of servers treating beer with respect, and as a result, more people would drink better beer. The idea of trained beer-service professionals ran counter to how most Americans conceive of the drink.

"In our culture, we tend to think of beer as extremely simple," he said. "You pick up a bottle of beer, pop the top off, and drink it. What could be any simpler?" But, he went on to say, beer is complicated. For one, it's perishable like bread. And it's dispensed in ways that can alter its flavor, texture, and aroma.

Ray named the program Cicerone (pronounced *sis-uh-rone,* or *chee-cha-rone* if you're Italian), because it means "guide." The word derives from Cicero, the famous Roman orator. In Italy, cicerones are informed locals who speak to the history and integrity of a place, especially as tourist guides. The writer Henry James referred to cicerones in many of his works about Brits visiting Italy. For example, he said one of his characters was like a cicerone when he provided a "bird's-eye view" of his early years abroad. When I told my Italian friend Ciro about the title of cicerone, he said, "In Italy, we would say you speak for the beer."

Much like the Court of Master Sommeliers program for wine, the Certified Cicerone program offers different levels of certification. Each level requires a certain depth of understanding of beer styles, brewing techniques, beer ingredients, tasting, serving, and food pairings. The first-level exam is an accessible online multiple-choice test, while the Master Cicerone certification anchors the other end of the spectrum. There are only 11 Master Cicerones, which means 109 people have taken the Master exam since 2008 and not passed. The grueling two-day exam includes tasting and describing the technicalities, characteristics, and history of certain beers for a panel of beer-industry luminaries.

I wanted to become a Certified Cicerone, which at the time was the middle level, one below Master. (Since I've taken the exam, an Advanced Cicerone level has been added between the two.) It wouldn't be easy. Only about 40 percent of people who take the test pass on their first try, a lower passing rate than most bar exams. The test takes four to five hours to complete and has three parts: a written portion with fill-in-the-blank and essay questions, a tasting section that requires test takers to blind taste and evaluate beers, and a demonstration section, during which test takers prove they can operate draft equipment and properly pour a beer. The tests take place at headquarters of beer distributors, hotels, culinary schools, restaurants, bars, and breweries in most major U.S. cities (plus a few in Canada, Australia, Ireland, and the United Kingdom).

While the Cicerone program offers a few five-day study camps in Chicago every year (for an investment of $1,995), most aspiring Cicerones study on their own, starting with the program's detailed syllabus and other official suggestions: recommended reading, tasting webinars, other certification programs, courses, apps, flashcards, and the recommendation to brew beer on an amateur or professional scale. That makes signing up for the exam the easiest part. The studying and prep? *Good luck,* the site whispers between the lines. *Let us know how it goes.*

Today, there are about 2,000 Certified Cicerones, many of whom pour, analyze, and educate the masses about beer as sommeliers, brewery consultants, festival organizers, authors, and teachers. Ray told me he considers Certified Cicerones "mature" beer professionals. "They're people you could give the keys to a beer program and they'd be able to operate unsupervised."

He recommends that people like me, who don't work in the beer industry, take a year and a half to study and prepare for the exam. After all, there's a lot of material to cover: hundreds of beer styles, the mechanics of draft systems, the chemistry of ingredients like hops, and beer's ancient history. Plus, the tasting section requires a unique kind of new muscle: the ability to conduct proper sensory evaluations, which takes time to develop.

I looked at a calendar. If I started studying in June, I might be ready to take the Cicerone exam the following spring. I could begin by focusing on brewing and ingredients. I'd make some homebrew and spend some time helping pros in commercial breweries. During the late summer, I'd visit hop farms during the harvest to learn about one of my favorite beer ingredients. In October, I'd go to the Great American Beer Festival in Denver, where I'd have access to every beer style imaginable, as well as the brewers who made them. Winter would be a good time to learn about draft systems and beer styles. And theoretically, I could squeeze in a trip to Europe, where I could learn about historical brewing traditions. By the time I received my test results, I would have experienced one whole year of beer immersion.

Even though I was shaving months off Ray Daniels's recommended study time, the plan felt necessary. Ever since I'd given birth to Oscar, who was now four years old, I'd come to understand time in that cliché way that's most obvious on birthdays and first days of school. There would never be a convenient time to study for the Cicerone exam. *At least I liked being a student,* I thought to myself as I scrolled through the Certified Cicerone syllabus, which began with a breakdown of the three-tier system for alcohol sales in the United States and ended with India pale ale as an ingredient in salad dressing.

The syllabus revealed I would need to set aside a lot of time for studying. While I certainly wasn't the first parent to sign up for a challenge while raising a small child, I was already feeling stretched by writing deadlines, which I carefully wedged around preschool hours, nap times, and healthy home-cooked meals. Tony owned a custom bicycle business, a demanding and stressful job that was a slippery component of our collective juggling act. I'd already come to terms with the fact that I wasn't a person who could go to every beer festival and bottle-release party. Being a working mom meant I had less access to the scene and, more important, to the beer. In some ways, that distance could help me. I already knew getting blotto and nursing hangovers isn't conducive to retaining information, which presented an interesting paradox: to pull this off, to become a Certified Cicerone, I'd need to approach beer—commonly consumed to blur and loosen the grip of perception—with my most sharpened senses.

———

Once, a woman in Chicago asked me to reveal my beer ah-ha moment, the time when one beer permanently changed the way I look at beer. I told her about the IPA in my kitchen, but it didn't seem like the right answer, mostly because I didn't believe in the question. For me, beer ah-has are more like Buddhist prayer beads. Not only are the moments connected, they inevitably lead back to each other. On the verge of a journey I hoped would deepen my understanding of beer, I wondered what experiences would slide into my fingers. Would my quest for knowledge reveal more mystery, romance, and allure or send me in the opposite direction, toward a more practical and mechanical understanding of beer? There was only one way to find out.

HOMEBREWED

You begin with the possibilities of the material.
—ROBERT RAUSCHENBERG

INSIDE MY KITCHEN, a long narrow room with a large picture window, dark wood cabinets, and mismatched appliances, the butter yellow walls glowed with the ambient light of the summer solstice, the longest day of the year. It was a Saturday, the day of the week that was mine to do with whatever I wanted. Usually, Tony spent most of the day with Oscar, riding bikes at an indoor mountain bike park, while I went to a yoga class then worked. Today, we would deviate from the routine: I would devote my work hours to beer.

At the ripe age of four, Oscar didn't sleep much during the day anymore, but today he succumbed to an afternoon nap. That left me and Tony alone together—a rare occurrence on any afternoon—with some plastic tubing, cloth sacks, buckets, a glass carboy, an airlock, a spiral of copper tubing, scissors, clamps, sanitizer, spoons, a hydrometer, Irish moss, carrageenan, salts, a long metal-handled brush, and a beginners recipe for an American Pale Ale. Tony wore a cotton cycling cap, a bike-related T-shirt, and cutoff shorts—his self-selected summer uniform that shows off his muscular forearms and calves while reminding me that, even when he isn't riding, bicycles are an integral part of his identity.

Many Christmases ago, I'd unwrapped a homebrew kit, a gift from Tony. I was thrilled. The idea of making my own beer seemed like an appropriate extension of other DIY food and drink projects we'd tried, from making kombucha and dashi to kimchi and mole sauces. The two of us had a history of exploring food and drink together. On one of our first dates, at a tapas restaurant, we spent hours tasting the food on plate after plate, comparing the textures and flavors of fried calamari to glistening beef tartare. I was thrilled to discover that the man who built a motorcycle from parts, and constantly had scrapes and gashes on his legs from mountain biking, was also an intrepid cook and gastronome. When we moved to Portland, beer became an extension of our epicurean explorations.

I loved how the homebrew kit reversed stereotypical gender roles, like a wife buying her husband a Crock-pot—an affirmation that, even though Tony shared my love of beer, I was the one who was professionally connected to the drink. However, even though the homebrew kit was mine, we always brewed together. The last time we had planned to brew a batch of beer was four years earlier, when I was pregnant with Oscar. The homebrew equipment was collecting dust, and since newborns spend most of their time sleeping, we reasoned, we'd have plenty of time to revisit a hobby we kept talking about doing again. Obviously, we were idiots. Tony tells me we did brew that new-baby batch of beer after Oscar was born, but I was so tired, I don't remember.

I do remember buying the ingredients while I was pregnant. I gingerly moved through the homebrew shop, careful not to bump my belly against shelves of glass hydrometers and carboys. Oddly enough, another pregnant woman was in the store at the same time. She and her husband were buying ingredients for a "lactation beer," a low-alcohol beer brewed with herbs that boost milk production in nursing women. I considered asking for a copy of the recipe, but I feared the herbs would taste medicinal. Even though it was hard to imagine what it would feel like to be a mother, I was already confident I'd want to drink a beer that just tasted good, something to connect me to my prior life as a person who wasn't responsible for keeping another human alive.

Today, I was a mother and an aspiring Certified Cicerone, two identifiers that were already making this brew day feel different. For one, I felt the pressing limits of time. Taking three or four hours to brew beer felt indulgent when I could have been doing something more productive like laundry, cleaning, writing, exercising, or some constructive and educational activity with my kid. Except this *was* productive. Deciding to take the exam meant that brewing beer was studying; what had once been a hobby was filled with new purpose. As a result, every object in the kitchen had become a study aid, a possible key to unlocking my greater understanding of beer. By brewing at home, I hoped to better understand how beer's basic ingredients come together, which included discovering how just one degree or extra minute on the boil would affect the colors, aromas, and flavors of the final beer.

I tried not to think about my homebrew history, which was disappointing on a few levels. First, there was the beer. My first bottles of homebrew looked amateurish, without labels, a science project that would either explode unexpectedly or fail spectacularly to prove whatever truth it was meant to illustrate. When I popped the caps, a reassuring *psssst* signaled that the beer was carbonated, as beer should be. Inside pint glasses, the beer didn't appear to have any blue or green strands of slime, what the homebrewing book said is proof of an infected beer that should be thrown away immediately. The beer was hazy and amberish. It had no head and tasted like the outline of a beer, devoid of any defining characteristics. I searched for a flavor, something I could mark as justification for all those hours near the stove.

"It's pretty good!" I said to Tony with forced enthusiasm.

"It's alright," he replied. "I can drink it."

Since I drank good beer, I'd assumed I'd make good beer: classic amateur hubris. Does someone who loves listening to Coltrane automatically play great jazz on her first try? Tony and I dutifully drank the bland IPA for weeks, as though it were a triple batch of chili that, for budgetary reasons, had to be eaten. I did reach a saturation point, and refused to drink any more. It would be a long time before we brewed again.

I was also disappointed by the infrequency of our brew sessions. Tony made custom steel bicycle frames by hand in our garage, which he'd converted into a shop. He worked long hours to sustain the business, which he and his business partner had named Breadwinner Cycles. I matched his work ethic and lack of financial stability with my own writerly self-employment. While I worked to meet deadlines and land my next big assignment, he brazed metal and courted customers. We had trouble finding the time to brew beer.

At its essence, beer is a simple thing. Malted grains are steeped in hot water, then the grains are removed. The water is boiled with hops, and the hops are removed. Yeast is added, and fermentation begins. Still, infrequent brewing sessions made every visit to the homebrew store an exercise in reacquainting myself with the basics. To prepare for the solstice brew day, I returned to my neighborhood homebrew shop, a spacious building with big windows and a sweet smell. Inside, a woman with a dark bob and a squeaky, high-pitched voice asked if she could help me. Her name was Miranda Karson.

"This looks like it's going to be a seriously hoppy beer," she said, eyeing the recipe. I'd decided to brew a pale ale, because the previous IPA had been so dismal. It would be a hoppy pale ale. Not only did I like hoppy beers, I knew hops could make average to poor beers actually taste good. In an era when craft breweries were popping up quickly, sometimes before they had the chance to dial in their recipes, hops had become a way to mask imperfections in beers. On the exam, I'd need to know how to detect those imperfections, a risky endeavor that might reveal a majority of beers I liked to be on par with my homebrew.

Miranda guided me to the bins filled with malt, which looked like the row of bulk foods at the grocery store. Most malt is barley, and it's the job of maltsters to turn raw kernels into useful ingredients for brewers, a process that begins by soaking and sprouting the grains, mimicking what happens in nature as the seed begins the cycle to produce a new plant. During that early stage of germination, the kernel produces enzymes capable of breaking starches into sugars. The maltster harnesses those enzymes by halting the sprouting process; he or she dries the kernels and roasts them in a kiln at various temperatures, depending on the desired darkness of the roast. Miranda and I were looking for Crystal malt, which is made by first steeping and germinating barley like other types of malt. But, instead of going straight into the kiln, Crystal malt is stewed along the way, which creates extra sugar inside the grain's hull. Crystal malts are famous for adding body, caramel flavors, and rich colors to beer.

My recipe called for Crystal 20L. Miranda explained that the "L" stands for Lovibond, which quantifies the level of roasting. The higher the number, the darker the roast. Somewhere between the shortbread-colored Crystal 10L and the roasted-coffee-colored Crystal 80L, Miranda reached into a bin and popped some malt into her mouth. I followed her lead. The difference between 10L and 80L was profound, a quick journey from crackery and sweet to bitter and smoky. She poured my 20L into a grinder that appeared to have just one setting. "You only want to crack it just a bit," she said. The machine spit out kernels that looked barely changed.

Near the cash register, Miranda opened a spigot on a giant plastic barrel to release a liquid with the viscosity of honey, which she caught in a small round tub. The goo was liquid malt extract, otherwise known as LME: a sugary syrup that's essentially concentrated malt. Malt extract, which also comes in a dry form called dry malt extract (DME), is a common building block for beginning homebrewers. Maltsters make it by creating a "reduction" of malt in water, which reactivates the enzymes in the grain, the same thing brewers do during the first step of brewing. By using malt extract, homebrewers can simplify the brewing process, reducing the brew time and creating less mess, but at a cost: by using malt extract, brewers relinquish some control of how the beer tastes. For that reason, malt extract divides the homebrew camp into two distinct groups: those who brew with it (dilettantes, like me) and those who don't.

Inside a cooler, I recognized the shining paperback-sized foil packages of yeast as well as smaller packets of dry yeast the size of a playing card. The larger packets held yeast suspended in liquid, but Miranda convinced me the dry yeast would work just as well. Either way, once the yeast meets the wort—the unfermented sweet liquid that eventually becomes beer and is pronounced more like "shirt" than "skort"—billions of tiny yeast cells will begin consuming oxygen before they start scarfing up sugars. The ravenous process of consumption, which we call fermentation, creates by-products, most famously ethanol (alcohol) and carbon dioxide (CO_2). But yeast also helps to create chemical compounds that greatly affect the flavors in beer. Esters create fruity aromas and flavors most common to ales, while phenols, another type of chemical compound that comes from yeast, create smoky, clove-like, or medicinal flavors. The type of yeast in any given beer determines whether the beer is an ale or a lager, and all beer can be categorized as one or the other. Ale yeasts ferment faster and at higher temperatures than lager yeasts, which prefer cooler temperatures.

Conveniently, packets of hops—the plant that adds aromas, flavors, and bitterness to beer—were stored next to the yeast; cool temperatures preserve their freshness. Some whole hop flowers were vacuum packed in plastic, and others had been turned into pellets. Like many people, I assume that the more a food is processed, the less flavor and nutrition it holds, and I had applied that same logic to hops, which made the whole flowers superior. I would only begin to question that rationale months later, inside a hop-pellet factory in Yakima, Washington.

Before I left the shop, Miranda told me she was forming a ladies' brew club that would meet once a month to brew a seasonal beer.

"I love men," she editorialized, "but they have a way of taking over when we brew together."

I nodded slowly, not sure if I was ready to concur.

"Men can brew with us," she continued, "but we're going to be the ones in charge."

I laughed. Even though the homebrew kit was mine and I was the one who worked with beer professionally, Tony always took charge during our brew sessions. It wasn't entirely his fault, of course. I let him do most of the work. But now, I wondered, what would it be like to be in charge? I realized, if I wanted to really learn about how beer was made, I'd need to take more ownership of my education. I told Miranda I'd see her at the brew club. Then I went home to brew beer with my man.

———

There was a moment in human history when the word "homebrewing" needed to exist, because at first, all beer was brewed inside the home; it was more like bread than anything else. Once beer began being made commercially, outside the home, the distinction was articulated.

During the Paleolithic period, hunter-gatherers subsisted by hunting animals and collecting plants. When they began to sow grains, they needed to live nearby to tend to the plants and reap the harvest. Agriculture led to human settlements and the domestication of plants and animals, events that happened independently in different parts of the world at nearly the same time: the beginning of the Neolithic period. Because of limited archaeological evidence from that period, scientists hotly debate what those early humans ate and drank. There's proof of early plantings: wheat, barley, and lentil seeds in the areas that are now Syria, Jordan, and Israel, plus tools that show these people were harvesting and processing grains. But what matters, at least to me, is whether or not those early humans knew how to ferment the grains.

"Suppose that the consumption of a food produced an altered state of awareness or consciousness that was noticeable, but that did not seem to have serious toxic side effects such as motor impairment," wrote scientists Solomon H. Katz and Mary M. Voigt in "Bread and Beer: The Early Use of Cereals in the Human Diet" (*Expedition* vol. 28, no. 2, pages 23–34). "Now suppose that this food also had a second, imperceptible effect, a substantial improvement in nutritional value over the unprocessed cereal grains. This is exactly what happens when barley and wheat are fermented into beer."

The pursuit of an altered but benign state—a beer buzz—would have been motivation enough, the duo argues. It is, after all, those altered states that have consistently created important social bonds and religious rituals throughout human history, but psychotropic plants are a sure way to waste an entire day. Still, beer might have also made those early fermenters feel good after the buzz subsided: B vitamins and lysine—a compound that makes it easier for the body to absorb essential minerals—are by-products of fermentation.

There's no conclusive evidence about which came first, beer or bread. Both are made by removing husks from grains, grinding them into flour or soaking them in water, then heating the mixture, which invites yeast and bacteria to join the party. There is evidence that Sumerians made bread from barley or emmer wheat, otherwise known as farro, for the sole purpose of turning it into beer. They'd partially bake the bread then mix it with water. Enzymes converted the starches into sugars, then the liquid would be strained and set aside in vessels, where yeast became responsible for the characteristics of a good beer: alcohol, CO_2, and B vitamins.

Scientists agree that mead, the fermented honey drink, probably existed before beer, but one of the first known written recipes for any food or drink was for beer. Written in Sumerian during the third millennium B.C.E., the recipe describes the brewing process in detail. Then there was the famous Code of Hammurabi from ancient Mesopotamia, a record of punishments and crimes carved into a basalt obelisk in 1780 B.C.E. One crime listed is the unfair pricing of beer, a transaction handled by women: "If a tavern-keeper [feminine] does not accept corn according to gross weight in payment of drink, but takes money, and the price of the drink is less than that of the corn, she shall be convicted and thrown into the water," the stone read.

Drawings and inscriptions show the Sumerians brewing in clay vessels with pointed bottoms and narrow necks. Frequently, people are shown drinking from straws inserted into these vessels, which archeologists guess was a way of filtering beer that was thick with grains and yeast sediment.

The Hymn to Ninkasi, a love poem from 1800 B.C.E. to the Sumerian goddess of beer, includes words like "sweetwort," "fermenting vat," "dough," and "beer bread."

> It is you who soak the malt in a jar; the waves rise, the waves fall.
>   Ninkasi, it is you who soak the malt in a jar; the waves rise, the
>   waves fall.
> It is you who spread the cooked mash on large reed mats; coolness
>   overcomes. . . . Ninkasi, it is you who spread the cooked mash on
>   large reed mats; coolness overcomes. . . .
> It is you who hold with both hands the great sweetwort, brewing it
>   with honey and wine. Ninkasi, it is you who hold with both hands
>   the great sweetwort, brewing it with honey and wine.

Since Ninkasi had her hands in every part of the brewing process, I decided to follow her lead.

———

On our brew day, I chose to worship Ninkasi, not only by brewing her a beer on the solstice, but by drinking a saison at the same time. Just like you're not supposed to judge a book by its cover, you shouldn't judge a beer by its label, but I couldn't help liking the look of the delicate, hot pink flowers on the label of the saison, Widmer Brothers Saison À Fleurs, a collaboration with Breakside Brewery. The beer had been brewed with jasmine, chrysanthemum, and Szechuan peppercorns. Drinking while brewing is a dicey activity that can lead to all sorts of missteps, from boilovers to missed hop additions, but I couldn't help myself. Since I was studying, as opposed to simply wasting my time drinking beer on a Saturday afternoon, I promptly looked up the saison beer style and wrote down its characteristics, which it turns out have nothing to do with exotic Asian ingredients. (Historically, saisons were brewed at the end of winter in the French-speaking region of Belgium, to be consumed throughout the summer.)

The recipe for the beer called for steeping a mesh hop bag filled with specialty grains in hot water for twenty minutes before slowly raising the temperature of the water. As I fished the bag out of the kettle, I had a flash of understanding. If beer was so simple, what would I possibly spend an entire year studying? In response to my hubris, something immediately went wrong. After I'd poured the liquid malt extract into the pot, I'd forgotten to turn off the stove's burner. Even though I had stirred it in aggressively, the extract seared to the bottom of the kettle.

"Look," I said to Tony with a note of defeat, when he came inside from the shop. "I screwed up." A storm of white particles followed in the wake of my moving spoon.

"It's fine," Tony said, squeezing my shoulder as he peered into the kettle. "Don't worry about it."

But it didn't look fine. I'd created a brown snow globe.

"That will teach you to put me in charge," I said sarcastically. Earlier, I'd told Tony what Miranda said about men taking charge during brewing, but I had a sense we were still falling into our stereotypical roles.

As the afternoon advanced—and miraculously, Oscar stayed asleep—I became convinced we'd screwed up the beer in multiple ways. I wasn't sure we'd properly sterilized everything that touched the beer after the boil, and I didn't know if we'd added the hops at precisely the right time. Even after we'd added the yeast to the cooled wort and transferred the mixture to a glass carboy using a siphon, there was still time to do something else wrong. Historically, the carboy always stayed in our kitchen, in the same spot along one wall across from the table, while the beer inside fermented. But this time, it didn't seem like a good idea.

"It's going to get really hot this week," I announced. Tony was bent over the carboy, slipping a bicycle T-shirt over its narrow neck, as though he were dressing Oscar for school. "Really hot," I said, firmly. "Let's put it in the basement."

"I like to have it up here so we can see it," Tony replied.

He had a point. If the carboy was in the basement, we would never remember to lift the T-shirt to watch fermentation in action. So the carboy stayed put. For the next few mornings, as birds chirped and garbage trucks grunted, the beer belched and bubbled furiously. Oscar would wake up and head straight to the carboy.

"Look mama!" he'd yell, excited. "It's moving!"

The floaties from the burn swirled through the beer as though they were magnetized or possessed, activity I'd assumed was yeast moving. But I looked it up, and it wasn't yeast we were watching move, but particles stirred by the heat the yeast generated as it consumed sugars. When the house was quiet at night, I could hear the beer belching and bubbling in the kitchen as it released CO_2, which traveled through a plastic tube and into a glass champagne bottle filled halfway with water, a system that kept the beer sterile, our homemade version of a tool called an airlock. After two days, the belching subsided and it was so hot we weren't sleeping. I convinced Tony to move the carboy downstairs.

We decided to bottle the beer one night after Oscar went to bed. It had been two-and-a-half weeks since fermentation stopped, and we probably should have bottled the beer back then, to get it off the trub, the cake of sediment at the bottom of the carboy. But we'd been going to work and school events, plus barbecues at friends' houses. Summer was in full swing. We simply hadn't made the time. My friend Rik, a longtime homebrewer who'd just opened a commercial brewery, said he'd recently left a batch of brew on the trub for three weeks. But without the T-shirt and the 70-plus-degree air temperatures, his beer was probably going to taste good. He also said that because we'd left the beer on the yeast for so long, we'd probably created some off-flavors. So much for drinkability.

I embraced the big, slippery grenade of a carboy and carried it upstairs.

"Careful," Tony warned. "Don't shake it too much." If the beer was exposed to too much oxygen at this point, it might develop a new array of off-flavors. But every time I stepped up onto the next step, the beer sloshed back and forth in my arms.

When it came time to drink the pale ale, I had low expectations. But making homebrew is like buying a lottery ticket. There's always the chance of hitting the jackpot. Despite the floaties and temperature fluctuations, maybe we'd made something that tasted like a Sierra Nevada Pale Ale, the iconic, beautifully balanced beer invented in 1980 by the now-famous brewer Ken Grossman. Alas. Even though our beer was surprisingly clear (the floaties had dropped to the bottom with the yeast, it tasted too sweet and had an unpleasant note of bitterness that one would be hard pressed to describe as "hoppy." With each sip, I thought about the nuances that produced this beer: the day, the weather, the Asian-fusion saison, the burner's blue flame, and a near boilover. Every detail mattered. It all matters.

I realized I'd just dipped my toe into a big pool. I needed to understand how each nuance became a perceptible element of the beer, and that would mean getting this homebrewing thing down.

———

When I arrived at the inaugural meeting of Lady Brew Portland, seven women were gathered under a large shade tent in the parking lot of my neighborhood homebrew shop. Already, they were in classic brewing form, a state of forward progress disguised by doing nothing. Not that certain things weren't getting done. One woman was cutting a watermelon into slices. Another was adjusting the heat on a stand burner underneath a kettle filled with water. Someone else was arranging packets of yeast and hops next to pints of fresh blackberries.

I saw Miranda, who announced that we'd be brewing a clone of Deschutes Fresh Squeezed IPA. She'd created the recipe.

"It kind of tastes like orange juice," she said breathlessly. "It's so good!"

"Maybe we should try some?" said a woman in sporty sunglasses and cutoff jeans.

It was a little past ten in the morning on a Saturday, and temperatures were supposed to rocket into the upper nineties, the kind of heat that's considered a weather event in Portland. We would get thirsty. So Miranda left on foot to find her muse at the grocery store in the next block.

I was thrilled to discover the recipe was all-grain, the next step for me as a novice homebrewer. Instead of using malt extract, we'd take additional steps to extract sugars from the malt, which a brewer named John Harris once told me was the difference between making a cake from a box and making one from scratch.

"You're at the mercy of whatever the extract maker was doing that day," he said. John, who has a full and graying beard and always wears a ponytail and wire-rimmed glasses, was the brewmaster at Ecliptic Brewing, which happened to be a few miles from my house in North Portland. Since I'd committed to taking the Cicerone exam, I'd started stopping by Ecliptic during their brew sessions in the hopes that I'd learn something valuable about the brewing process while I was there. Instead, I started noticing insignificant things, like how John wrote his brewing recipes on sticky notes. I also learned how the muscles in my arms burned when I was tasked with pulling the wet, spent grains out of the mash tun with a metal rake. The other brewer at Ecliptic was Phil Roche, a guy with a huge grin who'd worked with John for about four years at Full Sail Brewing Co.

"People have been doing all-grain brewing for five thousand years," Phil told me one day as I watched him fill bourbon barrels with imperial stout that was being forced through a hose. "I don't know why books make it seem so hard."

Phil told me that, the first time he brewed a batch of all-grain beer, he had sterilized every pot and ladle in the kitchen and set them out on the countertop so they were ready, just in case. Because he didn't have a kettle large enough to make the entire batch of wort at once, Phil used his oven to keep half of the wort warm while he made the other half. The thought of his kitchen filled with sterilized measuring cups, spoons, and possibly a lemon zester reminded me that there's no one right way to do things.

For mashing in, the term for combining the grains with hot water, the Lady Brewers needed to decide on the ideal temperature for the mixture, a choice that affects the final flavor of the beer. That's because the temperature activates enzymes inside the grains, and those enzymes turn starches into sugars. A lower temperature produces more fermentable sugars, which produces a drier beer, while a higher temp makes more nonfermentable sugars and, therefore, a beer with more body. Miranda had written "155°F" on the recipe, but a woman who'd introduced herself as Sheila argued for 152 or 153 degrees instead.

"But I like drier beers in general," she demurred.

Something about the parking lot, kettle, and burner made it difficult to imagine we could control the temperature with such specificity. But being around these women gave me a Rosie the Riveter sense of can-do. If this job demanded temperature precision, we'd roll up our sleeves and figure out how to make it work. As brewing got underway, we talked about rules for the club. We'd brew once a month and share recipes online. Men could come to brew days, but a zero-mansplaining policy would be enforced. We were off to a good start. Men coming in and out of the homebrew shop paused to ask us what we were brewing, but they never offered additional suggestions, as though they'd overheard our conversation.

Miranda returned from the store with some bad news: she hadn't found any Fresh Squeezed. Instead, she filled that hoppy hole with a local IPA brewed with seven kinds of hops (a gimmicky overuse of hops, as one of our Lady Brew crew appraised it) and a Sierra Nevada Torpedo Extra IPA, a beer named after a special piece of equipment called a "torpedo" that allows cold beer in the fermenter to circulate through dry hops for extra hop aroma. Sheila pulled out a SMaSH, which stands for "single malt and single hop." She'd brewed it herself using Maris Otter malt, a barley that was invented in the 1960s in England on Maris Lane. During the 1990s, the malt almost faded into obscurity, but it's been experiencing a resurgence, especially with homebrewers. (In Portland, if you ever want to find a homebrewer, head to a performance by Maris Otter, an old-time string band.) Her single hop was Meridian, a hop with a lemony aroma that was developed in Oregon. The beer tasted crisp, clean, and straightforward. I felt honored to be brewing alongside the person who made it.

For the Fresh Squeezed clone, we added doses of Nugget, Mosaic, and Citra hops. After each hop addition, the kettle of roiling brown wort smelled intoxicating. Before we could add the yeast, we had to cool the wort to 70 degrees Fahrenheit, a temperature that wouldn't kill the organisms. *How hard could it be?* I thought, as Miranda held the thermometer in the wort like a nurse gauging the severity of a fever. It registered 160 degrees. She attached a garden hose to a wort chiller: copper tubing shaped in a spiral, a key tool for cooling the wort as quickly as possible. After she lowered the spiral into the kettle, we waited. And waited. Heat rose from the softening asphalt, seeped through the soles of my sneakers, and basically spit in the face of the shade tent.

We ate watermelon and blackberries. We drank more beer. I was surprised when someone mentioned that in ancient Norse cultures women brewed all the beer.

"From what I've read, as soon as commercialization happened, the men took over," Miranda added.

Even though I knew she was right, I did an internal eye roll. Having this conversation at a women's brew club seemed so predictable. Catching myself before I made a snide remark, I realized I'd never actually talked about these historical facts with other women: I had only brewed beer with my husband, and I spent most of my beer-conversation currency on men. From that perspective, what was happening under the shade tent felt slightly subversive.

I kept pulling the thermometer out of the wort to check the temp, but I was learning that a watched pot never cools. 130 degrees. 125 degrees.

"The last few degrees take the longest," Miranda said. Sweat rolled from my bra to my bellybutton. We weren't even close to the last few degrees. As the sun traveled west, we moved the tent to keep the kettle shaded. We reminded each other that everything that touched the wort needed to be sterilized. I wished we were all wearing hair nets. *At least we don't have beards,* I thought, as I leaned over the kettle to look at thermometer—again.

Finally, the red line hit 75 degrees, which we decided was close enough. If the beer tasted off, we could call it Heatwave Haste. Miranda poured the wort into a plastic carboy, where the yeast would spend the next few days being gluttons at an all-you-can-eat sugar buffet. I stayed to clean up, but all I really did was help take down the shade tent. I didn't want to be the person who left a mess, a role I'd already explored at home. A few weeks earlier, when we brewed the pale ale, Tony ended up scrubbing the kettle and wiping the floor and countertops while I took a shower. When I got out, he yelled from the basement, where he was putting away the brewing equipment, "Hey, beer master, where did you go?" Even though it seemed cliché, brewing with women felt different than brewing with Tony. Instead of being someone who does not take well to being told what to clean, I felt more like a team member.

Sadly, I never had a chance to taste our teamwork. I was out of town for the next brew day, and even though Miranda and I tried to connect so I could sample the beer, we failed to make it happen. The next time we saw each other, I asked her about the beer. "It was OK," she said. I paused, hoping for more. "Yeah, pretty good," she added. I realized, if I want to understand the outcome of my labor, I'll need to do the tasting myself.

PALATE PUSHING

The world is full of magic things, patiently waiting
for our senses to grow sharper.
—W.B. YEATS

IN A ROOM WITH A VIEW of a train yard and the sweeping span of one of Portland's twelve bridges, I sat down around an oval table with eight men, one of whom I recognized as Rob Widmer. I tended to confuse Rob with his brother Kurt, not because they looked alike or wore matching clothes, but because I usually saw them together. They are joined in my mind, and the minds of many beer lovers, as the Widmer brothers, two men who were part of the early U.S. craft beer movement. The brothers founded their brewery in 1984. Kurt had spent two years living in Germany, and when he returned home, he craved German beers but couldn't find any that came close to what he'd been drinking in Deutschland. So he took up homebrewing. Five years later, his recipes were good enough to inspire a business plan for a commercial brewery. Those were the days when Americans had very few choices when it came to beer.

I was at Widmer Brothers Brewing for their taste panel, a meeting that happens every weekday morning at eleven o'clock. I'd heard about these meetings from a brewer at Widmer, who told me they were an important part of the brewery's quality control procedures. Not only was I curious about the ritual of the tasting panel, I hoped that by observing what happened in the meeting I'd learn a few tricks about how to evaluate a beer like a professional.

Every brewery has its own ways of making sure the beer leaving the brewery looks and tastes the way it was intended, but so far I'd only seen the methods of brewers at smaller places. They usually tasted some of the beer straight from the fermenters and made mental notes. Because Widmer is so large (the brewery shipped more than 200,000 barrels in 2014), it makes sense that the brewery has a more codified way of evaluating beer. In addition to the taste panel, the brewery has its own laboratory, which is run by a technician who monitors the productivity of yeast strains and tests beer for unwanted bacteria. The lab looks like the corner of a chemistry department at a university, complete with vials and a computer that produces chromatograms of mass spectrometric data. Only larger breweries have quality-control labs like this. In an act of brewing industry goodwill, the Widmer lab also tests beer samples for any small brewery that brings one in.

Before I got to the tasting panel, Widmer Brothers Brewing's director of brewery operations, Doug Rehberg, told me that every beer that leaves the brewery has been approved by the panel. He also said that Rob Widmer is usually in attendance, a level of owner participation I imagined was unique for such a large brewery. In 2008 Widmer merged with Redhook Brewery to form the Craft Brew Alliance, which eventually picked up Kona Brewing. The resulting brewing group is a giant by craft beer standards, in part because Anheuser-Busch InBev has a 32 percent minority stake in the company. That partial ownership exiled Widmer Brothers from the craft beer trade organization called the Brewers Association, which mandates that a craft brewery have less than 25 percent nonindependent ownership. I wasn't sure if having Rob Widmer at the table made Widmer more or less "craft," but there was something comforting about seeing him there. It was like catching a glimpse of Mario Batali in the kitchen of one of his dozens of restaurants, tasting a dish when he could be doing something else, like drinking a daiquiri on a yacht in the Bahamas.

In addition to a regular cast of taste panel attendees—the taste panel administrator, director of brewery operations, quality assurance manager, director of brewing, director of quality assurance, and a few members of the team that have been trained to taste beer—one special guest always gets a spot: a Widmer employee who won a drawing. Today, the honor went to a guy from accounting. I imagined his colleagues giving him fist bumps as he switched off a screen filled with spreadsheets so he could go drink beer with Rob Widmer. Suddenly, I felt honored to be at the tasting panel.

In front of each of us were three small glasses, two empty and one filled with water, and a tablet computer. Today, the tablets weren't working, so we each received a piece of paper titled "Sensory Validation Ballot." The sheet listed nineteen flavors in alphabetical order, starting with "acetaldehyde" and "acetic" and ending with "myrcene" and "papery." Each "flavor" represented a chemical compound or quality that can appear in beer, along with descriptions of how humans perceive each one. For example, a compound called dimethyl trisulfide, or DMTS, is a standard compound in beer that is produced when the wort is boiling. The sheet described DMTS as "garlic, onion, rubbery." Caprylic, a fatty acid found in mammals' milk and coconut oil, was "goaty, waxy, crayons, roller rink."

I sat two people to the left of the taste panel administrator, who walked around the room filling everyone's glasses with predetermined beers. The panel tastes six to twelve beers during every meeting. I waited for someone to make a joke about drinking on a Wednesday morning, but nothing funny seemed to be happening here. The room went quiet as everyone peered at the samples, then swirled, sniffed, sipped, and jotted down notes. Beer number one was a Kona Longboard Island Lager, a pale beer I'd had in the past, but not for at least a couple of years because I had considered it unremarkable. Before I had too much time to think about why I didn't like this beer, the taste panel administrator blurted out "pass." Doug Rehberg, who sat to my left, whispered, "This is when we say if the beer is good enough to be sold." The panel wasn't judging beers for their deliciousness or drinkability, but for flaws. If a beer was flawed, for whatever reason, the panelists were helping ensure it wouldn't be sold. The guy to my right said, "Pass." I was next, but since I was just observing, I looked to Doug. He stared back at me. So did everyone else at the table. Feeling desperate, I put my nose in the glass, again, and inhaled loudly before taking a gulp of the beer, hoping to find something in the lager that would help me convert aromas and flavors into a greater understanding about the rightness of this sample. I fought my instinct to say it tasted like beer.

"Pass," I said. The word came out sounding less like a judge making a ruling and more like someone declining an hors d'oeuvre at a party. Because the beer didn't smell or taste offensive, it seemed like the right thing to say. If only two panelists voted to fail the beer, it would be considered acceptable and allowed to leave the brewery. If more than two people deemed the beer flawed, it would return to be tasted again the following day. Two fails, and it might wind up washing the drains.

A few panelists included descriptors to their pass/fail announcement. By the end of the panel, I would hear "metallic," "yeasty with an unpleasant astringency," "pear-like," and "hints of isoamyl acetate," which was listed on the sensory sheet as tasting like bananas and circus peanuts. Doug told me the panelists work as a team. Each person has specific strengths and weaknesses when it comes to perceiving compounds and other attributes of the beer, and everyone on the panel knows the others' superpowers. That's why the collective opinion is what matters.

Next up: two versions of Widmer Hefeweizen, the cloudy, German-style wheat beer that made the brewery famous. In the eighties, hefeweizen was a fairly unknown style in the United States (as were most beer styles aside from mass-produced lagers). The Widmer version, which was released in 1986, isn't authentically German. It's brewed with an ale yeast that doesn't produce banana and clove notes, some of the defining characteristics of the style. But Americans didn't seem to care. During the past thirty years, Widmer Hefeweizen has come to define hefeweizen for American beer drinkers.

The first hefeweizen seemed sharper than the other, which I guessed had something to do with its bitterness levels. In sample two, I thought I tasted a hint of butter, which could have been the result of a flavor compound called diacetyl that is common in beer because it's a by-product of yeast. Diacetyl feels slick in the mouth and tastes like fake butter or buttered popcorn. Someone once described diacetyl as an overly buttery Chardonnay, a description that made it easier for me to imagine how it might feel in my mouth. In fact, we're probably all quite familiar with diacetyl: the compound naturally exists in and is purposely added to many dairy products, especially butter and cheese. Yeast can reabsorb diacetyl if given enough time, which is why some brewers practice a "diacetyl rest" during fermentation, when they raise the temperature of the beer so yeast can scrub away any buttery notes.

When it was my turn to weigh in on the two beers, I gave them both a pass. As the other panelists weighed in, no one mentioned butter. I felt relieved I hadn't said anything. Finally, we reached the last person at the table: Rob Widmer.

"Two. Diacetyl. Fail," he said emphatically.

I wanted to jump up from my chair and yell, "I knew it!" I'd definitely tasted diacetyl. But it was too late. I'd had my chance. I vowed to do a better job of trusting my own perceptions and voicing them, even in a room of professionals. Even though my fail vote wouldn't have changed the outcome for the beer, my opinion would have counted for something. If nothing else, speaking the truth about what I tasted would have given me hope that, one day, I could be good at evaluating beer.

Our final beer was a "guest beer" made at another brewery. In tasting panel tradition, the guest beer was served blind, sheathed in a brown paper bag that made it look like a recent purchase from 7-Eleven. After everyone voted, the taste panel administrator would reveal what we'd tasted. The panelists sipped the beer, crinkled their noses and shook their heads, what I imagined was standard procedure for a guest beer, a chance for corporate team building at the expense of another brewery.

"It's a weird one all the way through," someone mumbled.

"Artificial citrus and bathroom deodorizer," Rob Widmer said loudly.

We went around the circle for the last time that day. Despite the negative reaction from the panel, everyone gave the beer a pass, because it didn't have any major flaws. When the paper bag came off, the beer was a Samuel Adams Summer Ale, a wheat beer brewed with what the label said was "lemon zest and grains of paradise."

"I bet they didn't zest many lemons for that one," Rob Widmer quipped.

We'd never know exactly how they added the lemon flavor, although I entertained a quick fantasy about infiltrating the Boston Beer Company, which makes Samuel Adams beers, to discover the exact recipe and brewing process. We just knew how it tasted. Pass.

———

That evening, as Oscar zoomed around the kitchen with his Matchbox cars and Tony brushed olive oil on a piece of salmon for the grill, I produced the piece of paper I'd taken from the tasting panel.

"Look," I said. "Whatever indole is, it tastes like 'jasmine, floral, fecal, barnyard, mothballs.' I love a good jasmine fecal beer, don't you?"

I put the paper under Tony's line of sight as he sprinkled some salt onto the fish.

"Ooh, cheesy sweatsocks," he said, reading one description.

"Cheesy sweatsocks," Oscar squealed. "That's awful!"

I looked at the paper. Something called isovaleric was responsible for the notes of cheesy sweatsocks. I was thrilled that these were things I needed to know.

I put the piece of paper front and center on the fridge—prime real estate for photos of family and friends, wedding invitations, baby announcements, and Oscar's artwork—a reminder that my studying could happen incrementally as part of my daily life.

"I like it," Tony said, glancing at the fridge.

While I'd started to unpack the nuances of how ingredients create flavors, from the crackery-to-roasty spectrum that malt creates to the citrus and pine notes from hops, that wasn't enough. I also needed to understand what tastes *don't* belong in beer.

———

Inside an air-conditioned meeting room at a beer distributor's headquarters in Northwest Portland, I stared at yet another clear plastic glass filled with Kona Longboard. With every passing second, the beer was losing aromas, flavors, and carbonation. And that made me nervous. I was taking an off-flavors class from one of my beer heroes, Master Cicerone Nicole Erny. In 2011, at just twenty-eight years old, Nicole became a Master Cicerone, which made her the first woman and youngest person ever to earn the title. At the time, she was the fourth Master Cicerone.

Nicole stood in front of the room wearing black-rimmed glasses, earrings, and a floral tank top, the kind of office casual that signaled she was in charge. All ten people who'd registered for the class had shown up, a first.

"You're all here to drink yucky beer with me. What's wrong with you?" she quipped.

Before we got to the beer, Nicole explained how humans perceive taste. We'd probably already figured out that the map of the tongue—the one that shows where we're supposed to perceive sweet, sour, salty, and bitter—is completely wrong. Just like phrenologists theorized that bumps on the head predicted intelligence, a notion that was widely accepted during the nineteenth century, the tongue map, which has roots in research by the German scientist D. P. Hanig in 1901, is still accepted by some as fact. But it's a myth: receptors for various tastes are located in distinct cells, but those cells are evenly distributed across the tongue.

Nicole said that researchers are working on creating a better model, and it's possible they'll add a few other tastes to the list of what we can perceive: fat, carbonation, and metallic. Those types of discoveries have happened in the past. Since the invention of the tongue map, another flavor has been added: umami, the "fifth" taste, described as meatiness in things like mushrooms and fish sauce. Kikunae Ikeda, a professor of physical chemistry at the Tokyo Imperial University, discovered glutamate as an element in seaweed in 1908, which was the beginning of the scientific exploration of umami. People taste umami through receptors for glutamate. Even after Japanese scientists created the Umami Information Center in 1982 and started holding symposiums around the globe, American and European scientists were slower to concur that umami exists. Although umami isn't present in most beers, it can show up to a small degree in some stouts and aged beers, where it comes off as a soy sauce flavor. Also, since umami is an important part of pairing beer with food, Nicole recommended buying some monosodium glutamate (MSG), which is commonly labeled as "accent seasoning," and mixing some into a glass of water and drinking it.

Most of the flavors we perceive are aromas, which make the millions of receptor cells in the human nasal cavity essential tools for recognition. Aromas enter our olfaction system either through the nose—orthonasal olfaction—or through the back of the mouth and throat: retronasal olfaction. When it comes to evaluating food and drink, retronasal olfaction counts for a lot. That's because our warm mouths begin to break down food (or drink), which helps release an array of aroma compounds. Those aroma particles are swept up through the throat into the sinus cavities. Without orthonasal capacities we can be taste-blind. "Try holding your nose while eating pieces of raw apple and potato with your eyes closed," Nicole said. "It's nearly impossible to tell the difference." I remembered doing that experiment during what was probably a junior high school science class. My inability to tell the difference between a fruit and a vegetable seemed magical yet disturbing, something I'd think about as an adult during a horrible few days with a sinus infection, when I lost my sense of smell entirely. Eating became an exploration of textures, which was of little comfort. I was terrified I'd never taste again.

Retronasal olfaction made me think about how beer evaluators and drinkers pride themselves on swallowing, not spitting. Once, I'd written a story about a walking wine tour in Sonoma. The professional wine writers in the group had impressive ways of spitting out wines they were tasting—they spewed with precision while standing, sitting, or walking. *Only drink when you're eating a meal,* one wine writer told me. I'd never met a beer person who admonished only drinking at meals. In fact, the only person I'd ever known to spit a beer was myself, while I was pregnant but still needed to taste beers for story research. John Harris told me he feels bitterness in the back of his throat, and because almost all beers contain some element of bitterness, fully tasting them requires swallowing. Also, wine and liquor tasters might prefer to feel the tasting benefit of a full swallow, but the higher alcohol content of those drinks probably rules out that option.

"We screw up aromas by forgetting what they're called or getting confused about what to name them," Nicole continued. I can't count how many times I've struggled to find a name for a flavor or a smell, and I know I'm not the only one. But I had a feeling I was clinging too tightly to the idea that there was one correct way to perceive a flavor or aroma. Maybe if I loosened up my ideas of rightness, I'd find more creative ways of approaching beer. If a porter tastes like a grandma's hat box, why fight it?

"Our parents probably didn't talk about tastes, so we didn't learn the differences," she said. "We're here to make up for lost time and create a lexicon of what beer flavors are." If our palates were a box of crayons, she continued, we were about to attempt to go from the box of eight to sixty-four.

We started analyzing the Longboard, first by examining its color and the appearance of its head, which had disappeared into nothing. Then we did a "drive by," a quick pass of the glass about six inches below our noses, a means of protecting our olfaction systems from any aromas that could temporarily destroy our senses of smell. We were protecting our key instruments. Then we put our hands over the top of the glass and swirled the beer, which warmed the liquid and released its aroma compounds into a confined space. That made it easier to perceive the smell, which Nicole recommended taking in with short sniffs, a more effective way to spark aroma recognition.

"If you're having a hard time," she said, "take a longer sniff with your mouth open."

Once, when I'd interviewed her for a story, Nicole told me she views tasting as an inherent talent—a disheartening idea for those of us who were just learning (she hadn't repeated that opinion here in the class). What if my hard time meant I wasn't physically capable of detecting certain things advanced tasters, like Nicole, could perceive?

It was important to give our sense of smell a break, to help create the kind of sensory longevity needed for judging a beer festival or homebrew competition, or taking a Cicerone exam. I read somewhere that you can easily reset your sense of smell by sniffing the back of your own hand, the olfactory equivalent of eating a Saltine cracker, so I tried it. Even though I felt ridiculous smelling my own hand, it worked.

Finally, we tasted the beer. I closed my eyes and let it sit on my tongue for an extra beat, in the hopes that the warm beer would spark some new neural pathways in my brain. Already, I noticed how the beer seemed more complex than it had during the Widmer panel. For comparison's sake, I held my nostrils closed with my thumb and pointer finger while taking a sip of the beer. And that changed everything. The bitterness I sensed on my tongue seemed muted, as if I wasn't tasting bitter but feeling it. I also felt a little claustrophobic.

Nicole instructed us to write down six words that described the taste of the beer. I wrote *grainy, lemon, cardboard, wheaty,* and *bitter.* I tried to come up with word number six, but nothing seemed right. I kept coming back to the texture of the beer in my mouth, and nearly wrote down "smooth," but I knew Nicole would bust me on choosing a word that had nothing to do with flavor.

We called out the words we'd written down, while Nicole scribbled them on the white board in front of the class. Each time a word was repeated, she made a tick mark next to it.

"Lager yeast," someone yelled out.

"What does that taste like?" Nicole fired back, before writing it on the board. "That's not a flavor. How about something like 'white wine' instead?"

"Bitter herbs," someone yelled. Again, she pushed for more. "Thyme or another kitchen herb?"

Instead of saying "malty" or "grainy," she said, we should take it a step further with something like "white bread that's barely been warmed in the toaster." At that moment I understood the beauty of being overly specific, even if it produced descriptors that sounded slightly ridiculous. I also realized that I'd better start paying more attention to smells and tastes in general. Becoming familiar with the scent of wet moss on a drizzly fall day could add the Jazzberry Jam or Aztec Gold to my tasting crayon box.

Nicole revealed her own list of words for the Longboard: grainy, bitter, lemon, sulphur, and apples. I did a quick count. She and I shared three words, which felt like my own minor victory. And, just like me, she'd failed to write a sixth.

"Corn," she said, to bring her list to six. "I'm surprised more people didn't say it."

A lot of people had written down "lemon," which came from noble hops, classic European hops that are responsible for many of the signature flavors in pilsners and other lagers. And a lot of people wrote down texture words. The astringency of the beer was derived from tannins, Nicole told us, which caused the grainy, drying feeling on the palate. That could have also been the sharpness some people described, she guessed. Almost everyone said "bitter," but Nicole pointed out that, on the spectrum of all beers, this wasn't a bitter beer. "Yet bitterness is a major aspect of this beer," she said. I let my mind muddle over this idea. On a desert island, the beer was one thing. But placed in the panoply of beers, it was something else entirely.

Next up, the yucky beers. Before we'd arrived, Nicole had spiked samples of the lager with various off-flavors. To get to know them, I covered one glass with my hand and madly swirled the beer inside, as though I was covering someone's mouth so they couldn't whisper a secret. Then I released the riddles and swooped them up into my nose. Wham. Corn. Not fresh corn, roasted corn, or corn fritters corn, but creamed corn, the kind that oozes out of a can and splats onto school lunch trays. The chemical compound responsible for the smell was dimethyl sulfide (DMS), which is known for creating flavors of creamed corn, canned black olives, tomato soup, and rotten vegetables. Sometimes, low levels of DMS are considered acceptable in pale lagers, where the chemical can come off as pleasantly corny or sweet. This smell was anything but pleasant.

In the next glass, I detected "cotton candy" and wrote that the beer tasted "very sweet, sour." Wrong. It was my friend diacetyl, the buttery, butterscotch, or fake butter flavor I'd started to think I could identify with my nose plugged. While I had detected diacetyl during the Widmer panel, I struck out today. "Everyone thinks they know what it is," Nicole said. "It's the most commonly abused word on BeerAdvocate." I hadn't thought about it until then, but it made sense that the crowd-sourced beer review site could be a litmus for beer geeks gone wrong.

As I smelled and sipped all the beers in front of me, I realized that my control beer—the nonspiked beer—tasted like fake butter, big time. I asked my neighbor if I could smell her beers, and indeed, her number two beer smelled like what was sitting in my control beer spot. Somehow I'd mixed up my glasses, but I was thrilled that I'd caught the error. Maybe I was learning something. The third sample tasted like something artificial, maybe plastic or paint. It was acetaldehyde, a chemical that exists in the last step before the yeast creates ethanol, or alcohol, and that lingers when the yeast is separated from the beer prematurely. Nicole made us say the word five times out loud (its pronunciation is not instinctual), and described it as "green Jolly Rancher" and "underripe crabapple." Acetaldehyde was showing up in beers more frequently as new craft brewers tried to pump out beer too quickly.

We tasted a few more off-flavors, then Nicole asked us to leave the room and wait. When we came back, she'd rearranged our samples, which gave us the chance to do a blind tasting. As I started smelling and tasting, some answers seemed obvious. But I wasn't always completely sure. Even so, I knew I'd learned a lot in just a few hours. I certainly knew more than I did at the Widmer taste panel just a few weeks ago, which made me feel like I'd just taken my first steps down a new path. When we went through the answers, I'd identified five out of the seven samples correctly. Not bad. Somehow I'd mixed up DMS and acetaldehyde. In what universe does a green Jolly Rancher taste like creamed corn?

I said good-bye to Nicole, not knowing that the next time I would see her, she'd be spiking beers for me to taste at the Cicerone exam.

———

Unlike many beer bloggers and other beer writers I followed online, I led the life of a shut-in, mostly because I wanted to be home for dinner and Oscar's bedtime. That meant I wasn't attending Portland's constant stream of bottle releases, tap takeovers, beer tastings, beer dinners, and beer festivals, which made me feel out of the loop. I realized that, since most of my beer drinking was happening at home, I needed to transform my afterwork beers into learning experiences.

I found the Beer Tasting Sheet online, which, despite its uninventive name, seemed like a good way to evaluate beer. Unlike the Sensory Validation Ballot at Widmer, this tasting sheet didn't focus only on off-flavors: it presented four categories—Appearance, Aroma, Taste, and Mouthfeel—each with subcategories and then a group of words you were supposed to circle to describe the beer. For example, the head could be: *none, diminishing, lasting, fizzy, rocky, creamy, no lacing,* or *lacing.* The words forced me to investigate. For example, I'd never heard of a rocky head, a descriptor that describes the dips and valleys of a super frothy head, the craters on the surface of the moon. The sheet did feel constricting at times. One beer I was drinking had a head that looked like meringue, but that word was not an option. The words were training wheels; at some point, I'd come up with my own descriptors. Besides, the sheet had a space for notes, where I could get creative. At the bottom of the sheet, though, was an area I'd start to resent. The *Overall Description of This Beer* had just six words—*Crisp, Balanced, Fruity, Malty, Hoppy,* and *Complex*—plus the aggravating instruction to "circle one." How was I supposed to describe an entire beer using just one word? "Malty" was never going to cut it.

The Beer Tasting Sheet was created by Rob Hill, a Certified Cicerone who works with an online retailer called Total Wine & More. I e-mailed Rob to find out how he had developed the particulars. He told me he started with a wine sheet Total Wine & More had developed, then tweaked it for beer, in the hopes it would become a tool for staff and customers in beer classes. He said the first draft of his sheet was rejected by the powers that be at Total Wine & More, who thought it was too "geeky." Rob pushed back and showed them other tasting sheets; the benefit of his approach was that it provided people descriptive words for beer they might not have known otherwise.

"The challenge was that the aroma and flavor sources, and obviously the words and adjectives used, were irrelevant to beer," he told me. He also said that by forcing people to categorize a beer with just one word, they could more easily figure out what types of beers they liked.

I got into the habit of filling out a beer sheet every time I drank a beer at home. The sheets forced me to do simple things like look up beer styles, breweries, and the proper glassware for whatever I was drinking. My friend Dusty, who was visiting from Utah, watched me go through the ritual of swirling, sniffing, then filling out the sheet.

"It's like a mindfulness exercise, only with beer," he said.

The exercise did remind me of a "meditation lab," part of a course on Buddhism I took in college. One time, the instructor instructed us to chew a single raisin for ten minutes. My raisin may have made it three minutes before it dissolved into sugary nothingness, but before then, I'd noticed its changing texture and saccharine quality. I'd even started to notice the interestingness of the mechanics of my own jaw.

What the beer sheets weren't teaching me were the right and wrong answers. Without a guide to tell me if what I was tasting was toasty or roasty, I was just guessing.

Unintentionally, my Beer Tasting Sheets chronicled the details of time spent with my favorite people. When I opened a Duvel, a Belgian golden strong ale Tony gave me for my birthday, it was a Friday night. On my tasting sheet I wrote that Oscar was taking "milk notes." (We would pour his milk in a special glass, and if he was in the mood, he'd comment on its attributes. "It smells like milk!" he once yelled.) As for the beer: "Crisp lightness meets total richness. Perfectly appealing. HEY Belgium!" Another sheet recorded a Monday night: "Oscar wants to play flashcards. Tony cooking hamburger mac (celery seed)." The beer, the Black Widow Porter from McMenamins: "Weird fruity, peachy thing. Seems cloying. Good aroma. Some tangy/tart, bitter notes. Nice light body. Chocolate milk." In hindsight, I can't imagine any brewery selling a porter with those attributes, but I give myself points for trying.

HOP HUNT

The hop gardens turn gracefully towards me, presenting regular avenues of hops in rapid flight, then whirl away.
—CHARLES DICKENS

SINCE IT WAS LATE SUMMER, it was time for the hop harvest, which begins during August and lasts into September. In the Pacific Northwest, Yakima, Washington, is hop-growing central, and for years, I'd wanted to witness the hop harvest there. I couldn't imagine the scale (or the smell), and there was no better time to immerse myself in one of beer's most important ingredients. I hoped a visit would help me begin learn to how to distinguish hop varieties by smell and taste, and understand more about how the plants were grown and harvested, all things I'd need to know for the Cicerone exam. Before I left, John Harris told me Yakima happened to be a famous stopover for drug runners traveling between Mexico and Canada. Not one to be deterred by drug traffickers, I set off, unarmed, to witness Yakima's hop harvest.

During six months of the year, a hop farm is an unspectacular tableau of barren soil washed with rain—the kind of place where soldiers could conduct boot camp exercises in the mud. Long, muddy ruts hold eighteen- or twenty-foot-tall wooden poles that rise from the earth at regular intervals. The poles are connected at the top with long wires. In March, the imaginary soldiers would exit as rows of hop shoots protrude from the soil. Farm workers string coconut-fiber twine from the high wires to the ground near the shoots, because as soon as the plants poke through the topsoil, they long to head skyward, like astronauts determined to defy gravity without losing any long-term connection to the earth. Charles Darwin once kept a potted hop plant in a warm room where he was confined with illness. He recorded how the plant spiraled while growing vertically, noting how the "internodes," the joints where the plant extends its arms, would "bend to one side and to travel slowly round towards all points of the compass, moving, like the hands of a watch, with the sun." That spiral helps the plant clamber up the strings with an uncanny relentlessness. In just a few months, a hop plant develops sixteen- to twenty-five-foot tall "bines," vines with stiff hairs that help a plant climb.

But it's the hop cones that have transformed modern beer making. Hidden underneath the tiny, fluffy green leaves of a hop cone, a yellow pollen called lupulin contains the alpha acids and essential oils capable of adding bitterness and an exciting range of aromas and flavors to beer. The flowers resemble marijuana buds, which isn't surprising. *Humulus* and *Cannabis* share DNA as members of the family *Cannabaceae*.

Hops are worshipped around the globe, not only for the range of flavors and aromas they bring to beers, but also for how they've altered the brewing landscape. Today, very few beers are brewed without hops. The plant is fetishized around brewers' kettles, at festivals, and in backyards. People wear hop bines as crowns and toss hop cones into French presses filled with beer for immediate infusions. Beer lovers jump into piles of dried hops, where they have their pictures taken. They buy hop soaps, hop cheeses, hop candies, hop sodas, hop murals, hop paintings, hop T-shirts, and hop jewelry. Some of them even eat pickled hop shoots, possibly on pizza.

I love hops, not only for what they bring to beer, but because, for me, they are a local product. Hops are grown commercially in dozens of countries, everywhere from Albania to South Africa. In the United States, about 70 percent of the country's hops are grown in Washington, with Oregon growing another 15 percent. A few years ago, I had the chance to visit some Oregon hop farms, including Goschie Farms in Silverton. The fourth-generation family farm is run by Gayle Goschie, one of the few women in the hop-growing business. Gayle was the first woman in her family to take over a significant part of hop-growing operations (the farm also grows wine grapes, but hops take up a greater acreage). "There was a certain nod from older generations to me," she once told me, "because they saw my sincere interest in growing hops."

On a sunny spring day, we walked among her rows of hop plants, which were just beginning to spiral around strings, and she told me how in 2008 everything changed for the farm. It was the year InBev acquired Anheuser-Busch, a corporate merger that led to a withering relationship with Goschie Farms. Anheuser-Busch's contracts had been the farm's bread and butter for decades. Gayle had been watching the craft breweries sprout up all over Oregon; she saw potential.

She decided to start planting the kind of aroma hops craft brewers were using in all sorts of beers, especially IPAs, a reinvention that not only kept the farm afloat but pushed Gayle into prominence.

Tony and I had planted hop plants in our front yard four years earlier, giving us some welcome natural summertime shade over a large south-facing window. But this year, the plants grew top heavy and began to resemble poodle tails. I asked Gayle what was happening. "So few hop growers ever complain or question top-heavy hop vines!" she wrote in an e-mail. Like a doctor making a diagnosis without seeing a patient, she guessed that my plants may have been suffering from a shaded base, because even the slightest loss of direct sunlight keeps hop plants from "putting out arms," which she said would prevent them from "hopping down to the base." She was right. To the south of the hop plants was a vegetable bed and an overgrown hedge. Gayle also explained that hop plants produce a full yield of hops during their third year, which the plant can maintain for as long as twenty years if it stays free from diseases and pests. Eventually a late-summer windstorm blew my hop plants into my yard, which made them look like tumbleweeds tethered to the ground with a string.

Before humans domesticated the plant and gave it a scientific name, hops grew wild. Since the plants prefer to climb, they would often overtake willow trees. That predatory nature inspired the *lupus* in *Humulus lupus,* because *lupus* is Latin for wolf. In Europe during the eighth century, when farmers were becoming serfs between the Romans' exit and Charlemagne's impending rule, hops began to be grown intentionally, possibly for medicinal purposes. Those were the days of gruit ale, which was brewed with herbs and spices such as yarrow and wormwood. Hops would replace those additions for a couple of reasons: not only do hops alter the flavor profile of beer, the alpha acids in the hop cones act as a preservative.

The first written record of a hop yard comes from Hallertau in modern-day Germany, in 786 C.E. In 822, Abbot Adalhard of the Benedictine monastery in Corbie, France, wrote that his monks were adding hops to beer—the first written record of the practice. By 1300, hops were widely cultivated in Europe, from Norway to Austria. Today, farmers grow hops everywhere, from the Pacific Northwest and Europe to New Zealand and China. In 2014 growers produced about 208 million pounds of hops.

———

When I arrived at a hops-processing facility in Yakima with Meghann Quinn, the willowy president and co-owner of Bale Breaker Brewing Co., something seemed wrong. A truck piled with long, stringy hop bines, still fresh with a crushing green mass of hop cones, sat on asphalt outside a processing building, baking in the sun as an invisible clock ticked. Hops need to be processed as soon as they are picked to maximize the potential aromas and flavors that will end up in a beer. Once a bine is cut from its base, every minute counts.

Meghann ducked into a building then reappeared to announce that one of the picking machines was temporarily down. She seemed nonplussed as she walked to the back of the truck, pulled a cone off a bine and broke it open with her thumbs. Inside, glistening wet leaves sprouted from a central stem in a pattern that reminded me of an artichoke. Packed between the leaves were nubs of bright yellow lupulin.

"Rub the two halves together," she instructed.

Rubbing one cone between my palms turned my cupped hands into a small bomb of piney and citrus smells mixed with an aroma I don't often detect in a beer, the scent of a plant with a freshly broken stem. That potent combination is why the mechanics of the harvest matter, why a migrant workforce arrived in Yakima every year for one intense month of labor. Everything revolved around capturing the aroma of this hop cone in its purest form.

Meghann owns Bale Breaker with her two brothers and her husband. One brother, Patrick Smith, wrote a business plan for a theoretical brewery on their family's hop farm as his master's degree thesis. After he graduated from business school, he handed the thesis over to his siblings, and two years later the brewery was up and running. Meghann confirmed my suspicion that Bale Breaker was one of just a few American breweries located on a commercial hop farm, a happy event that's bound to happen more often. Bale Breaker operates as a production brewery, which means the taproom adjacent to the brewery is more like an accessory than a necessity, a place to cater to visitors and build brand awareness, but not a key outlet for selling their beer. The brewery's two best-selling, year-round beers are a pale ale called Field 41, the name of the hops field that had to be torn out to build the brewery, and Top Cutter IPA, which was named after a key piece of harvesting equipment. When the family built the brewery, they designed the building so the back walls of the brewery could be removed for an expansion. Forward thinking and optimistic, I noted.

As we stood by the weighted truck, Meghann pointed to a farmhouse next door, the place where her grandparents once lived. Meghann had lived there, too, until she was in grade school and her family moved across the street into the house we could see on the other side of field, past a small group of cows swatting their tails. One night in the late nineties, when she was a middle schooler, she woke up to the sound of chaos. Outside, she saw flames rising from one of the buildings we were standing next to on this day, the kiln building where the hops are dried at high temperatures. Fires, I'd learn, are common in the world of hops. The possibility of roaring flames and devastating destruction lurks in the shadows and shapes many hop-processing procedures.

Barring disasters like that one, harvest progresses with a pressing orderliness from late August to late September. In the field, bines are cut by men and machines then loaded into a truck. The truck immediately delivers the hop bines to a processing facility, where the cones are removed and separated from leaves and other unwanted materials. The hop cones go into a kiln, where they are dried at high heat for hours. Once they're dried, the hops are pressed into large rectangular bales and moved into cold storage. From there, the bales go either to a pellet plant, where they are processed into dense nuggets that look like rabbit food, or straight to a brewery or broker.

Since the first point of contact for the bines from the field—the stripping machines—were stalled, Meghann and I skipped that step and headed to the kiln. At the top of one set of stairs was a room with a nearly Olympic pool–size floor covered in bright green hops. "Citra," Meghann said. The air was uncomfortably hot and humid, like a sauna, and the constant hum of machines and blowing fans made it hard to carry on a conversation. The floor was divided into subsections that were only visible because the hops in each section were filled to different heights that could be measured in inches. The sections that had been drying longer had lost more mass and were therefore more condensed than the fresher batches. Above our heads, fabric conveyor belts glowing green with hop cones whirred around the perimeter. Meghann's father, Mike Smith, the third-generation farmer to grow hops on this land, required that each of his three children work the kiln during the summer between high school and college. I mentioned how it must have been difficult to spend an entire day in the ambient heat of the kiln building, and Meghann said it used to be much hotter, around 140 degrees. Her brother had been working on improving efficiency in the kilning process, and he figured out some ways to bring the temperature down.

As Meghann described how fresh hops enter the kiln building then leave perfectly dried, I started to understand the importance of moisture content in fresh hop cones. Until then I'd assumed hop farmers had a magical sense of when the hops were ripe. Sure, they'd examine the plants with an exacting, scientific eye, but would also maybe do things like talk to the plants during certain phases of the moon. In actuality, the farm crew simply measured the moisture content of the hops with a digital probe. When the cones reach 75 percent moisture content, the hops are ready to be harvested. With equal precision, the kiln dries the hops to a moisture content of 8 to 10 percent, a process that takes six to eight hours. Then the hops are cooled, an important part of the process. If the hops are too hot when they're baled, they will spontaneously combust, which can produce building-flattening fires. The temperature of hop bales is so important, in fact, I'd later see inspectors inserting long thermometers into hop bales that had just arrived at a storage warehouse—the Smokey Bears of the hop industry. For the record, a hop bale was not what set this building on fire in the nineties. The fire was started by spark from an overheated kiln inside a building constructed entirely of wood.

———

Just like ranchers talk about head of cattle, not pounds of beef, hop farmers refer to acreage. The B.T. Loftus Ranches hop farm, the Bale

Breaker Brewing Co. family's farm, was established in 1932. These days, it farms close to 1,000 acres of hops. For reference, U.S. farmers grew almost 40,000 acres of hops in 2014, about 29,000 of which were grown in Washington. Since an acre of hops in the Pacific Northwest yields about 2,000 pounds, it's easy math. Brewers use an average of two pounds of hops per barrel in an IPA, which means a single acre could produce 1,000 barrels, or 2,000 kegs. Those numbers seemed highly abstract as I stood in front of two giant piles of hops on a warehouse floor. The mounds were shaped like perfect Dr. Seuss hills and almost glowing in an astonishing bright green. The hops were about to be baled in two-hundred-pound increments. After a loose pile of hops is smashed together inside burlap or plastic sheeting, someone hand sews the pieces of the bale together at the top. Someone else stencils numbers representing the hop variety, lot, and farm on the top of each bale. When she was little, Meghann said, she would run across the tops of the bales with bare feet and write the numbers on each one.

These days, a single baling crew works twelve-hour days, and each member of the crew is paid per hour. The following day the local newspaper, the *Yakima Herald-Republic,* would run a front-page story about the labor shortage that was affecting this year's hop harvest. Because the valley's hop farms had increased their acreage by 7 percent, the previous year's workforce simply wasn't sufficient, especially since the hop industry was competing with the local apple industry for workers.

By the time Meghann and I had returned to the picker building, where the hop bines are processed when they arrive fresh from the fields, the machines were working again. Two trucks had pulled into bays, and men wearing the reflective safety vests of road workers stood in the back of each one, feeding bines onto hooks that would whip the plants, which were clinging to each other for safety, across the two-story building in an unnatural, dangling dance. Not even the most agile Tarzan would have been able to swing through this fast-moving jungle. The hooks fed the hop bines into a vertical slot where a machine violently ripped off all the leaves and cones, a sound like five hundred bug zappers working in unison. The scene made me think of the kind of farm accidents you hear about only when someone heroically survives one, and has to learn to live without a limb. I had the urge to fold my arms, but I didn't want to put away my notebook and pen.

Next, the bug zapper fed the plant material onto conveyor belts, which separated the hop cones from the leaves, stems, twine, dirt, and other things that shouldn't go in a brew kettle. Eventually, one conveyor belt carried pure hop cones that were then whisked through a pipe to the kiln building. As Meghann and I walked along narrow wooden planks covered with lupulin and hovering between roaring machines and whizzing conveyor belts, I smelled engine grease underneath the overwhelming aroma of lemony, verdant hops. Lupulin seemed to cover every part of my body, including the insides of my nostrils, and when we walked outside into the glare of the August sun, I noticed a light layer of the powdery resin on Meghann's face, a hop farmer's face powder.

———

So I could see the origin of all the processing activity, Meghann drove me to a lot on her father's farm where hops were being harvested. We zoomed along a straight two-lane road covered with chunks of hop bines—Yakima roadkill—until we turned onto a dirt road. It led to a spot where dusty rows of plant stubble and empty wires were bordered by rows of leafy green walls, twenty-foot-tall hop plants strung up to wires hung between poles. "Citra," Meghann said again, which made sense. Theoretically, all the Citra hops would be ready for harvest on the same day, so the harvesting and processing crew would be moving Citra for hours. A truck, bouncing without the weight of a load of hop bines, appeared from a nearby row. Then the parade arrived.

First, a bottom-cutter truck moved down the row, cutting each bine at its base. Behind it, a truck with a large bed pulled a top cutter, a tall contraption with a spiraling bar that grazed the wires as it severed the attached bines and twine. Immediately, masses of green tumbled into the attached truck bed, which looked small among the acres of plants. The clanking, slow-moving machines seemed inefficient, like old-time farm relics.

Before the 1950s, when machines volunteered to do the hop picking, people did the job by hand. In 1931 George Orwell worked on a hop farm in Kent, England, and he kept a journal about the experience. He wrote:

[Hop picking] entails long hours, but it is healthy, outdoor work, and any able-bodied person can do it. The process is extremely simple. The vines, long climbing plants with the hops clustering on them in bunches like grapes, are trained up poles or over wires; all the picker has to do is to tear them down and strip the hops into a bin, keeping them as clean as possible from leaves. The spiny stems cut the palms of one's hands to pieces, and in the early morning, before the cuts have reopened, it is painful work; one has trouble too with the plant-lice which infest the hops and crawl down one's neck, but beyond that there are no annoyances. One can talk and smoke as one works, and on hot days there is no pleasanter place than the shady lanes of hops, with their bitter scent – an unutterably refreshing scent, like a wind blowing from oceans of cool beer.

These days, workers wearing helmets and orange safety vests do different work by hand. A few men moved among the rows of plants with machetes, chopping missed bines at the base, as though they were on an expedition through the deep Amazon jungle.

I felt exhausted on behalf of all the workers involved in harvest. Here, every part of the harvest process, with the exception of the bailing room, would operate 24/7 until every hop from the field had been processed. If the entire length of this year's harvest were a Monday-through-Friday workweek, I was there on a Wednesday morning. One harvest manager told me these middle days were a difficult time; the crew couldn't yet celebrate the nearness of the end. As harvest unfolds, managers rejigger the end date. Every day that gets added weighs on everyone involved.

Years ago, after I'd visited my first Oregon hop farm, I'd come up with a vision of an end-of-hop-harvest dinner, which I thought would make a great magazine feature. In *Kinfolk* style, the dinner would happen on a hop farm at a long table flanked with the beautiful people who'd made the harvest happen. Bathed in flattering light of a sunset, they'd eat a roasted pig that had somehow been seasoned with hops. I'd gone so far as to ask an Oregon hop farmer about the idea. He sounded skeptical. "Everyone usually just wants to get out of here by the time we're done," he'd said. Later, at a different farm, I noticed a charred spot at the end of a row of hops, an informal fire pit littered with blackened corncobs and husks. I guessed that was how workers were sustaining themselves during nighttime shifts, when the plants were illuminated by headlights, flashlights, and moonlight. I silently wished them a roasted pig.

—————

All the lupulin and dust had made me thirsty. At the Bale Breaker taproom, a bastion of craft beer in an otherwise parched valley, I ordered a sampler paddle of the brewery's current lineup of beers. The lighter end of the beer spectrum was perfectly refreshing, and I was surprised to taste a restrained use of hops in many of the styles. Meghann's parents sat with us on a covered outdoor patio. Her dad, Mike Smith, told me how the snowmelt from the Cascades made for good irrigation. Combined with the long days and cool nights of the forty-seventh parallel, Yakima had the perfect conditions for hop growing. Compared to Oregon, the Yakima valley had fewer fungal diseases and downy mildew, factors that could severely diminish yield. While this kind of information was studied and recorded by science, in Mike's case, it was also passed down. His grandparents planted nine acres of hops on this land in 1932, the year before Prohibition ended. Mike told me when he got into the business in the early 1970s, a few hundred Washington families grew hops. These days, only forty or forty-five families were hop growers.

The Smith family had been preparing for a visit from "beer royalty," some famous craft brewers who were in town for the harvest. The family marked the occasion with a big dinner at home, which of course included plenty of beer. Sure enough, as I lingered at the tap room, Vinnie and Natalie Cilurzo arrived. They were the owners of Russian River Brewing Co. in Santa Rosa, California, and I'd interviewed them both by phone years ago, so I said hello. Natalie and I talked about the Great American Beer Festival, which was coming up in a few weeks. I would be there for the first time. A brewer from Tröegs Independent Brewing in Hershey, Pennsylvania, came through the door toting a cooler filled with his beers. As I finished my beer, I listened to the brewers and hop farmer talk about the weather and other Yakima farms they'd visited. They discussed certain hop varieties, gossiped about industry folk, and reminisced about last year. In that moment, I sensed that next year's beers were being created at that very moment, thanks to a magical mingling of dusty heat, verdant bines, and creative juices.

═══════

A hop yard grows despite the land's naturally parched state during the summer. The towers of plants rise as victorious symbols of how humans successfully wrangle water. But the sun is relentless. The next day, as I walked through rows of experimental hops in a hop yard designed to foster genetic experiments, not even the pillars of leaves blocked the unapologetic sun, which seared my neck at every turn. Every plant around me was an original genetic creation bred to serve a specific need; this was a place I felt I needed to see if I was going to understand how popular hop varieties had come into existence.

Because of the scientific nature of this space, I'd imagined rows of plants identified by metal plaques, the kind you'd find in a well-curated arboretum. Instead, the rows of hops looked like any other hop yard, until I slowed down and really started to look at the plants. Unlike a regular hop farm, where a single variety is grown together in rows that make up uniform-looking lots, these plants varied wildly. Some were bushy and hedge-like near the ground. Others were stringy and leggy-tall. I couldn't tell from looking at them what I longed to know: which hop would become the next big thing.

Maybe, just maybe, one of these hop plants would drive brewers and beer drinkers wild a few years from now. They'd crave this single variety's flavors and aromas, which would forever change the craft beer landscape. It has happened before.

The only way I'd understand this place was to stay close to Gene Probasco, one of the most accomplished hop breeders in the world. I tried to match his stride. He wore a baseball cap and a crisp button-up shirt; the collar was proof he was accustomed to a hop yard's harsh sun. Gene works for John I. Haas, a hop company founded in 1914 in Germany. Through mergers and buyouts, its parent company, the Barth-Haas Group, is able to call itself "the world's largest supplier of hops and hop services." Earlier that morning, Gene had picked me up from my hotel in Yakima. As we left the lobby, where men wearing caps and shirts emblazoned with beer logos carried briefcases and clipboards, I heard trucks roaring along the nearby highway. The air smelled resinous and green.

"Does it smell like hops?" I asked him. Gene paused and squinted, his face upturned to the stark blue sky.

"I don't think so. But maybe I'm just used to it," he conceded, generously.

My logical self knew that, if a man who'd spent thirty-plus years in the hop industry wasn't smelling hops, I wasn't smelling hops. But I didn't want to believe it, because I was in Yakima. Later I'd look back on the moment as proof of the power of place to alter one's perception, a common aspect of how humans evaluate aromas and tastes. Right then, I wanted to romanticize the air in a parking lot next to Interstate 82.

As we drove to the experimental hop farm, Gene pointed out fields of other crops along the way, from apples to asparagus. I kept steering the conversation back to hops. Gene explained that, unlike plants that have male and female parts on the same plant, entire hop plants are either male or female. While both "genders" of plants produce hop flowers, the male plants will pollinate the females to produce seeds, which makes them undesirable for brewing. That's why every plant on a hop farm is female. When hop plants do reproduce, the male and female plants cross-pollinate to make unique genetic offspring, like humans.

During his decades of working for John I. Haas, Gene researched and invented nonbrewing uses for hops. Because the alpha acids in hops are antimicrobial—one of the properties that makes them a preservative in beer—they're also useful in substances like ethanol. In addition, the beta acids in hops can be used to sterilize surfaces. In sugar processing, hops can be used instead of formaldehyde to clean equipment. Beta acids can also help control parasitic mites that attack honeybees.

But those hop uses are still secondary for Gene. The main focus of his work is to breed new hop varieties that will wow brewers. To accomplish that task, he plants about 15,000–20,000 seedlings each year, of about 2,500 distinct varieties. He and his team expose all the seedlings to powdery mildew, one of the greatest threats to hop plants, which will kill about half of the seedlings. For the next three years, Gene monitors the survivors. By the third year, he selects twenty to forty of the most promising varieties, multiplies the plants for each one, and transfers the plants to a test plot, where they'll spend at least five years in the ground. In total, it takes about ten years to develop a new hop variety, which means Gene becomes intimately familiar with each plant that has promise.

"Are they like your children?" I asked, immediately regretting that I'd anthropomorphized the focus of his scientific career. But he played along.

"Yes, I suppose they're kind of like my children," he replied. "You start to learn their behaviors and characteristics." He does have favorites, he said, but among the thousands of new hop varieties he's created, "very few of them are actually special."

At this point in his career, Gene is most famous for breeding the Citra variety, the highly sought-after aroma hop with a distinct citrus aromas I knew intimately after my time at Bale Breaker. Gene told me he first bred the plant in 1990, but brewers weren't interested in its grapefruit characteristics back then. In 2007 he sent samples of Citra to Widmer, Deschutes, and Sierra Nevada. At the time, the hop was known as EXP 114. Eventually, Citra was renamed, and other brewers fell in love with the hop. Back then, Gene was surprised it took so long for brewers to latch on to the variety. "I'm not surprised by anything anymore," he said.

Like a fashion designer who debuts shocking silhouettes on the runway years before they become popular with a mainstream audience, Gene seemed like a purveyor of tastes, like somehow he knew what flavors and aromas brewers would want ten years from now. But he told me my assumption was wrong.

"We don't tell the brewers what they're going to want or need," he said. "They tell us."

As we walked through the experimental field, Gene would stop and pull a stack of stapled papers from his back pocket. He called it a map, but once I saw it, I called it a spreadsheet.

"We're here," he said, pointing at one of the sheet's horizontal rows. The line read: 60, 18-24, S169-78. Once in a while, he'd stop to pluck a hop cone from a plant and break it open to examine the juicy inside. Then he'd rub the cone between his hands and inhale the air inside his cupped hands. I followed suit, trying to notice the differences between aromas, but more obvious was the scale of intensity of what I smelled. Some didn't smell like anything but a raw hop plant, while others seemed more complex and nuanced. At one point, I said I smelled mint, and Gene confirmed that a nearby farm grew mint, which was most likely being harvested that morning.

Gene said he wanted to check on a few varieties with banana aromas. He checked the map. When he found his destination plant, he pulled a cone, smelled it, and said, "Yep, that's banana, but onion and garlic are coming through. It's overripe."

We heard laughter and tromped through the rows to find its source. A few rows to the east, Joe Casey, the brewmaster at Widmer Brothers, and Doug Rehberg, who'd sat next to me at the taste panel, were holding the same spreadsheet. When brewers visit hop farms during harvest, most of them also visit nearby experimental hop yards, because what grows here could greatly alter their future. Joe and Doug said they'd visited this plot a few weeks ago, but they'd returned to check on a few varieties, because they wanted to examine how those hops were maturing on the bine. Joe said that, when they identified an experimental hop as interesting, Widmer would order about ten pounds of the hop for an experimental brew. If the hop performed well in the kettle, the brewery would "sponsor an acre" of that variety, a minor financial gamble for a large, well-funded brewery like Widmer.

"We're not looking for a specific aroma," Doug said, "but something new or different."

"We also look at yield," added Joe. I'd already learned how greater yielding plants were the future of hop growing, considering the rising cost of land and the growing demand for hops worldwide.

As they talked, Joe and Doug pulled hop cones from different plants, rubbed them in their hands, and inhaled.

"I'm getting lime and cedar here," Joe said.

A few plants down the row, Doug yelled out that he found one that had notes of menthol and something fruity, something like Fruit Stripe gum. Joe sprinted to him and smelled the hop for himself.

"Yeah, totally!" he said shaking his head in disbelief. "Fruit Stripe gum." I wanted to think they'd just discovered the hop that would launch a thousand brews.

═══════

The main reason I was in Yakima was also the reason so many commercial brewers were in Yakima: hop selection, the hands-on process of choosing specific hops for the coming year. Because brewers buy hops through futures contracts, the quantities and varieties had been determined at least two years earlier, but the selection process allows brewers to customize their orders by choosing between lots. Brewers only missed out on hop selection for things like births or deaths in the family. Otherwise they spent a few nights in Yakima every summer, filling the gaps between appointments with growers and brokers with farm visits and beer drinking. I hoped watching a brewer do hop selection would help me better understand the nuances of hops and why those choices matter for a brewery.

I'd e-mailed a slew of brewers, asking if I could watch their hop selection, and I ended up making plans to shadow Cam O'Connor, brewmaster at Deschutes Brewery. As one of the largest craft breweries in the United States, the Bend, Oregon, brewery buys a lot of hops. Unlike most breweries, Deschutes and just a handful of others, including Sierra Nevada, brew exclusively with whole hops as opposed to the more common hop pellets. Whole hops, which are also called "leaf hops," cost slightly less than pelletized hops because they require less processing. I've heard brewers argue the merits of pellets versus whole hops, a technical nuance that revolves around brewing style and willingness to clean up wet, heavy, boiled whole hops. (Pellets usually dissolve during the boil and turn into particulates, which makes them easier to manage.)

At the John I. Haas pellet plant in Yakima, most of the twenty-three buildings onsite are chilled to below freezing, a welcome mat for the average of three thousand bales of hops that arrive every day during the four or so weeks of summertime harvest. A team tests every bale for moisture content and every third bale for temperature to ensure the bales won't spontaneously combust. (Building number 12 burnt down for this reason in 1999—and the next year, building 18 caught fire too.)

To make pellets, one thousand bales of hops a day are milled into a fine powder on machinery, most of which is chilled to prevent lupulin from sticking to its metal surfaces. Most of the machines used in the plant were originally designed to do other things. One was made to mix industrial portions of cake batter, for example. Brice Hiatt, plant manager of pellet operations at John I. Haas, said that pelletizing creates a "clean product," because the pellet-making process removes unwanted matter from the bales of hops, such as rocks, stems, and dirt clods. The hop cones and powder travel over a magnet, which removes any metal before being pressed into pellets. Brice mentioned the magnet had even snagged Capri Sun bags and screws. In the end, Brice said proudly, every carton of a specific variety is identical. From the moment the bales are opened to when the last box of pellets is sealed, the process takes seventy to ninety minutes.

Because the alpha acids begin to disappear the moment the hop cone leaves the bine, the pellet plant roars into action as soon as the first bale of hops arrives on the day after Labor Day. Then the pellet plant operates 24/5 until sometime in May, when all the whole hops from one season have been successfully pelletized.

Cam O'Connor and his four-person Deschutes team examine whole hops, not pellets, during the selection process at five different brokers during their five-day road trip. They travel in a hulking black Suburban that moves them from Bend to Yakima and back to hop farms in Oregon's Willamette Valley.

I was late to arrive at Hopsteiner, the first appointment of the trip for the Deschutes team, but everyone else managed to get there on time. Inside a meeting room, a table of somber-looking people were flipping through binders and glancing at a screen with a digital chart. I didn't see a single hop cone in the room, whole or pelletized, and hoped I hadn't gotten the wrong impression of what happens during hop selection. I gave Cam a nod and sat in an empty chair at the table. Someone from Hopsteiner was presenting a State of the Union–type overview of the hops industry. More hops were being grown and harvested in Yakima, he reported. Supposedly, there was a local farmer who had ripped up apple orchards to plant hops. "I'm not sure that's ever happened before," the man said with amazement. From what I'd already learned about the cost of land in the Yakima valley and the profit margins of hop growing, this story seemed unlikely, but I understood the implications. If hops became more valuable than other crops, farmers might shift the agricultural landscape here, which would mean more business for brokers and more hops for brewers.

Cam volleyed back with his own view of the hop industry. Deschutes's newest flagship beer, Fresh Squeezed IPA (the beer that inspired our recipe at Lady Brew Portland), was selling more than expected, a ringing endorsement of the consumer's preference for citrusy hops in large quantities. Veronica Vega, a former biologist who was now a brewer at Deschutes, added that she saw sessionable, low-alcohol beers as the latest trend, especially ones with a strong hop presence. "We're seeing more and more consumers who know their hop varieties," she said firmly.

After the meeting, a procession of air-conditioned cars—including the Deschutes Suburban, which looked like it was designed to transport a family of ten—headed to a nearby building used just for hop selection. Inside, a table was covered with brown-paper-wrapped rectangles of dried hops—what are known as "brewers bricks." The bricks were sealed with brass tacks and marked with three-digit numbers. Each member of the Deschutes team brought a three-ring binder filled with evaluation sheets to the table. I asked to see a sheet, which had blank spaces for notes on the appearance and aroma of each brick, which represented hops from a particular lot. Like any agricultural product, hops are affected by variations in soil, sunlight, wind, the timing of harvest, and processing. Everything, from the temperature of the air at the time the hop bine was cut from the ground to the length of time the hop cones spent in the kilning room, affects flavor and aroma. Theoretically, each brick captured those nuances.

The Deschutes team started with eight bricks on the table at one time, all of the same variety. They opened the brown paper packages to reveal loosely pressed, dried hop cones. The five of them stood around the tall table, where they'd systematically scoop up a handful of dried hops, vigorously rub their hands together, bury their noses in their hands, then inhale. After each "rub," they'd dump the hops into a hole in the center of the table before scribbling notes on their evaluation sheets. By choosing the right hops for the coming year— the ones that would help best execute existing beer recipes and bring new beers to life—these five people would help elevate the sales and reputation of the Deschutes brand for the next year and, most likely, beyond. Just as fermentation tanks empty and fill, so do brewery bank accounts, and the room felt electric with focus.

"It's so quiet in here," I whispered to one of the Hopsteiner reps.

"This is important," he whispered back. "It's how you build a brand."

Not all brewers worked in silence, though: Some arrived with portable stereos so they could analyze aromas to the sounds of AC/DC. Others verbally argued the merits of certain lots like a high school debate team. As I watched the Deschutes crew, I started to understand the genius of their method. After each round of rubbing and note taking, Cam asked if everyone was finished. Once all pencils were down, each person held up a pointer finger. On Cam's word, they pointed at the one brick they would choose from the eight. The lot with the most votes would be shipped to Deschutes in increments throughout 2015, in accordance with hop contracts created years ago. By having each person form an opinion before voting, Cam ensured no one person held too much sway, although he cast any tie-breaking votes.

After a few rounds, I approached Cam and said in a whisper, "Can I try?"

Even though I knew I wouldn't be held accountable for whatever messes or victories happened during hop selection that day—unlike the rest of the people in the room—I wanted to understand what making those big decisions felt like. Did I have the ability to detect the key differences between dozens of hops that looked exactly the same? "Sure," he said. "Go for it."

I took a place at the table and picked up a small handful of Cascade hops, which felt light and airy, like confetti. I started rubbing the hops between my hands, slowly at first, then faster, as though I were trying to start a fire with two sticks. Then I pushed my nose into my cupped hands and inhaled. The smell was so warm and familiar yet juicy, I wanted to stop and just enjoy the aroma. But the five other people at the table were pushing past any such simplistic reactions. A hint of lemon and fresh grass, I thought. I dumped the hops into the hole in the center of the table, just like everyone else, and grabbed another hand-ful from a different brick. The difference in aromas was immediately obvious. Hay sitting in sunshine. The next lot seemed smoky. Another reminded me of Earl Grey tea. I silently picked my favorites for each round, and a few times my choice overlapped with the group's.

I snuck a few peeks at their evaluation sheets, where I saw "nice, bright, herbal," "blah!," "tea," "bright orange," and "cat piss." Once in a while, the group would share descriptors after a vote. "Smoky bacon." "Rotten dairy." "Sulfur." The lead brewer, Matt Henneous, sneezed. Everyone laughed then quickly went silent again, as they continued to rub, sniff, scowl, and scribble. They were still evaluating Cascades, a variety that kept coming, an endless parade of nuances tacked in brown paper.

The group took a break and went outside, where the hot dry air smelled like car exhaust, warm asphalt, and dirt clods baked in the sun. When they re-entered the building, they wiped their hands with Hopsteiner-supplied hand wipes, which, Veronica pointed out with disgust, had a lemon scent despite their "scent free" label. She didn't have to say what I already knew: artificial lemon scent was the last thing anyone in this room needed on their hands. The Deschutes team came back to the table and started opening more bricks. I started to feel like hop selection would never end. Matt kept sneezing. They kept using words I never imagined could apply to hops: Red Vine, Twizzler, jammy. Coconut. Chocolate. Hop leaves fluttered across the table and onto the floor. Finally, the team closed their binders.

I'd given up participating rounds ago. Even so, my hands were covered with a sticky yellow-green residue that seemed to be turning black the longer it sat on my skin. When I clapped, my hands stuck together in an unnatural pause. In the bathroom, I scrubbed my soapy skin with a little plastic brush and regretted that I hadn't taken off my wedding ring before I scooped up that first handful of Cascades—just one of many moments that revealed I was an amateur.

Before everyone left, the Hopsteiner employees pulled a couple of beers from a minifridge. Veronica and Amanda Benson, the sensory manager at Deschutes, quickly identified off-flavors in every beer they poured, which made it seem like either the fridge had some bad juju or these two women had supertasting powers. I would put money on the latter. As soon as they said "canned corn" and "buttered popcorn," I smelled those aromas in a burst, but I could tell my senses were exhausted, worn down by round after round of Cascades. I longed to smell something neutral, and I remembered the back-of-your-hand trick. But when I put my nose to my hand, my skin smelled like oranges, lemons, and the broken leaf of an aloe plant. If only I could reset my senses by slipping into an oxygen mask, I thought. The Deschutes crew, on the other hand, was just getting going.

═══════

A few weeks later, back in Portland, I was standing under a tent at an old-timey amusement park with a rickety roller coaster on the banks of the Willamette River. The inside of my mouth felt coated with a dank, resinous residue verging on chewy. I was sampling dozens of fresh-hop beers, beers brewed with hops fresh from the field, not dried or pellet-ized. Soon after I had moved to Portland, I declared fresh-hop beers as one of the perks of living in the Pacific Northwest. Fresh hops must be added to a beer in progress within twenty-four hours of being picked, and since most brewers weren't yet chartering planes to carry fresh hops across states or countries, fresh-hop beers are still regional trea-sures. I looked forward to drinking them every fall; by November, the beers were usually gone or stale. You had to get them while you could.

Even though I'd tasted something like ten beers at this point—sip-ping each one then dumping the rest of it into a trash can so I could taste as many as possible—I had yet to find one beer that expressed my idea of the essence of fresh hops. I wanted to smell and taste the juiciness I'd seen inside the hop cones, along with some hint that the flavors came from a plant. My ideal fresh-hop beer hummed with the life of the bines, ladybugs, and harvesters. When I looked at the people around me, who were just drinking and relaxing on a sunny Saturday afternoon, I envied the way they seemed happy with what was in their glasses. But I'd had perfect fresh-hop beers in the past, ones that whispered the secret of the bine. They are rare, like a dish that expresses the personality of a fresh, ripe truffle. I kept searching. One beer took me tromping through damp grass. The next made my mouth tingle with spearmint and pine, like a mild toothpaste. By the time I unlocked my bike for the ride home, I felt just like I had at the end of hop selection: completely dull to all flavors and smells. So I put the back of my hand next to my nose and inhaled.

JOIN THE CROWD

The crowd makes the ballgame.
—TY COBB

SEPTEMBER MARKS THE END of one beer festival season and the beginning of another. Festival goers say good-bye to summer's shade tents and sausages grilled *en plein air*. They start to daydream about warm weather and begin eating sausages grilled indoors. September is the month of Oktoberfest in Munich and fresh-hop beer festivals in the Pacific Northwest. It also marks the annual Feast Portland, a four-day food and drink festival that includes gluttonous dinners made by famous chefs and workshops on how to butcher a pig and make your own cocktail ingredients.

This year, the beer programming for Feast Portland included a panel about lagers, and a woman named Sarah Jane Curran was listed as a panelist. Sarah had worked as the beer director at Eleven Madison Park, the famous Michelin three-star restaurant in New York City. The title of beer director is rare at fine dining restaurants not only in the United States but around the world. I had to meet her. Not only was I curious how a restaurant like Eleven Madison Park orders and serves beer, I wanted to meet a woman who'd made beer such an integral part of her career. I e-mailed her a few weeks before the festival, and we agreed to meet after the panel.

Sarah looked poised and professional on the stage as she fielded questions about how much water breweries use and the flavors of a Spanish beer. After the panel was over, I stood on the cement loading dock of the art museum drinking beer out of cans with Sarah and the other panelists.

"Come on!" brewer Van Havig said when he caught me and Sarah pouring our beers into a dump bucket before we left. "You're not going to drink that?" His teasing wouldn't prevent me from pacing myself. The Feast festival required endurance. As Sarah and I walked to a shaded bench in a long, rectangular park that stretches across the city like a green Band-Aid, the late afternoon sun illuminated the green canopy of hundred-year-old trees. After she graduated from the Culinary Institute of America in New York City, she told me, she got a job at Eleven Madison Park as a food runner, the starting position for everyone who works at the restaurant. That's when her fascination with beer blossomed. As she worked her way up the ranks, from assistant server to dining room manager, she joined "the beer team." Eventually she took charge of the beer program, which in my mind made her the ideal person to consult about beer and food pairings.

When I asked her how she'd recommend I study pairings for the Cicerone exam, she recommended challenging myself with unexpected pairings: an English bitter with Mexican food or a strong Belgian ale with pork.

"The Belgian ale is full of stone fruit flavors," she said, "so it's like peaches and barbecue."

I was starting to get hungry.

"Foie gras," she said bluntly.

"Really?" I replied. It was hard to imagine what kind of beer would work with such a rich food.

"Try it with a good gueuze," she said. "You'll thank me later."

Gueuze, a blend of aged lambics, which are spontaneously fermented beers that originated in Belgium, got us talking about travel. Sarah told me that, the one time she visited Belgium, she was there with non-beer drinkers. While she'd visited some of the world's finest art museums and eaten lots of waffles and exquisite chocolate, she hadn't visited a single brewery. I may have gasped. It was like she'd gone to Napoli and didn't eat the pizza.

Of all the countries in the world, Belgium has the strongest reputation for producing great beer with great variety, a result of the country's geography. Bordered by France, the Netherlands, Germany, and Luxembourg—and just ninety kilometers of sea away from the United Kingdom—Belgium is saturated by many cultures and traditions. The country had been a highway for soldiers, a sanctuary for monks, and fertile ground for brewers who have had the freedom to make beers with fruits and spices, wild yeast strains, and dark sugars, traditions that originated with Trappist monks and French farmers.

"Do you want to go to Belgium with me in the spring?" I blurted out, to my own surprise.

I hadn't been to Europe since I fell in love with beer, and when I came up with the idea of studying for the Cicerone exam, I dreamed about heading to The Continent, where I could learn about beer styles that aren't brewed in the United States and about a brewing history that goes back centuries before the Pilgrims ever arrived on Cape Cod—a landing spot historians say was chosen partly because the *Mayflower* was running out of beer. I considered going to England, Germany, or the Czech Republic, but I was leaning toward Belgium because I saw it as a place of contradictions. There, brewers seemed free from the strictures of German and English brewing traditions yet still tied to heritage beer recipes, antiquated equipment, and ancient hop farms. I also liked that Belgian brewers are notoriously rebellious and mock Americans' obsession with categorizing beers by style; I saw them as arrogant expressionists enamored with creation, not categorization. Also, there was one clear reason to choose Belgium: I love the country's beers, from tart lambics to spicy saisons.

But I'd wanted to visit Belgium by myself. Ever since my parents bought me a plane ticket to visit my grandparents across the country as a kid, unaccompanied, I'd loved traveling alone. As a journalist, I'd had all kinds of solo adventures, from hiring a guide to take me into the Ecuadorian Amazon in a dugout canoe to shadowing a truffle hunter in Istria, Croatia, who had four cell phones. But since Oscar was born, I'd stopped going on long trips. Oscar and Tony needed me at home. The few times I had traveled, I'd made my trips short, to New York City, Chicago, and some remote places in Oregon. So I'd been looking forward to my European beer trip as a chance to reconnect with everything I loved about traveling alone. Yet there I was, offering to sacrifice that experience to a woman I'd just met.

"Sure!" Sarah replied, before I had a chance to reconsider.

———————

Before the Belgium trip, I was planning one other solo excursion. On a sparkling October afternoon, I sat in the backseat of an airport shuttle van, between a tan man in a loud shirt that looked like it had seen a few Jimmy Buffett concerts and a twenty-something woman wearing librarian glasses and a hoodie. Normally, we'd have broken the ice by complaining about air travel—the delays and lack of leg-room—but since we were in Denver on the first day of the Great American Beer Festival (GABF), we had something else in common. Before I could find my seatbelt, the guy was showing me pictures on his phone of a broken glass carboy, a scene that should have included police tape: the innocent carboy looked like it had been slashed across its midsection. The guy, a junior high school science teacher from Pasadena who was attending the festival for the first time, said he hadn't dropped or even nudged the vessel when the top just came off, leaving murky brown wort pooling on his concrete patio.

"It was so crazy," he said, his face flushing with excitement. "I've never seen anything like it."

The woman to my left was a biology major who worked for a small brewery in the Upper Peninsula of Michigan. She told us that last winter the ground froze to a depth of eighty inches there. At first this fact seemed unrelated to beer, but she then revealed that the deep frost broke water lines, which prevented the brewery from making beer for a while. She too was a first-timer at GABF, but she seemed more experienced because she already had a hangover. Tonight, she told us, she'd be pouring her brewery's beers on the floor of the festival.

"I can't believe it," she said, shaking her head. "It's so exciting."

The Great American Beer Festival is the largest and most well-known beer festival in the United States, an event that has been happening since 1982. Like Renaissance fairs do for LARPers, GABF brings together people with a shared passion. In this case, celebrating that passion involves consuming a copious amount of beer. The

Brewers Association puts on the festival. The group planned to welcome 49,000 festival attendees this year, and Denver—already a craft beer hot spot—became a place of beer-pairing menus, shuttle buses with discounts for beer lovers, offshoot beer festivals, tap takeovers, and brewery tours. GABF felt like the perfect place to explore beer styles, something I hadn't yet started to really study. At the festival, I'd be able to taste dozens of styles of beer and have the chance to ask brewers questions about those beers right on the spot.

I was a bit embarrassed I still hadn't been to the biggest beer festival in the country, but I'll be honest: the idea of three days at this huge festival, at any beer festival, sounded like too much, mostly for my liver. In the weeks leading up to the event, I asked experienced festival goers for advice on surviving a multiday drinking event. One Portland brewer told me to drink lots of water between beers, the kind of tip that seems ridiculously obvious until a throbbing dehydration headache on day two. Another brewer told me to expect a GABF "bloated face" look.

"With the altitude and all the drinking, you just puff right up," he said.

"You mean Great American Beer Farts?" said Megan Flynn, former publisher and editor of *Beer West* magazine. Megan assigned me my first-ever beer story back in 2007, and since then we'd become good friends. "You'll see what I'm talking about," she said, without cracking a smile. I knew Megan wasn't a big fan of beer festivals ("She's more of a beer dinner kind of girl," one of our mutual friends had said), but I had a hard time imagining she'd invent a story about mass farting. There was only one way to find out.

━━━━━

Every year for more than three decades, the Great American Beer Festival has produced a timeline of the American craft beer movement, marking both superficial moments, like when brewers were allowed to put alcohol contents on labels (1995), and more profound changes, like when nearly 1,500 breweries showed up to serve beer at the festival (2001).

In the early 1980s, a Boulder resident named Charlie Papazian founded the festival. Those were the days when just a handful of domestic brewers were starting to produce small-batch beers, especially ales, marking a departure from the standard lagers that had built brands like Budweiser and MillerCoors.

When I called Charlie to hear his version of how the festival came to be, he told me GABF had its foundations in homebrewing. As an experienced homebrewer, Charlie helped create the fledgling American Homebrewers Association during a time when homebrewing was illegal in most states, thanks to residual legislation from Prohibition. In 1980, he told me, he heard a man with a British accent on the radio talking about Cascade hops as part of a Blitz-Weinhard advertisement. He asked around and discovered the guy was a British beer writer named Michael Jackson, the most important beer writer of the modern era. Charlie was already familiar with the writer; his girlfriend had gifted him Michael Jackson's book, *The World Guide to Beer*, which "blew his mind." Charlie tracked down Michael Jackson—a task that, without the Internet, took weeks—and invited him to attend the 1981 National Homebrewers Conference in Boulder. To Charlie's surprise, Jackson accepted, and he was present during a particular moment that Charlie told me stands out as important in the history of American craft brewing: American microbrewers stood on a stage and talked about their craft for the first time. (The term "microbrewer" and "microbrewery" dissolved in popularity during the 2000s, and became replaced by "craft brewer" and "craft breweries.") The two men became fast friends; later that year, Charlie visited the beer writer at his London home, and they went to the Great British Beer Festival together. A kernel began to germinate.

"If England could have a national festival that celebrates their beer culture, wouldn't it be cool to do something like that in the United States?" Charlie said, to which Jackson responded, "What beer would you possibly celebrate with?" It was a friendly joke, but one based in reality. Not many microbreweries existed in the United States, just a few pioneers, including Boulder Beer Co. and Sierra Nevada. But Charlie was determined. He and his homebrewer friends made a list of about forty beers that would be suitable for drinking at a celebration of small-batch, American-made beer, including Ballantine IPA and Narragansett Porter.

"Some of the breweries had beers called ales, which sometimes were not as distinctive as we would have liked," Charlie remembered. "We took what we could get."

The list included one beer made by a corporate giant: George Killian's Irish Red by Coors Brewing, which Charlie said was "really good in those days." Otherwise, the large corporate brewers didn't make beers the homebrewers deemed interesting, so the big boys weren't invited. The homebrewers publicized the new beer festival in their magazine, which postal workers delivered to three hundred people, many of whom had taken Charlie's homebrewing class in Boulder. A new beer bar sponsored the festival, as did a small organic market, which would be swallowed up by Whole Foods decades later. The first GABF was held in 1982 at the Harvest House Hotel in Boulder; eight hundred people showed up to drink beer from twenty-two breweries.

Until 1985 the Great American Beer Festival and the National Homebrewers Conference were one and the same. Even for the year after the festival moved from Boulder to Denver, the two were combined. Eventually, splitting the conference and the festival into two events, plus changing the location, proved problematic. "The reception [in Denver] was not as enthusiastic as it was here in Boulder," Charlie said.

Organizers worked hard to spread the word. In fact, until six or seven years ago, the GABF scrambled to sell tickets, even on the day of the event. Times have changed: tickets for the 2014 GABF sold out in thirty-two minutes.

Charlie told me the early days of GABF served an important purpose for commercial brewers, both today's pioneers and yesterday's weirdos. "You had to be persistent, psychologically," he said. "It's hard to do something when everyone thinks you're crazy."

The beer fest was a lifeline that gave new professional brewers support and what Charlie called "renewed energy," a reminder that they were part of something bigger. A new American beer culture was dawning.

Microbrewers of the 1980s struggled, not only with the cultural perception that their beers and business models were strange, but also with a jungle of laws and misconceptions about beer that had roots in one of the most radical pieces of U.S. legislation: Prohibition. Before the Eighteenth Amendment to the U.S. Constitution prohibited the production, sale, and transportation of "intoxicating liquors," a law that went into effect in 1920, the country boasted a full century of German-influenced beer brewing, especially on the East Coast.

John Wagner, a Bavarian immigrant, brought lager yeast with him on his voyage from Europe to the United States in 1840. He made his home in Philadelphia, where he started brewing with the bottom-fermented yeast, which ferments at cooler temperatures than ale yeasts, making beers that were a notable departure from the city's famous ales. Today, a plaque at the site of Wagner's house, where he did his brewing, reads: AMERICA'S FIRST LAGER. Then August Krug formed a brewery in Milwaukee, which became Schlitz Brewing Co., and George Schneider started the brewery in Saint Louis that would become Anheuser-Busch. Lagers quickly became popular all over the country.

In 1810, 140 breweries were operating in the United States. By 1873, 4,131 breweries were making beer. This would be the largest number of breweries ever to operate in this country. While the number of breweries declined in the years leading up to Prohibition as a result of consolidations and the creep of dry states, the thirteen-year ban on alcohol production would forever alter the American brewing landscape. When Prohibition was repealed in 1933 with the passage of the Twenty-first Amendment, breweries that had survived those years by producing things like ice cream and malt extract fired up brew kettles once again. But many of them wouldn't survive the next few decades; the beer brewing landscape had changed.

During the fifty years between the end of Prohibition and the first Great American Beer Festival, the U.S. beer industry became dominated by large corporate breweries, the model that still defines the American beer landscape today. But the craft brewing market share is inching into mass-market beer territory every year, which has prompted the recent spate of acquisitions of small breweries by larger corporate breweries, a trend that has beer lovers and journalists debating about the merits of the word "craft" and the concept of quality. What does it mean if a great beer is being made by a small or mid-sized brewery owned by Anheuser-Busch InBev? Does it make the beer less great?

When I think about mass-produced beer in the United States during the twentieth century, two images come to mind. One is an advertisement from 1952, an illustration of a young woman holding a smoking skillet and wiping tears from her eyes. Her dashing husband has his arm around her shoulder. The copy reads:

"Anyway, you didn't burn the Schlitz!"
There's hope for any young bride who knows her man well enough to serve him Schlitz Beer. For what man (or woman) can resist the taste of Schlitz Beer.

Two bottles of Schlitz sit on the table with two empty pilsner glasses and dinner plates. At least the young bride gets her own beer, I thought.

The other image, a photograph, shows Ronald Reagan standing among four men with perfectly coiffed hair and gleaming white teeth. The year was 1954, and the picture was part of a series of commercials Reagan did for Pabst, which explains why he is wearing a starched apron with a Pabst blue ribbon seal on the front. Reagan's biographer, Bob Woodward, described the commercials as a low point in the actor's career, which probably had no correlation with the quality of the beer. But Reagan's apron strings are untied and his hands hang limply by his side. For me, his posture of defeat encapsulates that era in beer.

Flash forward to the 1980s. Reagan was the fortieth president, and many of the one hundred or so breweries in the United States had names Americans will find familiar today: Miller, Anheuser-Busch,

Coors, and Pabst. But a nascent beer industry was bubbling under the surface, one greatly influenced by Charlie Papazian. There's no better place to witness what he started than on the floor of the Great American Beer Festival.

———

The inside of the Colorado Convention Center in Denver has the acoustics of an airplane hangar and the charm of a Costco. The main room was arranged to support a singular activity: serving 5,601 beers from more than 1,300 breweries to anyone who had a ticket and could hold a glass. I had a media pass, which came with two important perks: skipping the lines to get into the festival and the option to enter fifteen minutes before the public. Those things didn't mean much to me on day one. In fact, I didn't even arrive in time to use those extra minutes, a mistake I wouldn't make again.

The floor was organized by breweries' geographical regions, from the Pacific Northwest to the Southeast. Experienced festival goers advised me to enter with a plan, to know exactly which booths I wanted to visit before I stepped onto the floor. After all, this was my chance to try beers that weren't distributed in Oregon. For the most part, beer distribution in the United States is divided into east and west; it's hard for West Coasters to find most East Coast beers, and vice versa. Because Oregonians prefer to drink locally made beers, I was living in a strange beer bubble filled with wonderful Oregon beers and not much else.

Because I ignored the advice to have a plan, I was immediately overwhelmed. Should I immerse myself in one region or try all the beers of a certain style? I started wandering. Under the numbing glare of fluorescent lights, I noticed I was in the Oregon aisle, which felt like a relief. I saw familiar faces at most of the booths, and I saw familiar beers. I stopped at the Barley Brown's Beer table. The brewery, which is located in a rural part of the state, consistently goes home with medals from the festival's competition. This year's medal winners wouldn't be announced for a few days, but this was my chance to taste some superior beers that might catch the judges' attention. A volunteer filled my glass to the one-ounce tasting line, the specified volume of each pour at GABF. The beer, Hand Truck Pale Ale, a gold medal winner in 2013, hit my tongue with a burst of grapefruit and the sticky texture of resinous hops, the comfort food of beer for a Pacific Northwesterner. The brewery was pouring four other beers, and while I wanted to try them all, I reminded myself that there were hundreds of other beers to try. Even so, I asked for a pour of a wheat beer, another gold medal winner, before walking away.

I started pin-balling between Oregon booths. I'd chat and drink, then chat and drink. I came across brewer Van Havig telling another journalist about aging beers in gin barrels. I told Van I was already feeling overwhelmed by the number of beers I wanted to try.

"It's like being a shark surrounded by sardines," he said.

After Oregon, I ended up at the Firestone Walker booth, where I tried the Bretta Rose, a refreshing Berliner weisse (a tart and fruity style that originated in the Berlin area) fermented with raspberries and aged in French oak "puncheons," which are large barrels, or casks. Not only was I drinking beer, I was learning new words! I clung to my festival guide and pen as though they were golden compasses. I couldn't see any clocks, which made me feel like I was in a casino or a grocery store, and I started to wish they'd dim the fluorescent lights even a little bit. I mean, we were drinking beer!

My bag and coat felt heavy, so I headed to the Oregon Brewers

Guild booth and asked if I could stash my stuff behind some kegs. Before I left, I noticed they were pouring a couple of fresh-hop Oregon beers. How could I pass up the chance to drink those? After more wandering, I waited for Dogfish Head beer in a line two-people wide, a human barrier that would have made Greenpeace proud. I laughed out loud. There's something ridiculous about standing in line for a beer in a place where hundreds of beers are available without a wait.

Among U.S. craft brewers, Dogfish Head is like Kim Kardashian, a high-profile media darling who's loved or hated, depending on whom you ask. Sam Calagione founded the brewery in 1995 with the tagline "off-centered ales for off-centered people." The brewery has produced a range of interesting beers, many of which were created in honor of historical moments and rare ingredients. For example, a beer called Pangaea is brewed with ingredients from every continent, including basmati rice from Asia and crystallized ginger from Australia. Midas Touch was brewed in accordance with the chemical analysis of residues in clay vessels found in King Midas' tomb. The brewery's best-selling beer, the 60 Minute IPA, is an India pale ale named after the sixty hop additions made during a sixty-minute boil. The beer also happens to have sixty International Bitterness Units (IBUs). The brewery is highly successful, yet beer geeks deride many of the brews for being unbalanced and undrinkable, the product of a focus on concept, not quality.

I squinted to see the list of beers hanging behind the table. There was Beer Thousand, a collaboration with the band Guided by Voices, which was made with ten grains and ten hops and measured 10 percent alcohol by volume (ABV). The word *chicha* caught my eye. I'd tried chicha in Peru and Ecuador, so I already knew the fermented beverage is often made with saliva. People chew grains, usually corn, and the enzymes in their saliva begin to breakdown the starches in the grain into maltose, a type of sugar. To make the Dogfish Head version, which includes Peruvian peppercorns, yellow and purple maize, and soursop fruit, brewery employees chewed the purple maize and spit it out, then added it to the mash. A video on the brewery's website shows Sam chewing the stuff. (The corn was then sterilized by the brewing process, so anyone wanting to come in direct contact with Sam's mouth bacteria would have to find another way.)

As I got closer to the front of the line, I felt a gravitational pull, not only to the sloshing beer in pitchers but to Sam himself, a man with a slightly off-center smile, clean-shaven face, and the kind of life-of-the-party persona that seems appropriate for someone who makes beer for a living. He's been profiled in the *New Yorker*, and he starred in the Discovery Channel series *Brew Masters*. Tonight, he beamed as he poured beer and shook hands. If any babies were around, he'd have been kissing them. When my moment finally arrived, my glass was filled to the pour line with Dogfish's Chicha, which tasted tangy and felt watery. Its earthy aftertaste made me want to brush my teeth.

I couldn't resist saying hello to Sam. I'd interviewed him by phone a few years earlier for a story on how terroir—the French notion that an agricultural product, particularly wine, holds a perceptible expression of place—applies to beer. From where I stood, terroir in beer was just beginning to be acknowledged. A few brewers were growing their own hops and barley, and some were fermenting beers with fruits grown near their breweries. To my surprise, Sam, a man who brewed beers designed to capture places and moments in time, told me that, because beer is a collection of multiple ingredients that are usually sourced from a wide geography, it's the brewers that are the

common element. "For us *terroir* has less to do with the dirt underneath the breweries where we make our beer," he'd said, "and more
to do with the gray matter in the brewers' heads." If terroir is an expression of the brewer, Dogfish Head beers are a product of Sam's
terroir of self.

He remembered we'd talked about wine.

"What are you drinking?" he asked.

"The Chicha."

"Oh, try the Black and Blue," he said, filling my tasting glass almost to the top.

He was right. I should have been drinking the Black and Blue, a
tart and rich beer that was so heavy with blackberries and raspberries, I wanted an accompanying tart crust and a dollop of whipped
cream.

"Do you want us to take your picture?" said the guy who'd been
waiting behind me in line.

It took me a second to realize that he wanted to take a picture of
me and Sam, which felt strange. I wasn't a run-of-the-mill fan; I was
a journalist who was studying for a serious beer test. What business
did I have taking a picture with Sam Calagione? I could always blame
the photo on my sister-in-law, who had a fermenter-sized crush on
the brewer, a holdover from his reality-show days.

"Uh, sure," I said. Sam and I put our arms around each others'
shoulders and smiled at the back of my phone, as though we were
long-lost friends.

"If you need more beer, come to the side," he said, nodding at my
glass. Just as quickly as he'd said hello, he was hugging a woman with
a red bob and reminiscing about the time they did something they
both found hilarious.

I walked away from the booth feeling disoriented. My glass felt sticky in my hand. I had planned to peruse the floor of GABF like a serious student, someone with a plan and a rigorous system of note taking and photo documentation. Instead I was getting drunk on whatever beer ended up in my glass and taking fan photos with Sam Calagione. I paused to send the photo to my sister-in-law, with the caption: "Just ran into your boyfriend." A few minutes later, my phone buzzed with an "OMG!!" At least someone thought I was doing it right. I could always redeem myself tomorrow, I thought as I waited in line for a Belgian-style beer from Austin, Texas. Its geography made me pause. Sure, Belgian yeasts produce a distinct set of flavors, but if I believed a beer was the sum of its parts, including the place where it was made, a Belgian beer made in Texas would be like a Swiss watch made in New Jersey. But I let the Texas beer fill in a new area of my mind. After all, we are living in a liquid world, where Texas and Belgium can harmonize in a single brew tank.

As the night went on, I started to feel affection for the thousands of people who were getting rowdy on the festival floor. They loved beer and weren't afraid to express their devotion to the drink. For starters, they'd each paid eighty dollars for a ticket that bought them an unlimited amount of one-ounce pours. But the beer was only part of what they'd purchased. They wanted to commune with their ilk, people who wore comfortable shoes in anticipation of a day of beer drinking and maybe even waxed their beards to resemble a hop cone. These were people who wore Mardi Gras beads in October, necklaces strung with stale pretzels, foam hats shaped like beer steins, and all manner of authentic and inauthentic lederhosen. They weren't afraid to make out under the convention center's florescent lights or do karaoke on a stage. They were loud, happy, and without a doubt, they farted. More obviously, they belched a lot. The more beer I drank, the more I started to hear their burps as signs of appreciation.

These beer lovers possessed an impressive ability to wait in long lines. They waited in lines to enter the convention center, to buy brewery T-shirts, and to use the bathroom. (The festival is one of those rare places where the men's bathroom line vastly out-snakes the women's.) They waited in lines for beer—the ones they'd tell their friends about later—and convention center hotdogs and pizza, which would never again be mentioned. As I waited in a slow-moving line for some samples of cheese, I chatted with a man who made six-pack holders that were also wooden puzzles. That's when I realized my time in the hall had transformed me from an impartial observer of an amped up, magnified arena of beer to a member of a welcoming community. I liked meeting people while I waited in lines, where we talked about which festival beers were worth trying and which were overly hyped. As I looked down at my comfortable boots, I gave myself credit for choosing proper beer-drinking shoes. For a moment, I even had a vision of myself wearing a bier stein hat at next year's GABF, an event I vowed not to miss.

En route to the exit minutes before the festival would close for the night, I noticed a booth with the Cicerone logo. I stopped at the booth and flipped through some sobering study booklets, one of which covered beer styles of Germany. Instantly, my bubbly feeling of inclusion evaporated. Not only did the book remind me of everything I didn't know, which made me feel like an outsider, it also reminded me that, by committing to taking the Cicerone exam, I'd signed up to make beer less fun. Right then, it was obvious what was fun: drinking beer at the GABF with a bunch of beer-obsessed strangers. Memorizing a technical primer on beer styles I didn't usually drink would feel more like scrubbing a bathtub or filing my taxes. The lanky gray-haired man behind the table was wearing a GABF pass that said RAY DANIELS, who is the man who created the Cicerone program.

I told Ray I was studying for the Certified Cicerone exam, and he told me about a man who, while preparing for the exam, developed severe test anxiety.

"It got so bad he had to see a therapist!" he said, laughing loudly as he tilted his head back. I mentally recorded the sound so I could replay it for hints of sinister motives while I made flashcards during the coming months.

"Wow," I said. "That's crazy."

"On the day of the test, it's pretty simple," he said. "Either you know it or you don't."

"So, there's no faking it," I said, as I wavered between buying the German beer booklet and remaining blissfully ignorant.

"Nope."

———

On Saturday morning, the last day of GABF, I prepared to reenter the convention center by tromping around downtown Denver in search of a green juice or something else that would make me feel ready to drink beer for a whole day, yet again. Along the way, I walked through air pockets of pot aromas, a pungent reminder that I was in Colorado. As I entered the windowless auditorium in the convention center, I was surrounded by throngs of bearded men wearing their best brewery-logo gear. Many of them scanned the crowd expectantly and laughed with a forced laugh, a sure sign of nerves. We were about to learn who won this year's GABF medals.

A majority of GABF medals are awarded by beer style, in categories such as American-Style Pale Ale or Oatmeal Stout. Over the years, the gold, silver, and bronze medals have become important marketing tools that help garner media attention and boost beer sales. Sometimes medals have helped open the checkbooks of deep-pocketed investors. In other words, medals matter. Some breweries strategize to make beers that could win. For example, a beer in the American-Style Dark Lager category will compete against fewer entries than a beer entered for American-Style Pale Ale, so entering the dark lager category creates better odds.

Charlie Papazian told me the idea of the festival as a marketing tool for brewers began in 1985, when festival attendees were asked to vote on their favorite beer from the event. "There was a lot of maneuvering by breweries to get as many votes as possible," he said.

Two years later, the festival switched to judges handing out medals for specific styles, which was a milestone. "We created a paradigm shift in the way people thought of beer," Charlie explained. "Before that, competitions weren't organized by style but by alcohol content, dark or light, and draft or bottles." Even a year earlier, the concept might have fallen flat, he said, but by 1987, craft beer consumers knew enough about beer to accept the idea of excellence within style categories.

Since then, the general idea of classifying beers within style parameters has blossomed, especially in the United States. Unlike the periodic table, which receives additions based on quantifiable scientific discoveries, the beer-style framework varies by organization, brewer, and beer drinker. While beers can be identified using science to quantify color, carbonation, bitterness, and so on, your idea of an IPA might be someone else's American pale ale. One of the most well-known sets of style guidelines is produced by the Beer Judge Certification Program (BJCP), an organization that certifies beer judges for homebrew competitions. The organization was founded in 1985, and it's produced style guidelines ever since—an accomplishment based not only in a knowledge of the technicalities of brewing but also in the ability to corral various beer professionals into consensus on thousands of debatable parameters, including the aroma, appearance, flavor, mouthfeel, ingredients, and history of more than one hundred styles. All the beers at the GABF would be judged by style according to a similar set of parameters that were created just for the GABF competition.

Ever since I'd arrived in Denver, I'd been noticing the judges who'd choose the winning beers. (They were easy to spot, because they always seemed to be wearing lanyards with nametags that announced their title.) I saw judges early in the morning, in the elevator of my hotel, and late at night, shuffling around the city. They always looked tired and slightly forlorn, like security guards at an amusement park who have to work while everyone else is having fun. For the fifteenth time, John Harris was one of the judges at GABF.

A few weeks earlier, I'd ridden my bike to Ecliptic to ask John about judging. Not only was I curious about the process as a beer drinker who was trying to come to terms with importance of the medals, I had also developed a strange new fantasy: I wanted to be a GABF judge someday, something I wasn't ready to admit out loud. Being part of a professional beer-judging panel at this point felt highly aspirational. As we sat the bar and I drank a Belgian-style pale ale brewed with raspberries and cacao nibs, John told me the first time he'd judged the competition was in 1992, three years after he'd entered his first beer in the competition. When he talked about the seven GABF medals he's won for beers he made at various Oregon breweries, he sounded unapologetically proud, which correlates with his experience as a judge; he knows it's hard to win. When judges enroll, they're asked to disclose any conflict of interest, which includes listing any beers entered into the competition that they made. Brewers never judge their own beers, but John said it wouldn't matter if he did. He'd never recognize his own beer in the lineup. I was shocked. If he, the creator, couldn't recognize his own beers by taste, did that make those beers run-of-the-mill? I hoped he didn't mean what he said. Maybe he was just trying to help me understand the palate-dulling process of judging.

To apply to become a judge, you have to submit recommendations from people who are familiar with how you evaluate beer. If you qualify, you're put on a waiting list that's a few years long. Judges aren't in it for the money. They're paid in meals and lodging, and they must share a room with another judge. John usually shares a room with Garrett Oliver, the dapper brewmaster at Brooklyn Brewery who's known for wearing tailored suits and bow ties. I'd never seen John in anything other than T-shirts and shorts. But just because they are style opposites doesn't mean they aren't simpatico roommates. "He knows if I snore, and I know if he snores," John told me.

Every year, judging happens according to precisely the same schedule. Judges evaluate beer during 3.5-hour sessions—two a day on the Wednesday and Thursday of GABF, and one on Friday. They eat breakfast and lunch together at a supplied buffet. "It's all about getting your base," John said, patting his stomach.

That base is no joke. To evaluate dozens of beers without eating could lead to drunkenness and foolish errors in judgment. The final four-hour judging session took place on Friday morning, the judges were let loose to enjoy the festival, if they had any desire to drink beer ever again.

When beers are received for judging, a team sorts and boxes the entries quickly in order to protect them from light, which can create off-flavors. (For that reason, the judging room has low light, just enough to see the color of the beer.) All beer is stored at 38 degrees until the moment of judging. It's up to judges to warm beer that should be served at a warmer temperature by holding the cups in their hands. A team of stewards pours and presents all beers to the judges based on instructions from brewers, such as "Do not rouse this beer" or "Rouse this beer." Stewards pour the beer samples and serve them to a table of judges on a tray in less than twelve minutes. The instant a beer leaves its bottle, its flavors and aromas begin to change.

Judges taste by style, in a sequence determined by palate fatigue. They begin with the least palate-wrecking beers—beers with lower alcohol and less bitterness—and end with heavy hitters like Russian imperial stout. Creating the schedule for the judges takes one person forty hours. As though it were 1972, judges write first-round comments and tasting notes on carbon-copy evaluation forms. Eventually one copy of each completed form is mailed to the brewer, and one is filed in GABF competition archives. Judges are identified by numbers so they remain anonymous. The judges sit at tables in groups of six or seven, and a Table Captain keeps everyone on schedule. Judges caught using smartphones during judging, even in the hallway during breaks, are asked to leave for the day. "You could be communicating with another judge across the room, or someone outside," explained John. "You don't want anything to compromise the integrity of the process."

John told me the judging room is a high-pressure environment. Not only do judges need to stay extremely focused, they need to be aware of their own sensory fatigue. "Your brain gets shot," he said. "It's like, 'Oh, I taste caramel again.'"

Interacting with fellow judges can be another challenge, especially since most have divergent opinions and annoying habits, like writing slowly or breathing heavily.

But what I really wanted to know, especially when I thought about being a judge myself, was: what made a winning beer? How did John know when he'd found a winner?

"You have to have the most boringly unique beer possible," he replied.

He explained that a medal winner usually has a middle range of attributes for its style, which helped the judges agree that the beer was brewed to style. At the same time, the beer needed to stand out. I tried to imagine what that meant for the India Pale Ale category, which had 279 entries this year. An extra dose of pine aroma? The kind of bitterly dry finish that would scrub a tired palate clean?

The preface to the BJCP guidelines notes to "allow for some flexibility in judging so that well-crafted examples can be rewarded." Their rules are suggestions, not hard limits. The guide also mentions that not every beer in the world falls into a style category. Those are the beers that wear black leather jackets and smoke cigarettes under the bleachers during Friday night football games, outliers that refuse to be categorized. While I enjoy encountering those rebel beers, which inspire other brewers to create their own mash-ups and contradictions, such as a "hefepils" or bitter gose (an unfiltered wheat beer made with coriander and salt), I knew that my quest to become a Certified Cicerone would require knowing, and respecting, at least one beer-style canon.

Learning so many beer styles by spring seemed daunting, so before leaving for the GABF I had decided to form a study group. I was inspired by my friend Ryan, who'd studied for the Master Sommelier test. He'd told me how in his wine study group, which met every couple of weeks, one group member presented on a single style each meeting. Then everyone tasted examples of that style together. Unfortunately, I didn't actually know anyone who was studying for the Certified Cicerone exam, and I had a hard time imagining anyone else would take the group seriously if a test score wasn't hanging in the balance (because that's how I function). Then I remembered Portland beer writer Adrienne So, who'd mentioned months ago that she was considering getting her certification. At the time, she said she was interested in being my study buddy. I was a fan of her work, especially a story she wrote for *Slate* called "Against Hoppy Beers," which outlined how craft brewers were alienating beer drinkers with their overzealous use of hops. The piece generated the kind of uproar you'd expect from an editorial on abortion or gun control, complete with reactionary pieces including "Lazy Beer Writers Are Ruining Craft Beer for the Rest of Us." Obviously, she'd presented a theory that was an affront to the beer geek's way of life. I liked that she'd stirred the pot.

By the time we finally got together, Adrienne was three months pregnant.

"One of the side effects is that alcohol and caffeine taste like sulfurous fish barf right now," she'd told me in an e-mail. "But that shouldn't get in the way of the studying and research part."

I was relieved she still wanted to study with me, because I desperately needed some accountability. When she arrived at a beer bar we had chosen in North Portland wearing an oversized hooded sweatshirt and carrying a backpack, I had a flashback to some ill-advised college study sessions in bars, which were never remotely productive. Even though this was a different situation entirely, beginning with the fact that one of us was pregnant, I was reminded of the inherent conflict that comes from having to approach beer, something consumed to diminish one's perception, with heightened senses. We asked the bartender for a few tastes of beers on tap, including the Imperial Doughnut Break from Evil Twin Brewing, an inky porter made by a famous Danish gypsy brewery.

"Interesting," Adrienne said, smacking her lips. "It really does taste cakey."

The beer was fermented in barrels stuffed with actual donuts, an ironic preface to our discussion of beer styles. We were hoping to better understand how beers belong in well-defined categories, but unless there are "pastry ale" parameters, this one surely landed out of bounds.

I ordered a pint, payment for the table space we'd occupy for a few hours, and we started making flashcards packed with acronyms— OG (original gravity), FG (final gravity), ABV (alcohol by volume), and IBUs (International Bitterness Units)—and the numbered ranges of each that define different beer styles. After about thirty minutes, my hand was cramping and my cards were slightly illegible. Even though Adrienne was in her thirties, her cursive handwriting made it look like she grew up without a keyboard. Making the flashcards had me thinking about how the evolution of beer styles corresponded with the development of an increasingly complex world.

During the Middle Ages, women brewed in their kitchens as part of their standard domestic duties. They weren't trying to create specific levels of bitterness or color; they simply brewed with what they had, the available ingredients of the day. (I like to think they had the capability to finesse their brews to suit their own tastes.) The development of commercial brewing helped delineate styles, but even so, brewers made beer based on available ingredients. As ingredients became more refined, brewers had the luxury of tailoring recipes to meet the public's tastes.

In the city of Plzeň in Bohemia, where commercial beer was first brewed in the early 1300s, the mid-1800s finally revealed a problem: the town's brewery made horrible beer. City officials came up with a solution: they tore down the brewery, built a new one, and recruited a German brewer named Josef Groll to take the helm. He started brewing a lighter-colored beer using a pale malt now called pilsner malt, Saaz hops, and a lager yeast. The new style, pilsner, became a worldwide sensation thanks to the happy blend of available ingredients and the public's thirst for a lighter-colored beer. Brewers in other parts of Europe began recreating the beer, with variations caused by things like the levels of carbonates and salt in their local water.

Money influenced the development of beer styles, especially taxes. In eighteenth-century England, the new availability of coal meant brewers had more access to malt that was free of the smoky flavors and aromas that pervaded malts made in wood-fired kilns. But for a while, high taxes on coal made the lighter, less smoky malt a more expensive ingredient. I imagined a British brewer poring over handwritten ledgers before pounding his fist on a rough wooden pub table: "There must be a way to make lighter beers!" he'd cry. Still, some brewers paid for the more expensive, lighter colored malt, which resulted in early versions of British pale ales and bitters. Since breweries had to charge more for the lighter beers, porter— made with the malts dried over straw or wood—became the working man's drink.

As Randy Mosher explains in *Tasting Beer*—the quintessential study aid I was now carrying with me everywhere—British beers became weaker once the malt tax was abolished in 1880. At that point the British government began charging brewers based on the original gravity of their wort, the amount of residual sugars suspended in the liquid, a number that portends how much alcohol the final beer will contain. The less residual sugars, the less brewers were taxed, a system that led to the rise of English "bitters," essentially pale ales with low alcohol.

As Adrienne and I made more flashcards, I flipped through my *BJCP Style Guidelines,* which mentions some of the reasons why specific beer styles are being made today—either as interpretations of historical styles or modern inventions. But the full equation, which takes into account the cost and availability of ingredients, production methods, and government regulations, isn't spelled out entirely. If every influence were listed, Great American Beer Festival medals would most surely be mentioned.

Even though it wasn't yet ten o'clock in the morning, a lot of people at the medal ceremony were drinking beer, which was being served just outside the doors of the convention center's auditorium in a frenzy. The rest of us clutched cups of coffee. I ended up sitting between two men: a beer book publisher and a brewer from Columbus, Ohio. Colorado's governor, John Hickenlooper, delivered the welcome address, not only because of his political rank but also because he was a bona fide member of the craft beer community. Hickenlooper cofounded Denver's Wynkoop Brewing in 1988, and as he told the crowd, he brewed his first batch of homebrew in 1971, "only a few months after Charlie did." Last year, Hickenlooper said he'd had four beer taps installed in the governor's mansion, a fact that could only help his current reelection campaign. (He'd eke out a win four weeks later.)

"This is based off a quote by writer Damon Runyon, my father's favorite writer," he said, raising a festival glass filled with amber-colored beer. "The race is not always to the swift nor the battle to the strong, but that's the way to bet. And I'm betting on all of you."

Finally, the announcement of the medals began. Out of 5,000-plus beers, 271 beers would win medals in ninety-three categories.

"271 medals?" I muttered.

"Yeah, it always takes a while," the book publisher said. Now I understood the frenzy in the beer-serving area. We were going to be here for hours.

The protocol went like this: after winners were announced, they'd head to the stage, where Charlie Papazian would hand them their medals and they'd pause for a photo. Charlie warned brewers not to shake his hand but instead go for a fist bump; excited brewers had nearly crushed his hand in the past. I remembered how he'd told me he always sensed the nerves in the audience. "You can feel the vibrations of all those people in the room, stressing out about if they're going to make it up on that stage," he said.

I saw a bunch of Oregon brewers sitting together, a nice show of camaraderie, although I suspected they hadn't left their competitive spirits at the door. I felt my heart race for a brief moment. For the first time since I had learned about GABF medals, I understood how important the medals were to brewers, people I knew and hoped would succeed. When winners were announced, there were hoots, hollers, cheers, and celebratory dances to the stage followed by fist bumps with Charlie Papazian and photos. After the announcement of each Oregon win, the state's brewers hugged and high-fived each other.

Then it was time for the American-Style India Pale Ale winners. With 279 entries, it was the biggest category ever at the Great American Beer Festival. I didn't need to calculate the odds to know it was also the most competitive category. Oregon's Breakside Brewery had just won a bronze medal for American-Style Strong Pale Ale, so brewmaster Ben Edmunds and his crew were close to the stage. Before the announcer had the chance to break the news, the name of the gold-medal winner for the American IPA category flashed on the screen: Breakside Brewery. The crowd went wild.

When the ceremony finally ended, I walked alongside the brewers who'd stuck it out for every last medal as we followed a troupe of bagpipe players (another storied GABF tradition) to the festival floor, which was already buzzing with beer drinkers when we arrived. That's when I saw John Harris, who hadn't won any medals. "It would have been nice to win," he said, shrugging off disappointment, then wandering down the aisle toward the Oregon section.

Volunteers were adding medal stickers to the booths serving the winning beers, and the lines at those booths seemed the longest. Those kegs would soon be emptied. Even though beer judging isn't a science and style categories are debatable, medals do matter. Because, when it comes down to it, everyone wants to drink the best.

———

The next morning at the airport, where presumably everyone had dumped their legalized weed in favor of air-friendly edibles, the greasy clamminess of a collective hangover hovered over the check-in areas and security lines, as haggard-looking and foul-smelling beer lovers endured the last lines of the weekend. It wasn't yet eight o'clock, and I was one of them. I could almost hear John Harris's voice, echoing from some distant place. "Always leave GABF on Saturday night," he'd admonished. "You do not want to be at the airport on Sunday morning."

At the Pizza Hut nearest to my gate, while I ordered a box of wedge-shaped, seasoned fries and a Pepsi, I vowed to follow all of John's advice in the future. A bunch of Oregon brewers were on my flight. Before we boarded, they filled their water bottles with shaky hands and kept conversations brief. "I may have overdone it," one told me, avoiding eye contact.

As our tube of stale, sweaty air roared across a few Western states, I closed my eyes and tried not to notice the distinct smell.

CONTAINED AND DRAINED

An empty vessel makes the loudest sound.
—PLATO

CHRISTMAS WAS APPROACHING, and my dream of being the person who arrives at holiday parties, not with a plate of home-made cookies, but with a beer I'd brewed myself, was being silently squashed by a glass carboy wearing a T-shirt. Filled with the beer I'd brewed almost two weeks earlier, the carboy was a near-constant re-minder that I needed to get its dark, murky liquid into bottles before the tan layer of sediment on the bottom started to create strange fla-vors in the beer.

I'd come up with the vision of being a holiday beer fairy after lis-tening to my industrious DIY friends talk about the knitting and can-ning gifts they'd be doling out to friends. Until then, Tony and I had brewed only hop-forward pale ales and one red ale. I was ready for a deviation. What if I could create a beer that embodied the season—the fruitcake of beers—without tasting like cinnamon or cloves, the typical "holiday ale" flavor profile? Ever since Lady Brew Portland, I'd been thinking about how I would make a conscious effort to be in charge of our next brew session. After all, I was the student of beer. I'd start by going to the homebrew shop and choosing the recipe.

"I'm going to the homebrew shop," I yelled to Tony over the heavy bass line vibrating from the stereo. I was standing in the doorway of his shop, bundled up for the five-minute bike ride. He was holding Oscar up to the milling machine, so he could see the levers.

"Mama," Oscar squealed as he craned his neck to try to see me. I was relieved to see he was wearing a pair of Tony's safety goggles. "We're cutting metal!"

"Sounds good!" Tony shouted at me. "Did you see if we have Star San?"

"Oh right," I replied. In fact, I hadn't checked any of our staple supplies, including the sanitizer. If I was going to be a successful brewmaster, I needed to remember these details.

At the homebrew shop, I plopped down in a comfortable armchair and set a thick binder of recipes in my lap. The recipes were organized by style, and almost by accident, I turned to stouts, the style that many historians consider to be the progeny of porters. In England during the 1700s, porters were the hearty, unrefined, brown, and smoky beer that quenched the thirst of the working class in that country. Because the porters of the day were so rough and inconsistent, most breweries blended different batches of the beer to create a single, palatable beer with a suitable strength. By 1799 a brewery in Dublin called Guinness began brewing a "stouter kind of porter," a clear connection in the shared history of the two dark styles.

I liked the simplicity of one stout recipe in the book, but the beer it produced would have just 3 to 4 percent ABV, which seemed like a cruel Christmas gift. The gift receiver would drink one and just want another. Then I saw it: an oatmeal stout with a few kinds of malts, which offered the promise of complexity, and with a 5-plus ABV, a better gift. The oats were in a bin between dozens of kinds of malt, which made them look like just another granular food in a variant shade of brown. I scooped some oats into a plastic bag as though I were planning to make oatmeal. In late Medieval times, oats and spices were common in beers brewed specifically for the poor, but as time progressed, healing properties were attributed to the grain. In England in the late 1800s, oatmeal stouts were sold as nourishment for invalids and the chronically ill. These days, we know that, because oats contain high amounts of proteins and oils, they create a creamy mouthfeel in beer, plus a foamy head. The trick is not to brew with too many oats, which can turn into a gluey mess in the mash tun.

Later that afternoon, Tony and I pulled out the brewing equipment from the basement and started the slow process of bringing a giant kettle of water to a boil on our stove. I poured the cracked grains and oats into a cotton mesh bag and tied a top knot. I'd decided to deviate from the recipe, a first in my homebrewing history. In order to make the beer drier, I replaced a malt that would have created nutty and biscuity flavors with some Crystal 120L, a less bready and more chocolatey malt I hoped would add notes of bittersweet chocolate dipped in caramel. It was the holidays, after all.

Oscar wanted to help. He pulled a chair over to the stove, and we lowered the mesh bag into the water together. On impact, a black cloud seeped from the bag.

"Look!" he said excitedly. "It's turning into beer!"

After the grains steeped for awhile, I pulled the bag out of the water with metal tongs and held it, dripping, over the pot. "Now pour the water from the teakettle over the malt, slowly," I told Tony.

"Whatever you say," Tony replied, as he gently poured the water, which had just boiled, through the steaming, water-logged mass of malt. "You're in charge."

The guy at the homebrew shop had told me about this teakettle technique, which he said would add an extra boost of roasted coffee flavors to the beer.

In keeping with our brewing tradition, it was time to drink a beer, and I was happy to find a stout in the fridge. But this stout wasn't so plain as to include oatmeal. Stone Xocoveza Mocha Stout is a milk stout brewed with chocolate, cinnamon, nutmeg, chili peppers, and coffee. The description of the beer I read online mentioned it was created by a homebrewer, which made it seem like a good-luck charm. Somehow, despite all the science homebrewing requires, I'd become irrationally superstitious. Next thing you know, I'd be brewing in my lucky socks. One sip of the stout transported me to Oaxaca, where during our honeymoon Tony and I had visited a chocolate shop warm with the pungent smell of cinnamon. I remembered watching a chocolate maker pouring a huge vat of granulated sugar into oozing melted cocoa. Because the stout incited such a sweet memory—combined with the fact that I'd altered the recipe I was using instead of following it to the letter—I had hope. This homebrew had promise. But now all would be lost if I didn't get that beer into bottles.

———

The history of moving beer begins long before bottles were invented, during a time when beer was transported in whatever container was most convenient: bowls, buckets, mason jars, troughs. Medieval monks were forced to face the problem of beer storage when they began brewing more beer than they could immediately consume. So they started storing the beer in barrels, which became the standard way to store and transport beer for centuries. That standard came to define how beer was fermented as well as stored, especially in Great Britain.

Barrels, otherwise known as "casks" in England, have helped the British develop their reputation for drinking weak, flat, warm beer. Since I have yet to set foot on British soil (a travesty for someone with an English last name), I've learned about these ales from friends, books, and inside a small brewpub about five thousand miles from London. In the town of Oakridge, a depressed former logging town in central Oregon, a brewpub called Brewers Union Local 180 serves imperial (twenty-ounce) pints of beer from "firkins," or casks, that are tilted slightly on their sides in a room adjacent to the bar. The modern casks are made of a breathable plastic instead of traditional wood, and they're slowly tilted by an automated system as the beer empties from their insides. Bartenders use hand pumps to get the beer into glasses. The last time I was at the pub, I was in the middle of an ambitious bike tour with Tony and Oscar, who was a good-natured toddler at the time. Starting in Portland, we rode the length of the Oregon Cascades with Oscar in a trailer. I'll never forget the perfection of the fresh, hoppy pale ale I drank during our stop at the pub. The beer didn't seem warm or flat, which meant the beer wasn't all that traditional, stereotypes about British ales are wrong, or thirsty bike tourists don't care much either way.

In 1971 a group called the Campaign for Real Ale (CAMRA) worked to save traditional cask ales in England, which had nearly been pushed into obscurity by modern kegs and corporate beer.

They started by creating a name and a definition: "real ale" is "beer brewed from traditional ingredients, matured by secondary fermentation in the container from which it is dispensed, and served without the use of extraneous carbon dioxide." The group's definition has become the standard way to talk about these beers, even in the United States, where cask ales remain a bit of a mystery. (Not only does the 175,000-plus-member group run the campaign to save real ale, it also works to save British pubs, which the group reports are closing at a rate of twenty-seven per week.)

Even though cask ales make up a minority of the beers in England, they still exist, and those that are CAMRA approved were made using a centuries-old process of fermentation and service. (The cask ales at the Oakridge brewpub are CAMRA approved.) After a beer is fermented, it goes into a cask along with some sugar or wort, which spurs the yeast into action for a secondary fermentation that creates carbonation and flavor. When it's almost time to serve the beer, someone called a cellarman—a person I hope to meet when I go to England for the first time—taps a porous peg into the bung, the plug or stopper in the hole in the top of the cask, which releases some of the pressure built up inside. At that point, the cellarman might add finings, such as isinglass (the nonvegan ingredient in beer that's made of the dried swim bladders of fish), to help the yeast drop and thereby clarify the beer. Or the cellarman might add dry hops to infuse the beer with more hop aromas and flavors. When the publican decides the beer is properly carbonated, a nonporous peg, called a spile, replaces the porous version, and the beer is ready to be served. Using a rubber mallet, the cellarman drives a tap into a hole on the side, hopefully without producing an unbecoming and unprofessional spray of beer. If the beer isn't poured directly from the cask, a hand pump at the bar pulls the beer from the cask through beer lines without the use of any carbon dioxide, the common means of pressurizing a keg. Since cask beer is exposed to oxygen once it's tapped, it's more fragile and starts to go bad within a day or two. It's the job of pub goers to drink the beer quickly enough to keep the ales fresh.

Cask ales are usually served at room temperature or, more accurately, cellar temperature, which is about 55 degrees Fahrenheit, warm for Americans' tastes. And since the beer is naturally carbonated by the yeast, cask beers usually have less carbonation than their counterparts in kegs and bottles, the essence of the flat beer reputation. Aficionados argue that because the beer is slightly warmer and less carbonated, it's easier to taste all the flavors the beer holds, which means brewers can't hide behind bold hop flavors or fizziness. Science supports their claims; the tongue perceives fewer flavors at colder temperatures. That means it's hard to brew a good cask ale, which reveals flaws like a magnifying mirror under fluorescent lights.

It's likely that by the sixteenth century, beers were being forced into a fresh human invention: the glass bottle. Early bottles were made of handblown glass, which was extremely fragile. That made storing beer inside a risky proposition, especially since most bottled beers were undergoing secondary fermentation in the bottle, which creates potentially explosive levels of carbon dioxide. In *The English Housewife*, a book from 1615, the author Gervase Markham gave housewives advice on how to do everything from preventing bad breath to growing flax and brewing beer, a pedestrian activity for many women of the day. Markham wrote that, when bottling ale, "You shall put it into round bottles with narrow mouths, and then stopping them close with corks, set them in a cold cellar up to the waist in sand, and be sure that the corks be fast tied in with strong pack-thread, for fear of rising out, or taking vent, which is the utter spoil of the ale." In other words, take precautions to keep those bottles from blowing, or bad breath will be the least of your worries.

Glassware came in various shapes: squat with embossing; cobalt, aqua, and green; smooth necks, tall necks, wide necks. At the time, commercial bottling was expensive, which made bottled beer something for the wealthy; drinking beer at home instead of at the pub was considered a luxury. The pattern of poor people drinking in public while the rich stored and consumed beer in the privacy of their homes continued into the twentieth century. One of the earliest commercial bottlers was a London brewer named Whitbread. In 1868 the brewer was using corks to seal bottles of beer, including a London stout called a "Family Ale," a feat executed by a workforce of more than one hundred "corkers," who were paid to hammer corks into bottles. That human labor was a selling point. WHITBREAD & CO. ARE THE ONLY LARGE BREWERS WHO BOTTLE THEIR OWN BEER, reads an advertisement.

Screw-top bottles and caps came next, before the creation of the game-changing crown top—the reason many of us have bottle openers attached to our keychains. The crown top was invented by the American mechanical engineer William Painter, who filed eighty-five patents during his lifetime, including one for a safety ejection seat for passenger trains. "I have devised metallic sealing-caps embodying certain novel characteristics which render them highly effective and so inexpensive as to warrant throwing them away after a single use thereof, even when forcible displacement, as in opening bottles, has resulted in no material injury to the caps," reads the patent for the crown top, which was filed in 1889.

Pasteurization helped brewers increase the shelf life of beer, which also pushed bottled beers to become the norm after World War I. While stronger, nonexploding glass bottles and well-preserved beers helped delay the need for kegs, the American public's thirst for highly carbonated lagers created a demand for the metal keg, which kept the beers in better condition for longer. In the 1950s, steel kegs began to replace wooden casks, and just ten years later, lighter weight aluminum alloys became the standard keg material. These days, homebrew forums are filled with people trying to figure out if their kegs are made of aluminum or stainless steel, because keg manufacturers use both materials. Supposedly, aluminum kegs scratch easily, weigh less, and make a "dong" sound when you bang on them (as opposed to steel's "ding").

Because kegs kill the need for bottles, which require washing and sterilization, more experienced and environmentally sensitive homebrewers keg their beers. But what kind of holiday beer fairy lugs a keg from party to party? Not this one. On another Saturday afternoon, while Oscar napped, Tony and I sterilized the bottles, caps, and a siphon. We added a priming sugar, which the yeast would consume to produce carbonation, then we put the oatmeal stout into bottles. I placed a cap on the top of each beer and squeezed the capper that seals the crimped edges around the bottle. We put the bottled beer back into the basement and waited.

After our oatmeal stout had been in the bottles for a week, I couldn't wait any longer. I put one in the fridge for an hour or so and then popped the top. It was inky black in the glass, and a gorgeous tan head appeared on top. The beer tasted like dark chocolate or good coffee, with a strong and dry bitterness and a creamy softness, the perfect blend of substance and lightness. If I'd been filling out a beer sheet, I'd have gone with "Balance." In effect, I'd made what I set out to create, a first for this homebrewer. The beer was so good, it deserved a name, so I called it Short Days Stout, in honor of the dark days of winter, and made some pen drawings on white mailing labels and stuck one to every bottle that went out the door. We took the beer to holiday parties and gave some to Oscar's preschool teachers and friends. I even mailed one to Tony's brother, back east. It was official: I'd made the first batch of homebrew I'd ever felt proud to share.

―――

I'd learned the basic mechanics of bottling beer in my kitchen, but how to serve beer on a larger scale, more specifically, from multiple kegs in a draft system, would require some research. To pass the Cicerone exam, I would need to know how to store kegs, clean draft lines, and troubleshoot problems, like taps that only pour foam— things I wanted to learn through hands-on experience.

One damp Sunday evening, inside a walk-in cooler chilled to a bracing 38 degrees, I stood between a metal tray filled with bloody flank steaks and eight squat kegs of beer. Denver Bon, a wiry thirty-nine-year-old, gently tugged and examined a mass of black, red, and beige tubes protruding from the kegs, like the protagonist of a dystopian science fiction novel. Denver was the brewer at Hair of the Dog Brewing in Portland, and he'd invited me to learn about draft systems by helping him clean the brewery's tap lines, something he did every two weeks. I'd asked Adrienne So to join me, which meant our study group was on a field trip.

I quickly calculated that I'd watched hundreds of people pull tap handles, made of everything from corrugated steel to chainsaw carvings, in order to serve me beer. Like magic, the beer arrived in my glass cold and carbonated, but I'd never thought about why. I was looking forward to replacing that ignorance with a new language, one that included references to pressure, gas blending, vinyl lines, jumpers, couplers, and ball lifters.

Hair of the Dog was an unlikely place for a lesson on draft systems, since the brewery's most famous beers are bottled. In 2013 twelve twelve-ounce bottles of Hair of the Dog Dave, a barley wine brewed nineteen years earlier, sold for two thousand dollars each at a charity event. But the brewery also kegs beer, much of which is served on tap in its pub.

Earlier, Denver told me he went through bankruptcy to work in the beer industry. When he moved to Portland from Pasadena, California, in 2009, he figured he'd quickly find a job serving beer or brewing. After all, he was a Certified Cicerone. But no one knew what the title meant. He finally landed at Hair of the Dog, and was promoted from server to brewer. These days, he does both jobs. Once he told me he gets annoyed when people ask for samples of beer before ordering one.

"It's not like you're shopping for shoes," he said. "Just order a beer. If you drink an entire beer you don't like, that's how you learn."

"But what if you love shopping?" I replied.

Most of my experience with draft systems was limited to the kind of keg-plugged-with-a-vertical-hand-pump setup commonly found at college parties. Those "temporary" systems can easily be operated by anyone capable of opening a tube of Solo cups. One of the main differences between those temporary systems and the one at Hair of the Dog is that the beer comes into contact with oxygen, an enemy of beer because it degrades flavors, and CO_2 is allowed to escape, which can result in flat, bad-tasting beer. While the hand pump pressurizes the beer with air, and therefore oxygen, the Hair of the Dog setup uses carbon dioxide to accomplish the same task.

"CO_2 in, beer out," Denver said, tapping a gauge that showed how much CO_2 pressure was being applied to a single keg. Eight beers on tap meant eight beer lines snaking from the wall to each keg, and eight CO_2 lines running from a vertical metal tank in the corner. He tapped another gauge and explained how he adjusted CO_2 pressure depending on the beer.

"Since you're trying to deliver the beer exactly as the brewer intended, right down to the serving temperature, you don't want to add or take away carbonation."

If there's not enough CO_2 filling the headspace of the keg, the beer's CO_2 will dissolve into the oxygen, which means a loss of carbonation. If there's too much CO_2 in the headspace, the beer will be pushed out too fast and pour foamy.

Draft systems are like closed ecosystems. Changes in temperature and atmospheric pressure can throw them out of balance, which is bad for the beer inside. At Hair of the Dog, beer travels from the kegs to the faucets through chilled tubes fifty feet long, an inefficient distance that's fairly common at commercial breweries. Ideally, beer in a long-draw system travels at a rate of seven feet per second, Denver said, the same number I'd read in the *Draught Beer Quality Manual*. The publication is put out by the Brewers Association, and despite having the soporific qualities of the Bible, is recommended reading material for aspiring Certified Cicerones. As Denver spouted more numbers—including the diameter of the coupler that attaches the beer lines to the keg—I had a momentary flashback to family road trips of my childhood, when my father, a former high school math teacher, would ask me to calculate the car's tire rotations at various speeds. *Science, not poetry,* I wrote in my notebook.

Before Adrienne and I had arrived at Hair of the Dog, I was worrying about her safety. Once I'd been told how a single drop of line-cleaning chemicals will eat an eyeball, which made them seem like something a pregnant woman shouldn't be handling.

"Should we be wearing safety goggles?" I asked Denver, who was filling a keg with warm water and the cleaning solution we'd eventually pump through the beer lines. Adrienne seemed too busy taking notes to hear what I'd said.

"Nah," he said, "we use an environmentally friendly cleaner." The cleaner was called PBW (Powdered Brewery Wash), a nontoxic alkali solution that's biodegradable and "user-friendly." I was relieved.

To prove I didn't need to worry, Denver suggested I touch and smell the solution. Between my fingers, the clear, warm liquid felt slippery and smelled faintly tangy, like artificial strawberries.

"If it feels slimy and smells like fruity yogurt, you know it's PBW," he said.

The exercise reminded him of a bigger idea.

"You have to use all your senses while brewing," he mused.

Technically, line cleaning isn't part of the brewing process, but for Denver, making beer and delivering it to the customers on the other side of the wall were part of the same continuum. Not only did he brew the beer that filled the kegs, Denver emptied and cleaned those containers, forming a complete cycle. I liked the idea of brewing as a full sensory experience, which includes the sound of roiling liquid and the feel of hot metal. I was trying to cultivate a similar awareness while drinking beer.

Denver cleaned the lines every two weeks—sometimes three, he admitted, if he was really busy. He told us the beer tastes different toward the end of the two weeks, which made sense to me.

———

Draft systems introduce flavors into beer, a concept I first encountered inside the bar of a classy bowling alley in Portland, where Jeff Bell, an "on-premise quality specialist" for MillerCoors, was teaching a class about how to properly clean draft lines. He was the one who told me about the dangers of the line-cleaning chemicals, which he illustrated with the unforgettable story of a guy who failed to wear safety goggles while cleaning beer lines and lost vision in one eye.

At the line-cleaning class, I sat with Megan Flynn and a lot of men who cleaned lines for a living. The sun gleamed off our table, which made me wish I were doing something outside instead of being stuck inside a bar. Jeff asked us to pretend we'd gone to a bar to celebrate meeting each other in class. We each had three beer samples in numbered cups in front of us. "Pretend you were served your first pint of beer, and try beer number one," he directed. "Cheers." We all took a sip. The beer was wrong, very wrong, with a buttery aroma and sharp tang. It also seemed watered down, just one of the factors that made it disgusting. We continued with our imaginary night on the town. "Let's go down the street to another bar, since no one was excited about their pints at the last place, and try beer number two," Jeff continued. "Cheers." The second beer was even more offensive than the first, with a strong odor of vinegar. "It's like a cider," one of the professional line cleaners said loudly. Beer three—our control beer—put it all in perspective, with its refreshing and slightly grainy quality. Beer three tasted like beer. It was Coors Light.

The sensory lesson, the result of chemical spikes added to Coors

Light, revealed the pitfalls of not properly cleaning beer lines. The rest of the presentation felt like a driver's education course. Instead of bloody heads stuck through windshields, we saw pictures of kegs oozing brown and yellow goo where the lines attached. Then there was a video of brown chunks of bacterial muck being flushed from a tap system the owner thought was clean. Unfortunately, no one has ever come down with an illness as a result of dirty tap lines, which places the issue outside the purview of health inspectors. That gives bar and restaurant owners little incentive to keep their tap lines clean; it costs money to hire a line cleaner or have staff members do it properly. In most cases, unless beer sales decline as a result of dirty tap lines, the beer still flows. One of the only ways to encourage better and more frequent draft line cleanings is for consumers to point out when beer tastes off, something I'd never seen anyone do in public. At that moment, I vowed to become, not only someone who knew what dirty-line beer tasted like, but someone who'd alert a server about the problem—a member of the undercover draft police.

———

Adrienne and I tried to keep up with Denver, who sprinted from the bar, around tables and chairs in the dining room, past a server mopping the floor, through swinging doors into the brewery, and then into the cooler—at least five times. We created two closed loops of four taps each, which meant we'd run the cleaning solution through the system twice. Denver let us take turns unhooking the beer lines from the kegs, a motion that required a swift turn of a handle, then a quick twist and pull, and, if done right, prevented beer from spewing onto the floor. Wasted beer translates to money down the drain. We had flushed the beer from the system and filled it with cleaning solution that we were letting sit, then we'd flush out the cleaning solution with cold water. The water would stay in the lines until morning, when the first person in the brewery would reintroduce the beer.

While we waited for the cleaning solution to do its job, Adrienne and I sat at the bar, across from the taps. Denver unscrewed the faucets and handed one to me and one to Adrienne. I immediately felt disdain for the faucet, with its gaskets, mysterious openings, and singular ball bearing. It felt as foreign as my Honda's engine the one time I tried to change its oil.

"You pop the ball out, like this," Denver said, his hands moving with sureness. He used his fingernail to pop off a black rubber washer that was lodged between the ball bearing and the faucet's body.

"Examine the washer," he instructed. "If it's gross or torn up, we need to replace it."

Any scratched or uneven surface is a place where bacteria could colonize and create off-flavors. Cleaning the faucets is like flossing the teeth of the draft system. We plopped each part into a bucket of hot water and cleaning solution. After the pieces soaked, we put them back together. As we worked, I thought about the thousands of draft beers I'd consumed over the years—at movie theaters, in restaurants, and at dive bars. There was no way every one of those beers traveled through lines and faucets that had been cleaned every two weeks. Jeff Bell had said regular line cleaning was a rarity, even in beer-centric Portland. That meant the world was awash in mishandled beer, and sadly, most consumers didn't know any better.

At the end of the three-and-a-half-hour cleaning process, we did not drink a beer: the draft lines were filled with water. In the morning, Denver would open the taps and allow the water to flow into buckets before reattaching the kegs to the lines. When beer began to come through, Denver said, he'd count to four, then pour himself a sample of one of the beers from each group of coupled lines. If the beer tasted like yogurt or water, he'd know something had gone wrong. If it tasted like a Hair of the Dog beer—poured with the perfect amount of carbonation, zero off-flavors, and at the perfect temperature—we'd done it right. Even though I wouldn't be there to see the beer flow, I felt the warm sense of having made the world a better place, as though I'd just picked up litter or returned a lost puppy.

Months later, on Superbowl Sunday, I'd pass up guacamole and hot wings to return to Hair of the Dog. The brewery was closing early because it didn't have a TV, and as soon as the last beer was poured, I started running between the cooler and the bar, trying not to slip, waste beer, or do anything destructive. This time, the cooler didn't seem as foreign and the lines didn't look menacing, a reminder that first impressions can't be repeated. While the cleaning solution did its work in the lines, I sat at the bar disassembling faucets and plopping the parts into the hot water bucket. My hands turned sticky and smelled like stale beer, but something had happened since the last time I was there. Tonight, the faucets seemed ordinary and my hands dismantled the pieces with an innate understanding. At the end of the night, Denver gave me an old faucet to take home, so I could practice. Later, I showed the faucet to Tony.

"You should be like a soldier with his gun with that thing," he said, sounding impressed. "You should be able to take it apart and put it back together blindfolded."

I was pretty sure blindfolds weren't part of the Certified Cicerone exam, but he had a point.

Eventually, instead of running back and forth with Denver like I'd done last time, I sat at the bar on a cushy stool. I'd brought a copy of the only Certified Cicerone exam ever released by the organization. (As far as I know, no tests have been leaked.) I'd been carefully filling in answers over the past couple of weeks. Tonight, I had the benefit of being in a room with a Certified Cicerone. When I got stuck on a question I didn't know, I asked Denver for hints.

"How about this one," I said. "A draft pale ale with a bit more flavor than ordinary, but still generally less than four percent."

"Think about the spectrum of English ales," he said, steering me toward a country with beer styles I hadn't yet studied. Then I remembered that "ordinary" was also the name for a subset of "bitters," a broad category of English pale ales. Now, the question made sense.

Sometimes he told me my response was right, or he would say, "I like that answer." A few times, we resorted to Google. I hoped doing the practice exam would make the real exam feel like this second line cleaning, something familiar I could do with ease, even with sticky, stale-beer hands.

———

There isn't any manual on how to prepare to serve beer to the public for the first time, so I considered stretching, hydrating, carbo loading, and elevating my feet. Instead I just stood quietly with about a dozen volunteers under a small white tent next to other tents where hundreds of beer drinkers were, well, drinking. The annual Holiday Ale Festival in downtown Portland was in full swing. At some beer fests, brewers or brewery employees pour the beer, but more often the beer is poured by beer lovers who do the job for free. For beer geeks, volunteering at festivals is like building a house for Habitat for Humanity, a way of giving back that, in this case, happens to be rewarded with free beer. Somehow, I'd never done my duty. Not only did I feel like it was time to enlist, I thought I might learn something useful about beer during my shift.

Behind a plastic picnic table in the corner of the volunteer tent, two beefy men watched us.

"Move closer!" one of them bellowed.

"Even closer!" the other one commanded.

We shuffled in.

"It's Saturday night at a beer festival," the first guy said. He sounded like he was using a megaphone. "That means you'll be on the right side of the table." A loud roar went up from the adjacent tent, where more than four thousand people would be drinking beer over the course of the night. "Those people are all totally sober, I swear," he quipped.

"We only have fifteen beers below seven percent," he continued. "That means people will be getting drunk."

During its nineteen-year run, the Holiday Ale Festival has become famous for serving an array of beer with high alcohol contents. That translates to high amounts of drunkenness, especially on Friday and Saturday nights, which are commonly considered beer-fest amateur hours. No one I knew—and I mean no one—would attend this festival on Saturday night. But seeing as I was a beer-service amateur, this was my night. The organizers assured us that a security brigade would help identify drunk people, escort them to an exit, and strip them of their wristbands. We were told to pay close attention and only serve people who were wearing wristbands and could hand us noncounterfeit tasting tickets. (During past festivals, counterfeit tickets began appearing in the tent within hours of opening on the first day.)

If I had been an unarmed gladiator about to enter the arena, my only weapon would have been an Oregon Liquor Control Commission pamphlet titled, "What Every Volunteer Alcohol Server Needs to Know." I'd printed, signed, and stuffed the publication into my back pocket; I was required by law to have it on my person while I served—theoretically so I could refer to the list of indications that someone's intoxicated.

I marched with the other volunteers down a beer-soaked plywood walkway behind about twenty jockey boxes: rectangular picnic coolers fitted with two beer faucets on the front and dispensing coils that are usually bathed in ice water inside. One of the bar managers showed me to my taps, where a woman with dreadlocks was finishing her volunteer shift.

"You're going to be serving one of the most popular beers at the festival," she yelled in my ear. "Are you ready?"

She poured some coffee-colored beer from a plastic pitcher into a tasting mug.

"Now it's my turn to drink!" she said jubilantly, before bounding down the plank.

I'd already realized that signing up for the six-to-ten evening shift meant I wouldn't enjoy the same perk—the festival ended at ten o'clock. Obviously, other volunteers had done the same calculation, because by the time I signed up, this was the only shift available.

I looked over the top of my jockey box at a line of serious-looking people waiting for beer. Every time I moved, two want-ad-size pieces of paper fluttered on the table, descriptions of the beers I was serving that had been ripped from the festival brochure. The beer everyone wanted was called Hopworks Incredible Abominable of the Enchanted Barrel Forest, a tongue twister I would enjoy watching people try to say over and over again. The beer was a variation of the brewery's Abominable Winter Ale, a popular canned beer.

———

Once upon a time, I was a canned beer skeptic, which was one of the reasons I would visit Hopworks Urban Brewery one weekday afternoon. The brewery canned about 60 percent of its beer, so I was surprised by the small size of the canning line. The canning system at Hopworks operates only one to three days a week, at a rate of about sixty cans a minute, which qualifies it as a midentry canning line. On the other end of the spectrum, a canning line at the Anheuser-Busch brewery in Catersville, Georgia, packages seven million cans a week. At the end of a row of fermenter tanks, I watched long, leggy ramps moving bumbling empty cans, which were inverted as though they were on a nauseating amusement park ride. Then a sweep arm pushed the cans onto a conveyor belt, where they were inverted again and rinsed with hot water. Inside a glassed area, which reminded me of the airport security booths that blast travelers with air, the cans received a squirt of CO_2 then their shot of beer. A robot hand topped and sealed the can, then the closed cans were inverted again, rinsed with more water, and blow-dried. A machine printed a "canned on" date on each one, then the cans traveled through an X-ray machine that reveals the volume of beer in each can. Variations in foam mean some cans won't have enough beer inside. Those lightweights were unceremoniously dropped down a plastic ramp, where they would become free beer for the staff.

Aluminum became the standard material for cans following the repeal of Prohibition, and in 1935 the first canned beers were sold in Richmond, Virginia, by Gottfried Krueger Brewing Company. Later that year, Pabst, Schlitz, and Anheuser-Busch started selling canned beer, the drinks that helped raise soldiers' morale during World War II. During the past decade, canning made a comeback as craft brewers realized its benefits. Cans are superior to bottles for a couple reasons: they better protect beer from light and oxygen, and because aluminum is lighter than glass, shipping them costs less money. I'd questioned canned craft beer in part because of the sound—a can opening reminded me of my Busch-drinking days in Utah and, therefore, that bloated, bad-beer feeling. I also assumed cans would make the beer taste metallic, but that's not the case. Thin plastic linings in cans prevent the beer from touching any metal that might alter the beer's taste.

—————

I thought about the canning line as I prepared to pour the Incredible Abominable of the Enchanted Barrel Forest. At 100 IBUs, the Enchanted Barrel Forest was one of the hoppiest beers at the Holiday Ale Festival, which explained the line in front of my jockey box. Humans are capable of perceiving as few as 6 IBUs, but somewhere around 100 we lose the capacity to detect a difference in scale. Most beer drinkers don't take into account how a beer's maltiness affects its overall hop bitterness; instead they turn to numbers. Hop hunters who seek out beers with maximum IBUs are like people who eat naga jolokias, the peppers that are listed near pepper-spray intensity on the Scoville scale: masochists looking for palate-destroying experiences. The other beer I would serve was the BridgePort Up in Smoke Lager, the sad trombone next to the hop trumpet. Not only was the beer a lager and smoked—two unpopular traits—it had just 5.4 percent ABV and 14 IBUs.

As I started pouring beer from the pitchers into people's glasses, I had some regrets. At every beer festival I've ever attended, I'd asked the volunteers to tell me about the beer they were pouring. With so many choices, I wanted some advice, or maybe a few guiding adjectives. But since I hadn't had come to the festival until that night, I was pouring two beers I'd never tried.

"What's it like?" people asked when they finally reached the front of the line, usually after they struggled to say the entire name of the Hopworks beer.

"People really seem to like it!" I answered cheerily, an attitude I maintained for at least thirty minutes. At that point I realized, if I was going to survive the remaining three-and-a-half hours of my shift, I'd need to tone down my enthusiasm—I was already starting to lose my voice. Still, I focused on each pour, trying not to create too much foam, which really pissed people off, while creating some head, so the drinker could experience the beer at its best. A beer's head holds aromas, which, as I'd learned in Nicole Erny's class, affect flavor, and makes foam atop any beer an essential part of tasting it (an inch of foam on a pint is a good standard). While some beer styles aren't conducive to producing foamy heads, these two beers wanted to foam. I also tried to keep the glass from touching the pitcher, and keep the pitcher from touching the faucet. Keeping that space is key, said one of the orientation guys. "Otherwise it's like kissing everyone at the festival."

"Don't touch that glass with the pitcher," a woman in the line next to mine shrieked as a volunteer poured her beer. She sighed and shook her head disapprovingly.

"OK, OK!" he replied.

I was impressed she knew to make the demand. Maybe she'd contracted mono after last year's festival.

When someone in line asked the same guy about the beer he was pouring, he told them it was "really sweet."

"When you said it's really sweet," I said to him, as I poured beer into a glass (which felt like an advanced multitasking move), "did you mean you didn't like it?"

"Nope, I've never tried it," he replied bluntly.

That's when I came up with my description for the Hopworks hop bomb, a factually accurate line I'd deliver over and over again: "It's really hoppy, at 100 IBUs."

Fifty minutes into my shift, a thin stream of foam poured from the Hopworks faucet into the pitcher. "The Hopworks beer is kicked," the bar manager yelled at the crowd. The guy who got the last pour bounded gleefully into the crowd, and everyone else groaned. Immediately, things got a lot easier. I had time to wipe up beer that had dripped from the taps onto the tables. I filled the pitchers with the sad trombone beer and created games for myself. Now were there more inappropriately intoxicated people, ironic holiday sweaters, waxed mustaches, or foreign accents? No one who came to my line was inebriated to OLCC-brochure standards, but I did see "alcohol monitors" escorting festival goers to the door, outside of which I pictured a shameful wristband-cutting ceremony.

When the BridgePort beer ran out at 9:55 P.M., I lamented I wouldn't have the chance to try that beer, either. The only other person who seemed disappointed that the smoked lager was gone was the guy who'd been standing nearby to have his mug refilled with the smoked beer every five minutes; I'd refused to give him bigger pours (he wasn't the only one who'd asked). Even though it seemed ridiculous to be refilling his glass with two ounces at a time, I was being watched, and there was no way I wanted to be booted from volunteering without getting my free beer at the end of the shift.

When the clock struck ten, I walked down the plank I'd come

up four hours earlier. Inside our gathering tent, the other volunteers seemed giddy. We'd survived, and were about to drink for free. Organizers delivered whatever beer was left in the pitchers when the clock struck ten. There wasn't much. A few brewery names were written on pieces of tape stuck to the pitchers, but most of the beers were unmarked. It didn't matter. We started pouring beer into our mugs in a frenzy.

"This one tastes like maple," one volunteer announced.

"This has to be a barley wine," said another.

"This sour is so disgusting it reminds me of vinegar."

It was like eating from a dim sum cart, a jarring range of flavors united by a common theme. Twenty minutes later, the beer was gone. I'd just survived my first beer-service challenge, putting me one step closer to Cicerone status, but I didn't feel satisfied. Not only didn't I have a chance to really taste the beers and enjoy them, all night I was separated from the beer drinkers by a jockey box, which felt like a barrier to understanding the beers and the scene. Even though I was volunteering, it was still a job, I thought as I walked out onto the street, where the lights of the city's two-story Christmas tree twinkled overtop the white festival tents—Portland's version of a white Christmas. A few people at the light rail station were wearing Santa hats. The train was the sleigh that would carry us home.

———

I knew that before I could take the Certified Cicerone exam I would first need to take the Level 1 test: the Certified Beer Server exam. Compared to the Certified Cicerone exam, this test was highly accessible: you just had to pay a fee and take it online. But I'd been putting off the easy exam.

"Oh, that test?" Megan Flynn told me one day over lunch. "It's so easy! You could pass it anytime, no problem."

But I wasn't so sure. The syllabus made the test seem like a serious challenge to my knowledge of beer styles and draft systems, in particular. I worried I wouldn't pass on my first try, and if I couldn't pass the "easy" level on my first attempt, how would I psych myself up for the Certified Cicerone exam? Feeling the pressure to get to the Level 2 exam, I decided to take the test the next day. I would have thirty minutes to answer sixty multiple-choice questions, a pace that eliminated the option of looking up answers online. I did some last-minute cramming by watching a video about draft systems, and I tried to memorize the specs for a few more beer styles. Before I sat down with my laptop to take the test, I made sure Tony and Oscar wouldn't be arriving home from the indoor mountain bike park during the next thirty minutes, the kind of interruption that would most definitely lead to a fail.

"Go for it!" Tony texted. "Good luck!"

The multiple-choice questions appeared one screen at a time, and once I answered one there was no going back. Some I knew right away, while others gave me pause. The ticking clock in the corner of the screen made me nervous, but I finished the test with a few minutes to spare. The next window revealed the news: *You got 51 out of 60 possible points. Your score was: 85%. Congratulations, you passed!* I was relieved. Before I closed my laptop, I looked at the list of questions I'd missed: beer styles, glassware, storage and serving, and keg mechanics. I had some studying to do before spring.

When Tony and Oscar walked in the door, I said, "You're looking at a Certified Beer Server." I had proof. I'd printed out my Certified Beer Server certificate, which had my name and the number 177863.

"Whoa!" Oscar said. "That's cool."

"I'm going to put it on the fridge," I said.

"Yeah, yeah," he chanted. "Right here!"

We made a clearing in his magnetic alphabet letters.

"You should definitely serve me a beer tonight," Tony said, as he pulled some salami and cheese out of the fridge for Oscar's lunch.

"Only if we have the proper glassware," I replied.

The following week I received a small cardboard box in the mail. Inside was a rectangular, black and gold lapel pin that said "Certified Beer Server." "Congratulations on passing the Certified Beer Server Exam from the Cicerone Certification Program!" read a typed note inside the box. "You are receiving a lapel pin to commemorate your achievement, we hope you wear it with pride." Maybe I'd wear it to the exam in April.

SUGAR RUSH

I make a mean cup of coffee, if you give me the right ingredients.
—ICE CUBE

WHEN THE NEW YEAR ARRIVED, I came up with some resolutions. In the past, I'd vowed to wear more lipstick, listen to more rock 'n' roll, and bake a pie a month. This year, I would brew more beer, drink more beer, and learn more about beer—all in hopes of passing the Cicerone exam in the spring. In many ways, I felt like I hadn't started studying yet, which felt unsettling. Sure, I'd been going through the steps of my master study plan, from making homebrew to attending the Great American Beer Festival. But many of those experiences felt like extra credit: I'd enjoyed them too much. The idea that I could actually enjoy studying felt at odds with the experience I'd imagined. Then again, there were still more than three months until the test. Maybe I just wasn't feeling the pressure yet.

On the second day of the new year, instead of doing burpees at the gym or juicing kale, I was shivering outside Breakside Brewery under a blushing winter sunrise. Breakside's head brewer, thirty-three-year-old Ben Edmunds, finally opened the door, wearing a woven hat, sagging Carhartt work pants, and an orange T-shirt. Ben had graduated from Yale with a bachelor's degree in Spanish and taught high school Spanish in rural Colorado for four years before he decided he wanted to become a professional brewer. Instead of tinkering with home-brewing, a typical path for commercial brewers, he enrolled in a six-month brewing program at the Siebel Institute, a respected brewing school, that included some training in Munich.

Ben and I walked across this newer brewing facility, and I remembered the last time I had watched him brew, in the original Breakside space—a cramped nine-hundred-square-foot basement room that requires a lot of ducking and polite I'm-coming-throughs. The new brewery was a fifteen-thousand-square-foot complex that made me feel like I was no longer standing inside a startup, but something touched by a benevolent angel investor.

"What are we brewing today?" I yelled over a mechanical hum.

"The IPA!" he shouted back, without slowing his stride.

I couldn't believe my luck. It had been three months since Breakside won the GABF gold medal for its IPA. Today, I'd see what went into making the beer that had received the most coveted medal at the festival. As the mash tun filled with fifty gallons of steaming hot water—which seemed wasteful, because this water wasn't an ingredient for the beer but was just a way to warm the stainless steel— Ben explained how the medal had altered their future.

"I always suspected we'd grow," he said, "but now it's a foregone conclusion."

At this point, in 2014, Breakside was brewing 7,400 barrels of beer a year. A year from now, Ben said, they planned to be making 16,000 barrels. Three years later, 25,000 to 30,000 barrels (which wouldn't bring Breakside even close to the maximum of six million barrels a year the Brewers Association uses to qualify a brewery as "craft").

I was surprised to hear Ben say they hadn't yet ramped up production of the IPA since winning the medal. Even though Breakside's distributor was struggling to keep the IPA in stock, the brewery didn't have enough hops to make more IPA; Ben had contracted all the hops for 2015 five years earlier, the standard length of time for hops contracting. If he were to order more hops that day, he'd receive them in 2019. Ben mentioned how brewers at 10 Barrel Brewing—a craft brewery that started in Bend, Oregon, and that had recently been bought by Anheuser-Busch InBev—could get whatever hops they wanted almost immediately.

"Awards are great," he said, "but when you're trying to compete with the big boys, money talks."

The only way to make more Breakside IPA in 2015 would be to change the recipe. "That's not really an option," Ben said with a confident grin.

I followed him up the grated stairs to the brew deck, which sits suspended between the mash tun, kettle, and whirlpool, the vessel that allows the next batch of beer to start brewing while the first one is still in progress. From the brew deck, I could see almost every corner of the brewery, which made it a good place to see if entry-level brewers were "dinking around," Ben said. Above a metal work sink hung a brew log neatly covered in plastic, with blank lines for writing everything from the cell count of the yeast slurry to the gravity of the wort before it boils. While I understood that accurate record keeping is key to understanding a final beer, I'd never seen a brewer track this many items.

"We could make a beer without recording the details," Ben said, "but we couldn't do it as consistently." To prove he wasn't the most rigorous, he explained how another a brewer records the barometric pressure on brew days.

Despite my down coat and hat, I felt like I was back inside the Hair of the Dog walk-in cooler, which made it hard to move away from the warm lip of the mash tun, where a steaming mix of water and malt smelled like the bowl of Grape Nuts I would microwave when I was a kid. But we needed to move on to where the malt is ground, inside a sealed mill room, away from the brewing area. Before we went into the room, Ben handed me a dust mask, which reminded me of Tony, who wore the same kind of mask when he was grinding metal tubes in his shop. Once I had pulled the mask over my nose and mouth, it was already pressing lines into my cheeks. Inside the room, a mill fed by a plastic auger delivered American two-row malt, the brewery's standard and most frequently used malt, from a silo that loomed large over the building. Other types of malt had to be poured into the mill by hand. Today, by *my* hands. *Lift with your legs, not with your back,* I thought, as I struggled to hoist a fifty-pound bag of specialty malt into position so the roasted barley kernels falling out would land inside a machine vibrating with hungry, whirring blades. Once we'd finished that job, Ben asked me to retrieve two plastic buckets filled with vibrant green hop pellets, pungent with aromas of pine and grass. *That's right,* I thought, *we're making the IPA . . .*

IPA is the fastest growing craft beer style in America. It may have been the brewers of the West Coast who reinvigorated the style during the past few decades, but India pale ale originated in England, during the late 1700s. If you've struggled to justify your beer budget, imagine being a British beer drinker in 1695, when 28 percent of the country's annual per capita income went to beer. England had a long history of supplanting the dangerous and unreliable drinking water of London with beer: before meals, during meals, and after meals. These were people committed to hydration.

By the 1700s, the Industrial Revolution had begun chugging, cranking, and clanging into productivity in a soot-stained smock. The era brought a few key inventions that spurred commercial brewing, including thermometers and hydrometers (the instrument that measures the density of liquids, used to determine the amount of dissolved solids, or sugars, in wort). Steam power meant breweries could make more beer for less money by more efficiently boiling wort and heating water. Earlier, by the 1600s, people had started baking coal in ovens, a process that produced the highly efficient fuel called coke. Because the new fuel had less sulfur, tar, and undesirable gasses than coal, coke revolutionized malt making. Instead of making only the signed, smoky malts that fed the porter craze, maltsters could gently toast, roast, and coax barley into more refined malts, something they'd previously made in very limited amounts, using malt dried over straw fires. Brewers used those lighter, pale malts to make pale beers, and when the first pale ales debuted in London in 1620, they transformed the public's palate. Those pale ales were the beers that would morph into IPAs.

Even though brewers had new tools and better malt, they still didn't understand much of the science of their craft. They knew how to harvest and control yeast, to some extent, but they still didn't understand the science of the single-celled organisms; Louis Pasteur wouldn't theorize that yeast was responsible for fermentation until 1857. Beer was only brewed between October and April, when cooler temperatures seemed to decrease beer spoilage. Another thing seemed to decrease spoilage: hops.

Most people know the tale: in order for beer to survive the long voyage from England to India, brewers started adding extra hops to barrels of beer to better preserve it. A new beer style was born, complete with a geographic name that fits the origin story. Lately, I'd noticed how every retelling of the tale tended to receive strong criticism from beer historians, brewers, and beer aficionados—a tide of revisionism stemming from either a fresh historical discovery or the rise of Internet trolls, it seemed. To find out what was happening, I called Mitch Steele, head brewer at Stone Brewing Co. and author of *IPA: Brewing Techniques, Recipes, and the Evolution of India Pale Ale.*

"My understanding of the story was the same as everyone else's until six years ago," he told me over the phone. After years of research, which included an immersive trip to England, Mitch said he learned there's still a lot we don't know about the IPA story. "Anyone who claims to know is mistaken," he said.

An entrepreneur named George Hodgson, who owned Bow Brewery in London, usually gets the credit for dosing pale ales with extra hops for the voyage to India, but Steele uncovered an alternate reality. Bow Brewery was shipping porter, pale ale, and October beer (a strong pale ale) to India, but no one can find documentation that shows Hodgson created hoppier versions of either. Yes, British citizens living in India received beer that had survived a sloshing, four-to-six-month voyage that crossed the equator twice—temperature fluctuations that aren't good for beer under any circumstances. Even so, Mitch said, the beer that arrived in India wasn't all that bad. It wasn't that a hoppy pale ale was intentionally created for the voyage to India, he told me, but that the beer that did well on the journey, styles that were heavily hopped, became more popular over time. "Especially when Burton brewers got involved."

As early as the 1200s, when monks started brewing at the local abbey, the town of Burton-on-Trent became known as a magical place where brewers consistently made great beer. Located in the East Staffordshire borough of England, the town is cradled in the River Trent valley. Rainwater flows through deep layers of gravel and sandstone before it's captured in town wells. The bedrock exposes the water to a rare blend of minerals—high levels of calcium and sulfate—that do a few things for beer. First, it produces an eggy, fart-like aroma famously known as "Burton snatch." Local brewers weren't chasing the snatch, per se, but what the aroma-producing compounds did during fermentation: they promoted vigorous fermentation and caused protein particles and yeast to clump together, which produced beautifully clear beer, a defining attribute of English ales. (You should be able to read a newspaper through a good English ale, brewer Van Havig once told me.) The composition of the water also allowed brewers to add more hops, which made Burton beers slightly less perishable than beers from other parts of the country. Essentially, Burton beers were crisp, clear, and bitter. A new standard was set.

During the eighteenth century, the town of Burton developed a tight relationship with Russia; waterways threaded through Burton, the English port city of Hull, London, and the Baltics. Eventually, a canal became the pathway for transporting IPAs to Liverpool, a prime shipping port for India. Before Burton beers were loaded onto ships, most were aged in barrels for nine months. Then they sloshed their way around the Cape of Good Hope, a trip that took six months. When steam shipping became more prominent in the 1830s, the voyage shrunk to three months. Catherine the Great was "immoderately fond" of ales from Burton, and if I were to brew a beer for her today, I'd "Burtonize" my water by pouring Burton salts in the mash, a common homebrewing technique. The mix of gypsum, potassium chloride, and Epsom salt increases the hardness of the water, which would be especially important if Catherine were coming to drink in Portland, the land of otherwise-enviably soft water.

In the 1700s, Burton ales were strong, copper-colored beers that were slightly sweet, with flavors of dried fruits and the signature Burton hop bitterness, old ales that would eventually evolve into English barley wines. Burton pale ales were another beer entirely. By 1823 the town's most prominent brewer, Samuel Allsopp, created a recipe for a pale ale designed to mimic Hodgson's pale London beer. Two more Burton brewers—Bass Brewery and Thomas Salt and Co.—started exporting a pale beer to India around the same time.

Were those beers the first IPAs? While the bitterness in Burton ales increased, and the Burton exports became known as reliably high-quality beers, they weren't called India pale ales. That matters. Because, even though a rose by any other name would smell as sweet, a beer style's name is one key piece of its provenance. In 1817 the W. A. Brown Imperial Brewery advertised a pale ale that was "prepared for the East and West India Climate," and an advertisement in the *Sydney Gazette* in August 1829 touted an "East India pale ale." By the 1850s brewers were consistently using the name "India pale ale."

The Burton versions of IPA appeared in London more frequently than other IPAs, which helped the Burton brewers became known for the style. Like other beer styles, IPA was advertised as restorative, the chicken soup of beers. An ad for Hodgson's ale in the January 30, 1835, edition of the *Liverpool Mercury* described the beer as "Being brewed from the finest East Kent hop, it contains a particularly fine tonic quality, and is consequently much recommended by the faculty, even to invalids." (I couldn't help but notice that a copy of the paper cost seven pence, while a pint of beer at the time cost two.) For the healthy, IPAs were marketed as beers with extraordinary clarity and "sparkling lightness," with the "light body of a wine combined with the fragrance and subdued bitter of the most delicate hop." Champagne, anyone?

━━━━━━

Ben moved between the brew deck and other parts of the brewery at an exhausting pace. I tried to stay within conversation distance without getting in his way.

"You probably already know this," he said, before pushing some buttons and peering at a gauge, "but we're mimicking the German practice of step infusion mashing."

He explained how enzymes break starches into sugars, and that two types of enzymes are key for brewing: alpha and beta amylase. Each one creates different types of sugars and works at different temperatures. By bringing the mash temperature up in "steps," you can activate both kinds of amylase, which helps create a customized wort filled with variable sugars, some of which the yeast will consume and some of which the yeast will leave behind. Brewers who don't use step infusions—like me, when I homebrew—try to bring their wort to a temperature that activates both amylases in one swoop. Step or no step, never again would I approach the mash temperature as a general suggestion. Brewing is more like making a piecrust than I initially thought; the temperature of the chilled butter matters to the degree.

At one point, Ben disappeared among the long line of fermenters. When he returned, he was holding a clear plastic pitcher filled with about five inches of an obsidian beer with an espresso-crema-hued head. The beer was a stout, a new recipe that upped the body and hoppiness of the brewery's Irish dry stout, he said. Ben took a small professional sip then passed the pitcher to me. After his second taste, Ben looked at the floor, paused as though he were thinking, then looked at me and decreed, "Yep. Just right."

Two times, Ben produced a kit that looked like he was about to test the composition of chemicals in a hot tub. It was called a titration, which he used to measure the concentration of sanitizer solution that cleaned the brewing equipment.

"Standards are for everyone," he said loudly. I felt like he was talking not to me but to the assistant brewers working in the vicinity.

From the brew deck, I saw one of the brewers let out a loud burst of carbon dioxide from a hose before attaching it to a fermenter. He paused and looked around, which made it seem like he'd made a mistake, but he was actually following protocol and purging oxygen from the valves attached to the fermenter tank before adding the beer, which would help keep the beer tasting fresh.

"See," Ben said, nodding with approval. "It's those kinds of practices that keep the beer at quality levels."

Next thing I knew, Ben looked panicked. He'd just checked the temperature of the mash and something wasn't right. The mash tun's mixer paddle wasn't mixing, which meant sugars from the malt weren't being evenly extracted.

"It's just moving around!" Ben yelled at another brewer.

Three of them started attending to the gleaming steel vessel, moving through steam to reach into the small hatch that provided access to the mash and the paddle. I knew they were facing the possibility of a large batch of beer gone wrong.

The mash tun was new, and had only been installed a few days earlier. Now, mechanical errors were creating ripples of chaos, a disruption of the calm rigor Ben tried to cultivate. Before the brewers had figured out how to fix the paddle problem, Ben muttered that the temperature gauge appeared to be malfunctioning, which also had major implications. If the wort was too hot or cold by just one degree, the beer wouldn't taste right. But he knew that, if he had indeed followed his standard brewing procedures up until this moment, the wort should be the right temperature. "We have to trust our process over the readings!" Ben shouted, like the captain of a ship that just lost radar.

Once the ship was righted and the wort began flowing into the whirlpool, Ben sprinted up to the brew deck and began ripping open large bags of what looked like cocaine. DEXTROSE, said the red letters on the bags. If I'd seen Ben opening containers of premium raw brown sugar or bottles of agave syrup, I wouldn't have blinked. But this was dextrose, a sugar derived from corn that seemed more like something you'd find at a Budweiser plant than a craft brewery. I was shocked.

"Go ahead and pour it in without getting the stuff stuck to the sides," he told me.

I paused. Was I really about to pour dextrose into a GABF-gold-medal-winning beer? Around us, the hum of the brewery made communicating with Ben difficult, so I held back asking the question I longed to ask: why *were* we adding dextrose to this beer? Muted by our surroundings, I did what any good assistant brewer would do: I followed instructions. Each brown-paper bag weighed more than my four-year-old, and when I tried to lift the first one over the whirl-pool without dropping it inside, the bag slipped in my hands. I took a step back to stabilize my body. As the white powder billowed into the wort, the bag became lighter. For the second time that morning, I considered how the physicality of brewing must be a barrier for women in commercial brewing. Once I asked Whitney Burnside, the petite head brewer at 10 Barrel Brewing in Portland, how she coped with the physical demands of the job.

"I'll never stop asking for help doing things I can't do myself," she said bluntly.

With her in mind, I yelled to Ben for help. We wrestled with the bags. Every second counted. In brewing, like cooking, ingredients need to be added together, at the right moment, for even "cooking" and precise temperature control. As soon as the dextrose touched the liquid, the powder disappeared, becoming an invisible piece of an increasingly complex puzzle.

For days afterward, I thought about the dextrose, a sugar that is completely fermentable. Because yeast will ferment all of it, brewing with dextrose means adding no residual sweetness to the beer. I remembered that Tony and I had used sugar (dextrose, in fact) during homebrewing, but we added it after fermentation, when we were putting the beer into bottles. During that phase, the sugar gives the yeast a little extra boost, a bit of fuel to help it produce extra CO_2 to carbonate the beer. The way Ben had used dextrose was different.

Online, I found lots of homebrewers sharing their experiences using dextrose, good and bad. One site mentioned it as the cause of an off-flavor. "Try cutting down on the amount of corn or cane sugar being used," someone advised a brewer who was trying to deconstruct the origin of some off-flavors. "Using an alternative source of fermentable sugar can help to reduce cidery or winey flavors." A homebrew forum from the nineties referenced American craft brewing pioneer Charlie Papazian as having said sugar produces cider-like flavors, something I'd heard before. "I used no sugar," the homebrewer wrote, to which another replied, "Papazian simply got it wrong."

Eventually I e-mailed Ben. "Question," I wrote. "The sugar that was added to the kettle. Is that standard for most of your recipes? What are the pros/cons of adding sugar then? I'm guessing it cuts down on the size of the malt bill, but maybe there are other reasons for the addition."

He replied within the day.

"I should probably state up-front that it is a 'controversial' practice in that some people view it as a 'cheater's method' of getting more gravity/alcohol without having to foot the cost of more malt," he wrote. "While those things are true, I think there are important flavor impacts of using a small portion of simple sugars in hoppy beers: first, they improve fermentability." He went on to explain that by using less than 10 percent sugar as part of the total fermentables, he gets "greater attenuation," or more conversion of sugar into alcohol. That creates a drier beer with a lighter body, which "allows the hops to shine."

He admitted there are some downsides to brewing with dextrose, but cidery flavors wasn't one of them. If you use the sugar for more than 20 percent of the malt bill, the yeast will suffer, he said, and keeping yeast healthy, so you can reuse the same yeast in batch after batch of beer, is one way brewers keep costs down. Also, unhealthy yeast can produce undesirable flavors.

"We stand by the practice one hundred percent," Ben said.

I felt like I did when I heard David Chang defend cooking with MSG: a strange mix of thrill and disappointment. Later I'd learn my bias against sugar was common among homebrewers and craft beer lovers, who considered "adjuncts"—ingredients that include corn, oats, rice, and sugar—to be the stuff of big corporate breweries. Sugar, in particular, has been widely used in British brewing, not to save money on malt but to create the beers drinkers desire. During World War I, when sugar was rationed and therefore expensive, brewers in the United Kingdom continued to brew with sugar because it helped them affect a beer's color during an era when malt, and its color, was inconsistent. Sugar also helped reduce the nitrogen in beers made from nitrogen-rich malts, which could produce less haze. When I started researching sugar in brewing, I learned white sugar creates neutral flavors, while dark sugars—including dark candi sugar, turbinado and demerara—can add plumy and dark-dried-fruit notes to beer.

Weeks later, on an unseasonably dry January evening, Tony, Oscar, and I went to Breakside's brewpub for dinner. At one of the long sidewalk picnic tables, I peered through a pint of their straw-colored IPA, which was so transparent it would have passed the newspaper test. Even before I took my first sip, I'd convinced myself that this pint was from the batch of beer I'd help brew. Sure enough, it tasted better than ever, with an alluring zing of grapefruit zest and a fresh, palate-cleansing finish that made me want just one thing: more.

My trip to Belgium was six weeks away, and on my return, I'd only have one month until the test. I was starting to feel like every day counted. I'd been reading *Tasting Beer* by Randy Mosher during my train commute to work, but my study sessions with Adrienne So had fizzled. I felt like I wasn't making much progress studying alone. Plus, all the books in Powell's wouldn't prepare me for the tasting portion of the exam. So I signed up for a class.

One Monday night, after a long day at my copywriting job, I sat by myself in a suburban brewpub forcing myself to eat a French dip sandwich that resembled a crusty salt lick, while pro football players bashed heads on television screens. Tony and Oscar were at home having dinner together, and I wouldn't see Oscar until morning. I was fueling up for my beer class, which I thought sounded like a euphemism for getting drunk at the bar. (Once, one of Oscar's pre-school teachers asked him what I did while he was at school. "Go to her beer class," he replied, which may have given her pause.) The class was run through Portland Community College and taught by Bill Schneller, a man with wispy shoulder-length brown hair and a graying goatee.

We all introduced ourselves that first night: the students included a twenties-something homebrewer, a California transplant who loved wine, two admitted beer geeks, and a woman who planned to open a beer bar. Bill told us he got into beer through wine, an entry point I assumed had something to do with the saying, "It takes a lot of beer to make good wine." But I was wrong. After working some wine-related jobs in New York, he moved to Oregon to make wine. When those plans fell through and he lost a lucrative job, Bill found himself without the funds to buy the kinds of wine he appreciated. Starved for sauce, Bill accepted the invitation to brew some beer with a friend.

"It was a horrible brown ale, an extract beer with a ton of sugar in it, and I thought it was the best thing ever," Bill later told me.

He was hooked, and started brewing on a regular basis. In 2001 he attended a meeting of the venerable Oregon Brew Crew, one of the oldest and largest brew clubs in Portland. Bill climbed through the ranks of the Beer Judge Certification Program, which certifies judges for homebrew competitions, to become one of four master BJCP judges in Oregon.

One of the reasons I thought the class would broaden my knowledge was because we'd cover mostly European beer styles that I didn't encounter much in Portland. (Beer with lower amounts of alcohol and hops didn't move quickly in the City of Roses.) In a sense, I'd be forced to drink what I wouldn't normally order, which reminded me of one of my college journalism professors, who suggested reading the stories in the newspaper that didn't seem interesting. That's how you learn, he said.

Every week, Bill began the class by lecturing about whatever style we were studying that night—from pilsners and light lagers to English and Scottish beers. Then he distributed bottles and cans of beer to each table, so we could pour our own samples into clear plastic tasting glasses. We spent the next few hours tasting through them, together.

During one class about wheat beers, Bill explained how wheat kernels have smaller, less robust husks than barley kernels, which made wheat turn into a gluey mass in the mash tun. That's why wheat usually makes up 50 percent or less of the grain used in any particular beer.

"The taste of wheat is grainer," Bill said from the front of the room, over the sounds of a video game console spewing computerized bleeps. "It's not rich, but has a round feeling, like flour."

I wrote his words in my notebook, hoping to inherit his ability to feel a beer in three dimensions. "There's some smoke," he said, as he swirled his glass of Andechser Weissbier Hell, a German hefeweizen. Then he shoved his nose inside the rim of the glass and inhaled deeply. "More clove on the nose." He took a sip, closed his eyes for an instant and said, "Banana up front, but wow, this beer is crisp, light and dry. Is anyone else getting anything else from this beer?" Bill repeatedly told us that one of his motivations for teaching the class—besides the chance to hear himself talk—was the opportunity to taste with other people. "I always learn from you guys," he said.

Bill told us he drove all over town to find the freshest examples of the beers for class, but even so, the locally unpopular beers stayed on the shelves for a long time and, therefore, suffered from oxidation. While I lamented that the imports weren't at their prime, I noticed that, with each class, I was getting better at identifying the cardboard and papery notes of oxidation, which seemed to be less a set of flavors or aromas than a texture I felt in my mouth. If tasting was building muscle memory, I was bulking up on wet paper towels.

After one class, I asked Bill if he had any recommendations for learning to blindly identify a beer by style, something I'd need to do on the Cicerone exam.

"You can drink a beer here and a beer there," he said, "but that's not going to help you. Drink beers of the same style, side by side. It's the only way to really learn the differences." To prepare for class, Bill said, he would buy six or eight beers of the same style. One night, he'd taste three or four. The next night, three or four more. Then he'd decide which ones to bring to class. His side-by-side approach made sense. One time we tasted a Hoegaarden Wit next to a St. Bernardus Wit. The less cloudy St. Bernardus smelled like a floral perfume and tasted like a bowl of lemons tucked under a dishcloth.

If the St. Bernardus was layers of puff pastry and custard cream, the Hoegaarden was a plain biscuit begging for butter and jam.

Bill told me he played rock guitar until his wife signed him up for classical guitar lessons. "I'd always played with a pick, and as soon as I had to use my fingers, I couldn't roll a chord," he told me. "I'd try, and couldn't do it. I'd think about it and try again. I still couldn't do it." One day he rolled a chord naturally, without trying. "To me that's what beer judging is," he said. "You practice and work on it, then it becomes unconscious. Tasting is just a skill. It's a matter of doing it again and again and again."

The next week, my friend Danielle Booth, aka Badger, wanted to get together to talk about writing. But I wanted to taste beer. So we struck a bargain: we'd talk about writing while drinking beer. When she arrived, I produced a stack of beer evaluation sheets, two pens, and three bottles of different doppelbocks. Side by side, the beers revealed their differences with a lucidity that made evaluating beers one at a time seem like a failed lie detector test. The Ayinger Celebrator was hoppier than the Spaten Optimator and tasted like raisins or another kind of dried fruit. "The more you have, the better it gets," Badger wrote on her tasting sheet. One of the beers was Aecht Schlenkerla Eiche, a doppelbock brewed with 100 percent oak-smoked malt in the German town of Bamburg, a place known for its smoked rauchbiers. I've never been a huge fan of smoked beers; usually the smokiness makes me feel like I am inhaling a campfire. But this doppelbock was different. It smelled like smoked ham and tasted savory and complex, a bedrock for the smoky notes. I couldn't stop sipping the beer, as I tried to figure out how the sweet malt intertwined with the smoke. Badger wrote, "Aftertaste is icky." Badger indulged my tasting exercise for awhile, but our conversation drifted, and she started drawing diagrams of her memoir on the back of the tasting sheets. When she left, I realized I'd learned two lessons: not everyone wanted to study beer like I wanted to study beer, and Bill was right about side-by-side tastings.

═════════

One January afternoon, I stared at a recess in my basement where, behind a naked lightbulb with a pull string, two shelves packed with bottles of beer hovered. I called the space "the cellar," while Tony referred to it as "all those beers we never get to drink." Ever since I learned that certain styles of beer age well, I'd started to stash bottles with a hoarder's vision of the future. Slowly, the beer began to outnumber the wine I had started with. That afternoon, I was looking for a beer to take to a party at my friend Brian Yaeger's house, which he calls Beeradise. Brian, another Portland beer writer, has infused his surroundings with beer references, from the beer-themed bed and breakfast he and his wife run out of their converted garage, to his dog named Dunkel. Even though I'd never been to one of his beer parties, I knew they usually took place in his basement—near his beer collection—while his wife was out of town. It sounds like an invitation for scandalous behavior, but in reality, the parties were more like excuses for Brian to let his toddler stay up way past his bedtime. Each party had a theme, and this one was "old beers."

Even though the party would give me the chance to taste a bunch of potentially hard-to-find vintage beers, which sounded like a delightful way to study oxidation, I realized I was getting tired of all my recent forays into beer analysis. Between the Breakside brew day and the Bill Schneller classes, I felt like I'd shifted from fun study to more of the rigor I'd expected when I'd committing to taking the exam. I needed to remind myself that I actually enjoyed drinking beer. To that end, I invited Tony to join me for a date in Beeradise. Not only were we overdue for a night out together, I knew having Tony by my side would help pivot beer talk into bike talk, which sounded refreshing. Besides, if Tony came to the party, I could prove to him in person that I had the capacity to drink (and share) something from the cellar.

While a majority of beers are best drunk fresh, beers with high amounts of alcohol and yeast in the bottle have the capacity to change for the better over time. Unlike wine bottles, which are typically stored on their sides, which helps keep corks fresh, beer should be stored upright as it ages. The exception is beers capped with corks. Some beer collectors choose to store beers with corks upright, as well, which keeps the yeast in the bottom of the bottle and makes it easier to pour without letting the yeast slide into the glass.

It's not just the storage position that's disputed. A slew of online forums are dedicated to discussing when to drink specific vintages of hundreds of beers, subjective choices that are debated with relish. Did the 2008 Bourbon County Brand Stout peak last spring, or would it peak next spring? Forum participants demand thoroughly documented positions, complete with pictures of full or emptied bottles.

I'd been to bottle share parties before, the kind of party where people gather to share hard-to-find beers, many of which are aged. I had attended a bottle share called What Would Jesus Bring (WWJB). Each gathering had a theme, which ranged from beers made of breakfast ingredients—including oatmeal and coffee—to bourbon-barrel-aged beers. One focused on verticals, side-by-side tastings of the same beer from successive vintages. Usually verticals are hard to come by. Either you dutifully buy each beer the year it's released, then stash it away until you have enough years to taste them in a vertical, or you spend the time trading or buying beers from the years you're missing, an activity that may lead you to online beer forums or illegal trading sites.

Whether because of their rarity and lack of national distribution, some of the most vaunted craft beers in the world are being sold for exorbitant prices online, and not by the people who made them. Let's say you're a law-abiding citizen of Seattle, and you're thirsty for a bottle of Dark Lord, a Russian imperial stout made by 3 Floyds Brewing in Indiana. Good luck. Unless you can score a coveted ticket to the annual Dark Lord release in April, travel to Indiana for the event, then get the bottles home without breaking any shipping laws, your best bet is to find a neighbor who already has a bottle of Dark Lord in the cellar. Maybe she'll share. Or you could find and buy the beer online, which is illegal. Unless you're licensed, buying and re-selling beer isn't something state and federal governments allow.

In 2012, Westvleteren 12, a rare Belgian ale that's considered one of the best beers in the world, went on sale for the first time outside Belgium. Boxed six-packs (which included two glasses) sold for $85 but were being offered online and between friends, within hours, for $300 to $500. For a while, beer lovers were selling rare beers on eBay. They got around the U.S. website's policy forbidding the sale of al-coholic beverages by listing "collectible beer bottles"—insider code for selling the collectible beer inside. When eBay responded with a ban on the sale of "collectible containers that contain alcohol," other sites fielded the traffic. Beer even ended up on auction blocks in auc-tion houses more experienced with selling wine.

There are legal ways to get cult beers, which are commonly re-ferred to as "whales," "whalez," or "white whales" (references to *Moby-Dick*). First, there's beer trading, the practice of swapping similarly valued beers, which is entirely legal (except if you break alcohol shipping laws). Beer traders frequently meet online, everywhere from Craigslist to BeerAdvocate, which has a trading forum complete with a "Bad Traders List" and a thread where people post pictures of their latest hauls.

When I wrote a story about black market beer, most brewers told me they were upset by the practice. "When somebody is selling our beer for five hundred dollars on eBay, it's a falsely inflated price point and a bad representation of our brewery," said Natalie Cilurzo, the co-owner of Russian River Brewing, whom I met in Yakima during the hop harvest. Natalie told me she and her husband Vinnie Cilurzo, brewer and co-owner of Russian River, wanted their ales to be stored and shipped properly, which the average black market beer seller can't ensure. And they wanted to be the ones setting the prices for their beer. "Could we charge a lot more?" she said. "Sure. But it's beer. It's not gold."

Hair of the Dog's owner-brewer Alan Sprints says the aftermarket for his beers doesn't bother him. But he does try to quash some of the black market. At the Hair of the Dog tasting room, you can buy some of the brewery's vintage beers, but only if you're willing to drink them on-site. "If I allowed them to be sold to go," he says, "I wouldn't have any more beer."

Nothing about what we did at What Would Jesus Bring was illegal, though I can't vouch for how each beer was acquired. Twenty-five of us—friends and beer industry professionals—wore nametags with preassigned numbers. Every so often, two bartenders would fill rows of little plastic cups with one- or two-ounce pours of beer, which created a grid of dark circles. Our nametag numbers indicated which row we could drink. Whether or not the beer looked more like doses of medicine or some type of sacrament was a hot topic during the hours we spent sipping seven vintages of Goose Island Bourbon County Brand Stout, four years of Roots Organic Epic Ale—beer that is coveted in part because the brewery no longer exists—and seven years of He'Brew Jewbelation by Shmaltz Brewing. Bottles of these were beers were like individual pearls; in verticals, they became stunning strands. WWJB was Portland's version of a Davos penthouse party, with thousands of dollars of rare beer instead of champagne, and locally made cheese and charcuterie in lieu of a caviar bar. At the other end of the spectrum, some bottle shares are announced on Twitter and held in bars. BYOB: bring your own burrito.

After I'd rearranged some of the beer in my cellar, an excuse to ogle my collection, I finally decided on what to take to Brian's house: a 2011 Samuel Adams Utopias. Packaged in a ceramic container shaped like an old mash tun and with 29 percent ABV, the Boston Beer Company, owners of Samuel Adams, marketed it as the "strongest beer ever made." It was also one of the most expensive beers ever made: a twenty-four-ounce bottle cost $150 retail. (On the black market, Utopias can cost upwards of $300.) Utopias is a blend of beers that were aged in different kinds of barrels, some of which were brewed as early as 1994, which creates a drink less like beer and more like port or sherry. The Samuel Adams PR department had sent me, and other beer media, bottles of Utopias for free. I'd held on to mine, not only because I was waiting for the right occasion to drink the strongest beer in the world, but also because I wondered if the fact that the beer was free would alter its taste. My friends could help me find out. I tucked the beer into my bicycle pannier, hoping the ride across town wouldn't do any damage. Since the beer wasn't carbonated, I knew even a jarring, bumpy ride wouldn't cause the beer to spew.

At Brian's house, Tony and I settled into chairs in the basement while Brian's two-year-old son, Izzy, rolled around with a cooler on the floor. People started arriving, and so did the beer. A homebrewer named Rodney Kibzey produced a ten-year vertical of North Coast Brewing Old Stock Ale, which spanned from 2002 to 2014 but didn't include 2003 and 2005. He'd bought the beers one at a time at bottle shops over the years, and he would later lament that the 2015 was released just a few days after the party. Because I was trying to act like someone who hadn't been spending an inordinate amount of time analyzing beer, I purposely tried not to pay too much attention to what I was drinking. Instead, I let sips of Old Stock slide across my palate, oldest to newest, as I asked myself a simple question I'd started to forget to ask: *Do I like this beer?* Somewhere around 2008, I became distracted and started trying other beers on the table, including a sour from Upright Brewing and the ridiculously rich, barrel-aged Speedway Stout by AleSmith Brewing.

Tony, on the other hand, was deeply enmeshed in the Old Stock vertical.

"Oh wow," he said. "They're all so different." He looked entranced, and I remembered that tasting and talking about beer was something we used to enjoy doing together.

"This one doesn't seem right," he said, and passed his glass to me so I could try it. The beer tasted dusty and made me feel like I was cleaning out a closet, a sure sign of oxidation.

Then he found Goldilocks, possibly the 2008, 2009, or 2012. While the newer vintages seemed disjointed and jangly, the "just right" one was like the perfect dinner-party guest, a witty conversationalist who expressed both lightness and gravity.

At one point, I discovered I was sitting next to a Certified Cicerone, a guy who worked as a blender—someone who blends beers from different barrels—for a local brewery. I peppered him with questions about how he had prepared for the test, but to my frustration, he answered most of my queries with shrugs. I felt like he was withholding advice, but maybe he was just trying to relax. I tried to follow suit.

When I opened the Utopias and passed around the bottle, Brian suggested adding an oversized cube of smoked ice he'd brought home in a to-go bag from a restaurant famous for its cocktail program. I tried the beer straight up, then, even though I feared watering down the beer with the smoked ice, I tried it. The smoky dilution didn't even make a dent in the intense, sherry smoothness.

During the slow ride home, I took in gulps of cold air and felt the gentle slip of the pedals under my feet.

"They were so different!" Tony yelled from in front of me in the bike lane.

"The people?" I asked.

"No, the beer!"

GOING WILD

You can't just let nature run wild.

—WALT DISNEY

ON ONE OF THE LAST DAYS of February, during a rosy, gauzy sunrise in Brussels, my plane landed on a runway surrounded by soft hills punctuated with sharp steeples. With heavy eyelids, I rolled my bag from the airport to a hotel across the street, where I'd arranged to meet Sarah Jane Curran, my travel companion for the first half of my trip. I wasn't sure I'd recognize her again. We'd only met that one time at the Feast Portland festival, when I'd asked her if she wanted to go with me to Belgium. If I acted on every plan I made under the influence of a beer buzz, I would have climbed K2, written a dissertation on the wild desert truffles of Saudi Arabia, and spent a year working as a long-haul trucker. Yet there I was, on a frosty winter morning in Belgium, about to meet up with Sarah.

Because I'd been worried about giving up my solo travel time, I proposed a plan: Sarah and I would travel together for the first half of the trip, then I'd do the second half alone. Even though I worried I'd come off as ungrateful for her willingness to travel with me—a beer novice and a total stranger—she seemed excited about the idea, which wouldn't take her away from work and home for too long. I also started to realize that, if we traveled well together, I would've hit the Cicerone-study jackpot: Sarah was the real deal, an experienced beer industry insider who could teach me so much. Besides, as Megan Flynn had said, "It might be fun to have a buddy." She had a point: At most beer events, minus the rare night Tony and I got a babysitter for Oscar, I flew solo. Having a copilot might make Belgium more fun.

Arranging the trip had taken some work, starting with simply finding a time for Sarah and me to talk to make plans. She'd recently moved to Washington, D.C., and had landed a job at Birch and Barley, an upscale, beer-centric restaurant. Between her late-night hours and my copywriting job, our phone conversation took weeks to execute, which didn't seem like a good sign. When we finally talked, I was glad I'd trusted my intuition about her. She'd already made a Google map of all the breweries she wanted to see.

"I'm assuming we're both on a tight budget?" she said over the phone, before explaining that she wasn't picky about hotels, as long as they were moderately clean. I felt a surge of relief. Sarah was a budget traveler, just like me.

"So, this is kind of random," Sarah said, "but my co-worker told me about a great restaurant in a town called Ypres. The chef used to work at a Michelin-starred restaurant, so it's definitely a splurge. Want to go there for lunch one day?" My mind flashed to a vision of us eating juniper foam and *uni*.

"Absolutely," I said.

With just a few weeks until we would meet in Brussels, Sarah and I decided to each contact people who could help us arrange meetings with brewers at breweries, which fit with my vision of gaining firsthand knowledge of Belgium's beer culture and traditions among fermentation tanks and in brewery tasting rooms. There was no one brewery or town I needed to visit to accomplish this goal. I welcomed serendipity; whatever I encountered would teach me something. Sarah talked to the distributors she knew from working at Eleven Madison Park. I asked for contacts and introductions from fellow beer writers, from a sales rep for a distributor who'd recently let me sit in on a tasting of imported ales, and from two Portland friends who run bicycle beer tours in Belgium. I told the Belgian brewers I was a journalist who was studying for a beer test by visiting Belgium for the first time. (I didn't mention the word *Cicerone:* since it seemed to confuse most people in the United States, I could only imagine how obscure the program was in Europe.) Our approach meant that planning focused less on geography and more on just getting appointments. As our travel dates approached, Sarah and I e-mailed each other in a flurry as we tried to gauge distances and timing.

As our itinerary filled, I faced a few heartbreaks. I wouldn't have time to see Bruges, a city known for its reflective canals and medieval architecture. And I hadn't been able to gain access into any Trappist breweries, which wasn't a surprise; Trappist monk brewers were notoriously unreceptive to visitors of any kind. While beer geeks still flock to the cafés and nearby spots that serve Trappist ales, I was less interested in being a tourist and more interested in being on the inside, even if it meant missing the chance to drink some of Belgium's most famous beers. Lastly, I had scheduled only one day during my eleven days on the ground that didn't include a beer appointment, which meant I probably wouldn't be visiting art museums or chocolate factories. This trip was all about work, but it would be the best kind of work.

I was worried about being away home for thirteen days, including the two full days of air travel (but who was counting)—it would be the longest I'd ever been away from Oscar. Nearly a year earlier, when I first brought up the idea of going to Europe, Tony seemed skeptical. "Oh sure," he said. "You *have* to go to Europe to learn about beer." But once I'd committed to taking the exam, he'd fully endorsed the idea.

"Go," he'd said over and over again. "We'll be fine!"

I showed Oscar maps of Europe, and I told him about my new friend Sarah and what made Belgian beers so special. I told him I'd miss him. We agreed I'd take one of his beloved Matchbox cars, a black one, which would make it like he was with me all the time, I said. I'd heard of parents photographing their kids' objects on the road then sending the pictures home, so I thought I'd give it a try. After I tucked my toothbrush into its travel case and zipped up my suitcase, I decided to sneak into Oscar's room for one last chance to feel the warmth of his forehead and take in his sleep smell, an even mixture of milky baby and goaty boy. The sun wouldn't rise for at least a few hours. As soon as I opened the door, he rolled over and struggled to open his puffy eyes.

"Sunshine," I started, taking a deep breath. "I wanted to say goodbye one last time. My taxi is here."

"Mama!" he wailed. He threw his arms around my torso, as though we were lovers being torn apart by unjust forces. "I can't bear it!"

I cried during the taxi ride to the airport. I'd justified this trip as career development, but who was I kidding? I was going to Belgium to drink beer, which sounded less like a job and more like a vacation. I was selfish, and my sweet, innocent child couldn't bear it. But once I buckled my seatbelt on the plane, I felt an odd sense of liberation. I was by myself, about to explore the new and unknown, like I used to do before I had a child. I'd packed my dog-eared copy of *Tasting Beer*—a book I kept reading in nonsequential chunks—stacks of beer style sheets from my classes, and some blank flashcards. *Let the learning begin,* I thought, as the plane's engines roared.

———

In the lobby of a hotel across the street from the airport, I immediately recognized Sarah's long stride. Her straight hair was swept back, which made her look professional, as though she was headed to a meeting at the European Union. She'd flown in the night before and spent the night in the hotel. I tried not to resent her recent full night of sleep and hot shower.

"Hey," she said, smiling. "How's it going? I didn't check out yet because I thought you might want to freshen up. You know, brush your teeth and stuff."

"Ah," I sighed. "Thank you."

After I collected myself in the hotel room, we were off. I'd already warned Sarah that I hated driving. In foreign countries, I usually took buses, trains, boats, airplanes, taxis, and canoes, anything that would prevent me from having to navigate strange road signs, and do metric conversions, at seventy miles per hour. Unfortunately, as a New Yorker for the past five years, she also hated driving. But since our trip was centered on traversing a country the size of Rhode Island, many times, we rented a black Jetta. As we left the airport, Sarah gripped the steering wheel at ten-and-two and peered at the small GPS unit mounted to the dash. The console said "Klara," which we assumed was the name of the car. Later we would discover that Klara was the name of the classical music radio station playing at the time, but it was too late. We would address Klara by name from then on, as though she were the European goddess of safe passage.

Sarah cautiously drove us to Erpe-Mere, a sparsely populated area in Flanders, the Dutch-speaking area of northern Belgium that includes the capital city of Brussels and five provinces. Flanders is known for many styles of beer, most famously the fruity and acidic Flanders red ales, which writer Michael Jackson called the "Burgundies of Belgium." But that beer style wasn't why we were here.

In a well-manicured suburb with pointy iron gates and streets too narrow for most American cars, we'd found a modern, two-story garage with a sloped roof next to a well-kept vegetable garden. The air smelled richly fertile, making the frenetic aromas of cars, fried foods, and the perfumed people on the streets of Brussels seem like a dream. We'd arrived at De Glazen Toren brewery, named after the street it's on—Glazentoren, which translates to "glass tower" and was the name of a pub that existed on the street a century ago.

Inside, we were greeted by Mark De Neef, one of the brewery's three business partners, who was retired from his job as a librarian in the nearby city of Aalst. Our balding guide, who wore a diamond-print sweater, circa 1994, hunched over a bit. I guessed he was close to seventy years old. He told us the brewery made 1,500 hectaliters of beer a year, my first introduction to two weeks of nonstop conversions. (I later figured out that equals about 1,280 barrels, which made

De Glazen Toren a small, if not tiny, brewery.) The two brewers were the other business partners: Dirk De Pauw, a lawyer and the financial director of a hospital in Aalst, and Jef Van den Steen, a mathematician and one of Belgium's most famous beer writers. They'd both earned degrees from the Ghent Brewery School CTL (Chemie Textiel Landbouw), a three-year program they pursued during weekends so they could continue working their day jobs.

"Anyone can call themselves a brewer, but Jef and Dirk are *masters*," Mark said forcefully, as spittle flew from the corner of his mouth. This, I believed. Since the brewery's opening in 2004, it had developed a reputation for outstanding beer made from iron-rich well water from Jef's house, next door. Even though the demand for De Glazen Toren beer outpaces supply, the three men don't have plans for expansion, what seemed to me like a distinctly non-American approach. While I knew a few brewers in Portland who weren't interested in growing their breweries, they were outliers.

"We don't want to become rich," said Mark, "but it all needs to be paid for." He swept his arm around the brewery, which was originally built to be the garage for Jef's "camping car," which is now parked elsewhere. All the brewing equipment was designed by Jef, the perfect job for a mathematician. But he didn't do his own welds; he'd had the equipment constructed in Germany. After the beer ferments in stainless steel, it is bottled and moved to a small room heated to 25 or 26 degrees Celsius (78.8 degrees Fahrenheit). I'd heard about these "warm rooms," which are used to develop flavor profiles from certain esters during secondary fermentation, otherwise known as bottle conditioning. The rooms were standard in Belgium breweries. Inside the warm room, faced with case after case of bottled beer sitting upright, the balmy air kissed me once on each cheek, a greeting the people of Belgium would bestow on me many times in the coming days. Despite the warmth, I shivered from the thrill of finally standing in one of these famous rooms.

Mark told us he was in charge of wrapping each 75-centiliter bottle (25.37 ounces) with paper, which protects the beer inside from light and makes the beverage look like an elegant present.

"I'll do it blindfolded!" he cried out proudly.

I imagined him wrapping the bottles with the same swift care he took when shelving books at the library. Sometimes "students," or interns, helped with the wrapping on Saturdays, when they weren't in school. The good ones can wrap fifteen cases of twelve bottles an hour.

A man with a long white beard, a red fisherman's cap, a blue jumpsuit, and a carefully arranged scarf, looking like he could play a role in *The Life Aquatic with Steve Zissou,* opened the door. He gave us a nod and a dismissive wave, as he pressed a cell phone against his ear and spoke in a language I couldn't understand. It was Jef Van den Steen.

Eventually Jef led us to a table near the warm room, where he explained that, for him, brewing school was "absolutely necessary," a path many American craft brewers choose not to take. Jef said he and Dirk were making excellent homebrew, but they weren't always able to reproduce the results. Getting an education in brewing made it possible to consistently make the same great beer. When the brewers launched De Glazen Toren, they decided to make their own versions of classic beers they admired.

"We're too old and too wise to try to invent something new," Jef said.

When they designed Saison d'Erpe-Mere—one of the brewery's most famous beers—they based it on Saison Dupont, a Belgian saison brewed near the border of France.

"We went the direction of Dupont, but a little different," said Jef. "Dupont has a hard bitterness. You can feel it here." He gently tapped a segment of beard that cloaked his throat. "No compromises," he continued. "We make honest beer with simple ingredients. We don't look for experiments."

The idea gave me pause. American brewers were constantly saying they'd invented something new—a new use of hops, a new mashing technique, a new name, a new label—an attitude of individuality and self-expression that was being cultivated long before the Declaration of Independence came into existence. I realized I'd become immune to declarations of invention, and with one sentence, Jef had reminded me I was in a country with different values. This was why I'd traveled across the Atlantic, I thought, to see beer from the perspective of brewers with a different relationship to history.

Jef grabbed a bottle of papered Cuvée Angélique, a revival of Cuvée de l'Ermitage, a beer from Brasserie de l'Union, a brewery in the town of Jumet that went out of business. "It was the beer my wife loved very much," he told me. "For her I created this beer." He filled squat goblets of amberish beer until they formed a nearly two-inch-thick, unapologetic white head, and explained that a bottle of the beer cost 2.90 euros at the brewery's gift shop and 3.85 euros at a shop down the street. In the United States, a bottle of beer of this caliber would cost somewhere between $12 and $20. I'd quickly learn that, not only was this the land of great beer, it was the land of *cheap* great beer. The beer smelled faintly of fruitcake and booze, like a corner of a classic holiday party, but delivered a rich wallop of prune and toffee, plus a tingle of sourness. My first Belgian beer on Belgian soil made me feel heady with the possibility of drinking more beer like this during my trip. Even so, the beer had 8.5 percent ABV, so I was glad to have been presented with just one small goblet. Still, jet lag and excitement were making me feel slightly delirious, so thankfully, Sarah offered to drive us back to the city.

As I finished my beer, I glanced at Sarah, who was taking her last sip with her eyes closed; it wouldn't be the first time I'd see her relish a beer with total pleasure. Before we left, Jef mentioned that once he met a fan from Italy who gave him a T-shirt that said: *Simplicity is the ultimate complexity.*

"That's the taste of a good brewer," said Jef with a hearty laugh.

Sarah and I thanked the men profusely, bowed like Japanese tourists, and walked down the driveway. We looked at each other and grinned.

"That was amazing," she said.

I nodded. I was thinking about mathematical precision, repetition, profit, and care—the kind of exhilarating rush of thoughts that arises when I'm in foreign places. While I'd learned many lessons abroad before, never had I created the chance to look at a new place through the lens of beer. And I was just getting started.

———

The next morning, in a cobblestone plaza where a farmer's market was underway, I sunk my teeth into a divinely sticky and chewy waffle hot off the griddle. Sarah was eating a flaky *pain au chocolat,* and soon we were discussing breakfast foods.

"I know it's not cool for a food person not to like eggs," she said. "But I hate them, in all forms."

"What?" I mumbled, as I took another bite of waffle and contemplated buying another one. I was accustomed to hearing people say they didn't eat certain foods—I lived in Portland, land of dietary restrictions and cleanses—so her declaration wasn't shocking, but I imagined that someone working in the upper echelons of the culinary world would find it difficult to avoid eggs altogether. Even though I was just starting to get to know her, I sensed that, if anyone could pull off an upset, it would be Sarah.

While I'd assumed I'd be nursing a hangover that first morning in Brussels, the previous night Sarah had smartly suggested that I *not* drink liters of beer from the neighborhood bodega, which had a thrilling selection of bottled Belgian beers, many of which I'd never seen before. "Don't worry," she had said, "they'll be plenty of beer on this trip." She was right, of course.

We shared a room in a mid-range hotel in the Saint-Gilles neighborhood of Brussels, which, one shocked local told us, was home to the city's "prison." When I snored during the night, she politely snapped her fingers in front of my face until I stopped. "I didn't feel comfortable with a nudge," she told me the next morning. "We're still getting to know each other."

On day three, instead of driving all over the country in a mad dash to meet brewers, as we had been doing, we decided to park the car and explore the city by foot. In the morning, we would move Klara from the street to the hotel's underground parking just as street-parking enforcement went into effect. Ever the budget travelers, we calculated we could save twenty euros by not paying for hotel parking overnight, which defied advice from a woman at the hotel's front desk.

"What does she know?" I'd said.

In an act of solidarity, Sarah and I decided to set an early morning alarm and move the car together. Then we'd go back to sleep.

The next morning, we walked out of the hotel, bleary eyed and quiet.

"Where's Klara?" Sarah said, stopping abruptly on the sidewalk.

"Are we on the right street?" I asked.

"She's not here."

In her place was a dirty truck and workers destroying cobblestone. It turns out the temporary sign the size of a fire hydrant, a chalkboard with a handwritten message, meant "no parking." Klara had been towed. We tried to ease the pain with pastries: delicate *pains au chocolat* and a warm, flat pastry the size of a placemat. *"Un crêpe!"* the baker told me, excitedly. Then we steeled ourselves for the task of finding Klara in a city where we didn't speak any of its three official languages.

During the five gray and rainy hours it took us to retrieve Klara—a process that took us to multiple government buildings, an ATM for a budget-blowing withdrawal, and a warehouse filled with impounded cars—Sarah and I agreed we were being punished for acting like cheap old men. One thing kept us going. That afternoon, we were going to Cantillon.

Ever since I decided to go to Belgium, I knew I'd visit Cantillon, a brewery that produces some of the world's most famous lambics. Lambics are an ancient style of beer made with unmalted wheat, aged hops, and wild yeast and bacteria that naturally become part of the fermentation process (as opposed to the beer being inoculated with a culture, which is how most brewers spark fermentation). The resulting beers vary wildly, from vinous and tart to earthy and strange. Beer writer Michael Jackson called them "neither strong nor aggressive but they have a lean, firm wineyness that can shock at first sip—and seduce to the point of obsession anyone who truly loves sensory exploration."

Much like champagne is only made in the region of Champagne in France, genuine lambics are only produced in the Senne River valley, home to Brussels. But drinkers beware: lambic labeling laws in the EU do mandate that the beers be made using spontaneous fermentation, but labels don't have to specify where the beer is made. And while many American beer drinkers assume all lambics are made with fruit, only some contain the addition. *Kriek* is a lambic that was originally made with local Schaarbeek sour cherries, but today's brewers source cherries from elsewhere, if they use fresh cherries at all. Traditionally, brewers added real fruit to the beer fermenting in the barrel, but in modern times some breweries have resorted to a cheaper method of adding fruit flavors. For example, Lindemans, a popular Belgian import in the United States, brews spontaneously fermented lambics in a small town southwest of Brussels, in the Senne River valley, and uses fruit juice as a substitute for whole fruit in some of its *kriek*.

The nonfruit spawn of lambic is gueuze, a blend of aged lambics. There are few beer firsts I remember with as much clarity as my first gueuze. Five years earlier, a salesperson at a bottle shop had suggested I try Oud Beersel Oude Geuze, when I mentioned my curiosity about sour ales. Not only was I confused by the beer's name and its many vowels, I was convinced I wasn't going to like the beer. "Be prepared for something different," he'd warned. Drinking the cloudy, honey-hued beer was a form of culture shock. Its tartness was complicated: lemony, electric, and alive.

Many beer historians consider lambics to be one of the oldest existing beer styles. The oldest recipe for the beer is from 1556, but historians know the style existed before then. The beer was cited as having health properties, because it generally lacks residual sugars and has low amounts of alcohol. In 1941 the mayor of Brussels wrote, "I am recovering from a serious illness and to get me back on my feet again my doctor advises me to drink a glass of gueuze every day, or even better, a glass of kriek."

After we secured Klara in the hotel's parking garage, Sarah and I took the Metro to the Anderlecht area, a neighborhood that, despite the fact that it didn't house a prison, felt a little gritty. Next to a Laundromat and across from an empty lot surrounded by chain link, Cantillon didn't profess to be a landmark. But the brewery is an original. When Cantillon was founded in 1900, it was one of a hundred breweries in Brussels. These days, it's one of three.

On the other side of the two large wooden entry doors, we stood in a dark, cool cave of a space with low ceilings and a long hallway that tunneled into a beer-making womb. I smelled a dank mustiness, as though I'd just walked into a barn with baying livestock. Earlier, I'd tried to arrange to meet head brewer and master blender Jean Van Roy, who's considered to be one of the most famous brewers in the world. In an e-mail, a brewery employee said that, while Sarah and I were welcome to visit, Jean, a fourth-generation brewer at Cantillon, may not have time to speak to us. Sure enough, when he was summoned, Jean, who has high cheekbones, a fair complexion, and trim build, like a Norwegian skate skier on the verge of winning an Olympic gold medal, shook my hand tersely and clenched his jaw.

"There's a problem I must fix, I'm sorry," he said with a thick accent, before disappearing down the long hallway.

Sarah and I were left standing across a counter from Alberto Cardoso, a man whose long graying ponytail made him look like he was headed to an American beer festival. In the tasting room behind us, two young bearded guys wearing hooded sweatshirts were taking turns gently pouring beer from a bottle nestled in a traditional lambic basket. A wicker cousin of the picnic basket, lambic baskets cradle bottles of lambic on their side at a slight incline—the angle you'd hold a baby for bottle feeding—which allows the yeast in the bottle to settle in one corner, so you can pour the most beer possible without including any sediment. (A pour without yeast sediment is considered a "clean pour," which is commonly preferred over a cloudy "yeast pour." Some people, including me, enjoy the taste of the yeast pour, which includes a bonus dose of vitamin B. Others think yeast pours taste disgusting and act as a laxative.) Like the trope that sex appeal increases when someone lights your cigarette, men who pour beer from lambic baskets look refined, no matter how big their beards.

As a volunteer at the brewery's "museum"—which so far appeared to be a T-shirt sales area—Alberto launched into an exposition about the brewery. Cantillon brews only during the winter, he explained, the same schedule brewers used before humans discovered the science of fermentation. The brewing schedule is determined by the life cycle of flying insects native to the Senne River area. (The Senne flows through Brussels, a city that was built on the river's swamps, which made constructing the underground subway system a feat of engineering.) At first frost, when the insects stop appearing, Cantillon begins brewing. Near the beginning of April, when the temperatures warm up and the insects begin to buzz, the brewing season ends, and the staff shifts to nonbrewing tasks, such as adding fruit to beers in barrels or blending batches of lambics to make gueuze.

"We are always working with nature," he bellowed, "and nature is never predictable." Even though he must deliver the same speech hundreds of times a day, Alberto was enunciating his words like a Shakespearean actor performing a central soliloquy. "We are the perfect witness to declare that global warming is not a lie," he said loudly, over a symphony of clinks at the nearby bottling area. "We've lost six weeks of brewing time since the 1960s."

Alberto handed us a blue and white booklet and told us to follow the numbered Cantillon logos—an iconic outline of a man drinking a beer and falling over backward.

"So we just take ourselves through the brewery?" I whispered to Sarah.

"It appears so," she said.

Alberto had mentioned that public tours of the museum, which turned out to be the entire brewery, helped save the brewery from financial ruin in the 1970s, when Jean Van Roy's father came up with the idea of opening the doors to the public. In litigation-prone United States, I couldn't imagine any brewery giving visitors this kind of freedom, especially in a place filled with slippery hallways, hot brewing equipment, and creaky old stairwells. We walked down the same hallway Jean had gone down, a walkway lined with the butts of green bottles filled with fermenting beer. Small chalkboards showed the name of the beer inside and the date it was brewed. Within moments, we'd mis-guided ourselves to a stairwell to the bathroom.

Behind me, I heard an American drawl. "Can I help you guys?" A sweaty and flushed bearded man introduced himself as Brandon Evans. He was finishing the first day of an uncommon "internship" at the brewery: in exchange for a week of labor, which would allow him to learn firsthand about lambic making, Brandon vowed to help Jean improve his English. While Brandon's wife worked as a nuclear engineer for the European Commission in Germany, he traveled around Europe helping run beer festivals and brewing under his own label in France: Get Radical.

When I told him I was studying for the Cicerone exam, he told me why he wasn't studying for the exam.

"I don't need to take a test to prove what I know about beer," he said. "I learn in breweries."

The idea that the Cicerone exam quantifies knowledge that doesn't need to be quantified is a common critique in the beer community. Since I started studying for the exam, many people told me they thought the test was too expensive ($395 for the first go-round) or that certification didn't hold any real value for the titleholder; the program was just a way for Ray Daniels to make money. While I understood those complaints, Brandon's comment made me bristle. I hadn't asked why he was or wasn't taking the exam, which made his rejection of the program feel like an undercut of something I obviously found valuable. But I let his comment slide; the Cicerone program was the last thing I wanted to be dissecting right then.

Brandon led us past a wood-plank-sided mash tun with a lid that looked like a mad man's flying machine. Inside, I saw the hunched back of someone bent over scrubbing.

Some lambic blenders buy wort from nearby brewers then inoculate that wort in their own facility. A few others, including Cantillon, brew on-site. Jean was checking equipment, and he moved among the tanks, copper tubing, and rising steam with a smooth, professional swiftness. I wasn't sure what kind of problem he was solving, but I hoped the solution would throw cold water on the tired, wilting feeling of a brew day ending too soon.

Sarah and I followed Brandon up some narrow wooden stairs to a room with two hop boilers, one of which had a gleaming copper top.

Lambic brewers have a unique relationship with hops. Not only do they boil the hops extensively (which gets rid of the volatile oils that contain hop aromas and flavors, while intensifying the bitterness), but they also start with "aged hops," hop cones that are at least three years old. Rather than agents of flavor, hops function as the key preservative in lambics. Earlier, I'd asked Alberto what type of hop is used at Cantillon.

"We don't care," he said. "Any hops, as long as they're European."

To make a lambic, brewers create a thick mash with a high ratio of malt to water, a tradition with roots in a Belgian tax relative to the size of a mash tun. The tax forced brewers to make smaller, more concentrated batches of beer, a tradition that continues to influence brewing practices today. The turbid mash has a white froth from the unmalted wheat, which is removed and heated separately, then added back into the rest of the wort. Lambics boil for longer than most beer styles, and most braised meat dishes: three to six hours.

I heard a belt whirring, and the room felt damp, as if its surfaces were layered with the steam and the sweat of multiple generations of hard workers. A long wooden trough from the granary room hung empty, waiting for its next load of malt. As we shuffled around the room, trying to stay out of the way of Jean's brewing team, I felt the urge to look inside one of the boiling tanks. When I tapped the handle with my hand, the metal was too hot to hold. Without my asking, Brandon whipped off his sweat-soaked Cantillon T-shirt, revealing more skin than I'd ever seen inside a brewery, and, as though the shirt was an oven mitt, opened the lid. When I looked down into the hole, I saw only steam rising out of an eerie darkness.

Brandon said he'd meet up with us later, because he had to help clean now, so Sarah and I continued our tour, following the drunk-man logo to the base of another narrow stairway. At the top, under the slanted wooden beams of the attic, sat some battered and rusted barrels covered with tiny dots of white mold and decorated with delicate cobwebs. "A lambic brewer will never destroy a cobweb, and killing spiders is very much frowned upon," the brochure explained.

"They're the Zen monks of the beer world," I whispered to Sarah. She nodded silently.

Through the open top half of a Dutch door, I saw a flat, open-topped rectangular copper vessel—the coolship, or *koelschip* in Flemish—where the magic of fermentation begins. The gurgling sound of water filled the room, and steam rose to the ceiling; it was like a beer spa. Hot wort was filling the coolship, and as it cooled to between 18 and 20 degrees Celsius (64 to 68 degrees Fahrenheit), natural yeast and bacteria from the air would drop into the wort and begin to consume the liquid's sugars. Scientists have found up to two hundred different strains of yeast and bacteria in lambic, including acetic and lactic bacteria, which produce the acids that create the beer's legendary tartness.

Before 1857, when Louis Pasteur discovered yeast, brewers and bakers certainly saw the effects of the invisible (to the naked eye), single-celled organisms: bubbles in rising dough and alcohol in beer. Back then, all yeast was "wild." It thrived in certain places, including fruit skins and human skin. Even though they didn't understand yeast as we know it today, brewers figured out how, at the end of fermentation, to harvest the yeast that had made good beer so they could reuse that yeast in subsequent batches of beer. So began the split between wild and domesticated yeast.

These days, "wild" yeast has a few definitions. In one sense, wild yeast is something that hasn't been cultivated for human use, making it the Alaskan salmon of the beer world. In the scientific treatise *The Yeasts: A Taxonomic Study* by Kurtzman, Fell, and Boekhout, wild yeasts are called "contaminants from the environment, or genetic variants of the cultivated strain." It goes on to say that the most problematic wild yeasts are those that are similar to "industrial" yeasts but able to overtake the cultivated strains and spoil the product.

I'd been seeing beers described as "wild" even though they had been inoculated with cultivated microbial cultures. While scientists might get away with describing cultivated yeast as "industrial," brewers never could. (Who wants to drink something made with "industrial yeast"?) When I asked Ben Edmunds about the discrepancy, he said many "wild beers" were simply beers that used yeast strains other than *Saccharomyces*, the genus of fungi that includes all ale and lager yeasts, cultured or not. "It seems like there's just no better nomenclature that anyone has come up with yet," he said.

It's a gamble to rely entirely on the yeasts that naturally land in wort. At Cantillon, one hundred years into production, the gamble is less risky. Jean Van Roy knows that the right yeasts and bacteria will land in the wort, the ones that will make his lambics, lambic. Mixing yeast strains, cultivated or wild, creates uncertain outcomes; brewers who inoculate their beers using cultivated yeasts rarely use more than one strain in a single beer.

The first time I had thought about this fact was at Logsdon Farmhouse Ales (now Logsdon Farm Brewery), outside Hood River, Oregon, under the glare of Mount Hood's glaciers. Brewmaster David Logsdon is one of the founding fathers of the American craft brewing scene, mostly because of the yeasts he's harnessed. In 1986 he and his then-wife Jeannette Kreft-Logsdon opened Wyeast

Laboratories, which has become one of the most respected suppliers of brewing yeasts in the country. (I dare you to find a home or commercial brewer who hasn't made a beer with at least one of Wyeast's yeasts.) When he opened Logsdon Farmhouse Ales, he decided to brew beers fermented with a palate of yeasts he had personally developed by "borrowing them" from certain European beers.

He told me this fact as we lingered in the sunshine outside the brewhouse listening to his cows bay, and I immediately imagined a *Mission Impossible*–style heist, complete with laser-beam security systems and black-gloved yeast thieves. In reality, David flew to Europe then tucked his favorite bottles of beer between sweaters in his luggage for the trip home. He developed the yeasts contained in those beers, and started using them in his beers in Oregon. Because of his experience as a yeast wrangler, he knew how to combine certain yeasts in a single beer while avoiding mutations and contaminations. But David is the exception.

———

Through the thick steam, I saw fading daylight and the rooftops of Cantillon's neighbors through louvered horizontal vents, which were open so that the city's air—the provenance of the invisible life that would inoculate the wort—could enter the room. Among the wood and dampness, I'd forgotten we were in gritty Brussels, a humming city, another kind of organism that shaped the decay and life of Cantillon's beers.

At Cantillon, the wort rests in the coolship overnight. In the morning, the liquid is transferred to wooden barrels, where the porousness of the wood helps the bacteria and yeast thrive. While Alberto Cardoso told us the barrels didn't contribute yeast and bacteria to the wort (the barrels are steam cleaned, then filled with hot water and chains and shaken vigorously on a machine that Sarah said looked like something used to train astronauts), it seemed impossible that the cleaning would remove every single organism from the wood. *Brettanomyces,* a genus of wild yeast that naturally appears in lambics, gueuzes, and sour brown ales, thrives in wood. The yeast imparts earthy, savory, and funky flavors, which have become increasingly popular with American craft beer drinkers. While the beers at Cantillon are naturally inoculated with *Brettanomyces*—making them truly wild—many brewers intentionally ferment with "Brett," a calculated risk that has the potential to destroy an entire brewery.

Russian River Brewing intentionally adds Brett to many of its beers. For vintners, Brett is considered a menace that creates off-flavors in wine and permanently infects barrels, so a few local winemakers refuse to give Russian River any barrels on principle and won't even step foot inside the brewery. The brewery has a set of additional equipment that's used to make beers that contain Brett: a separate tank and separate pumps, hoses, valves, gaskets, and bottling equipment. And if a brewer works on the Brett side of the brewery one day, he or she is not allowed to wear those same clothes to the brewery the next day, in the hopes of preventing contamination of non-Brett beers and equipment.

Brettanomyces infections have happened at major breweries, a mistake most brewers hesitate to reveal to the public. In 2009, after customers began complaining, Deschutes Brewery went public with the news that a batch of Mirror Mirror, an oak-aged English barley wine, had been infected with Brett. Now the brewery flash-pasteurizes all beer from wooden barrels to kill any potentially present Brett before the beer is blended with unpasteurized beer from the tanks.

The yeasts in Cantillon's worts change the liquid during one, two, or three years in the barrels. After the beers age, they're combined with fresh whole fruit, which is shoved through bungholes, except for apricots, which are cut in half so they can fit. Sarah and I walked past rows of barrels filled with beer and stacked three-high, to the ceiling. On one support beam, a round barrel top nailed to a beam read: LE TEMPS NE RESPECTE PAS CE QUI SE FAIT SANS LUI. *Time doesn't respect what happens without him.* The hairs on my arms stood up, like the first time I saw the Duomo in Florence. I felt awed by this sacred space filled with art, liquid art.

Eventually, we made our way back to the tasting room, where Alberto was waiting to give us the end-of-tour beer samples. With a steady hand, Alberto poured a sweetened lambic called *faro* from a blue ceramic pitcher. The first sip was bracing and tart, but it gave way to an earthy mustiness that encapsulated the brewery: a mixture of the life of tiny spiders, mold spores, and dank wood—the ingredients a witch might throw into her kettle to make a magic potion.

"People who visit Cantillon don't always like the beer," Alberto said. "For the first time in human history, we have children eating sugar every single day of their life since they were born. The result: their taste buds are calibrated on sweetness. So people today hate two flavors: sourness and bitterness."

We moved to the tables where the bearded guys had been drinking, and he produced a bottle of kriek, a two-year-old lambic fermented with sour cherries, that had just been bottled. At two years, a lambic is considered young. The beer glowed a mesmerizing ruby color, and a soft layer of pink foam reminded me of strawberry frosting on a cake. The kriek tasted purely of cherry, only without any sweetness, like an eau de vie without the hot alcoholic heat.

If Alberto decides to wage a war on sugar, this beer should be his weapon.

Brandon arrived for his postwork beer, a spectacularly enviable way to end a day of labor, and Jean Van Roy appeared out of nowhere. In one hand he held an empty glass and, in the other, a bottle of lambic made with carignan, a black-skinned wine grape native to northern Spain. Later, I'd find out the beer was only available in the brewery, but right then its rareness meant nothing. After taking a sip, I wanted to preserve the moment so my future self could return to this first taste of its tart acidity, hay, animal funk, dark cherries, and sweet grapes. The beer brought together the wild and unkempt nature of the brewery, a place I felt infiltrating my skin, as though I was a porous wooden barrel, with a fruit from a place I'd never been. I was tasting two terroirs, and although the flavor of grape wasn't lost, it had been assimilated. For a moment, I was so focused on the beer, I forgot Jean Van Roy was leaning against a wooden support beam with his arms crossed, holding his glass with his pointer and middle finger. He sipped with a crisp sense of propriety.

"We produce the most specific beers in the world," he said with the staccato of someone in a hurry. "Yet we are totally alone here in the city." Belgian beer drinkers had lost interest in lambics. Of the 45,000 people who toured the brewery the previous year, 60 percent were there independently, like me and Sarah, and not on an organized tour. Only 7 percent of those visitors were Belgians.

As the brewery shut down for the night, Brandon and Alberto invited me and Sarah to join them at Moeder Lambic, a famous Brussels beer bar. Part of me didn't want to drink anything else that night, so I could hold on to the taste of the carignan lambic like a souvenir. But I understood the possibility that I could drink something even better, the type of greed that can lead to sloshy nights or delightful discoveries. The four of us walked outside into the dusky evening. Somewhere beneath our feet, the water of the Senne River seeped through the city's manmade barriers, evidence of the natural world's persistence.

"Looks like Brooklyn," Sarah said. We were facing the empty lot across the street.

"It actually looks pretty good today," Brandon replied. "Usually it's filled with trash."

Jean Van Roy appeared, again, with the quiet stealth of a ninja. He was straddling a bicycle so shiny it must have been fresh from the box. Unlike the common upright commuter bicycles nearly everyone in Brussels seemed to be riding, Jean was on what looked like a mountain bike. After Jean gracefully hopped the curb and pedaled down the street, Alberto said, "That bike came from the Americans." Before I had developed a full vision, of an American tourism board, maybe, gifting Jean a bike to thank him for making such special beers, Alberto added, "Americans are buying all the beer."

As we walked through a whole city pressing home from work, the lambics, gueuze, and kriek Sarah and I had bought at the brewery gently clinked in our bags, the glassy music of beer lovers leaving a world-famous brewery. Before we turned the corner, I glanced back for a final glimpse of Cantillon, and I considered taking another picture. After all, I was just your average American.

UNBROKEN CHAIN

When a language dies it is a vision of a world that disappears.
—KOICHIRO MATSUURA

SARAH AND I stood under a sable sky, huddled around a crackling fire pit with a group of Belgians we'd just met. "We have a saying," said a robust man with a swoop of highlighted hair. "A proper gueuze is like an angel pissing on your tongue." I wasn't prepared to endorse this metaphor, because the beer tasted too tartly electric to have been spewed from a sweet, celestial cherub. But after a hairy day of driving across the small country—which took us from a tour of De Dolle Brouwers in West Flanders, where we met some boisterous college-aged Boy Scouts clad in shorts and neck scarves, to some outstanding truck-stop *frites* and, finally, Klara's traverse of a narrow dirt road elevated above fields of rice paddies—the gueuze tasted like salvation.

The man was Dimitri "Dimi" Cockaert, a hair stylist and bon vivant I'd met through Kris Schamp, a Belgian native who lives in

Portland and leads bike tours in Belgium. His brother, Jan, had kindly invited me and Sarah to his house for a cheese and beer tasting, and Dimi was part of a welcoming cast of forty-somethings who liked to eat and drink well and ride bicycles. I felt at home. The evening unfolded into an elaborate spread of national cheeses and beers, including the Westvleteren Blond, a Belgian pale ale from the Trappist brewery that made the Westvleteren 12, which is consistently voted "Best Beer in the World" on community beer sites and by media. I savored each sip of the Blond, which would rank as my favorite beer that evening, knowing I wouldn't be visiting the brewery and tasting the 12 on this trip. Dimi arranged to introduce us to Armand Debelder, the man who'd crafted the angel piss. Armand was a famous lambic blender at Drie Fonteinen (also known as 3 Fonteinen, because *drie* means "three" in Dutch).

The following evening we met Dimi in Beersel, a small town thirteen kilometers south of Brussels in the Senne River valley. For decades, Beersel has been known as a hub of traditional lambic making. I'd heard of Armand, and I sensed his beers were as culturally significant as those from Cantillon, but I wasn't sure why. And even though I'd had a thorough lesson in the magic of spontaneous fermentation at Cantillon, I wanted to learn more about the art of blending. Outside Drie Fonteinen, Sarah, Dimi, and I shivered in the bitter wind as the sun unceremoniously sunk below the horizon. Inside, a videographer was interviewing Armand for a documentary. We waited our turn.

Eventually, the three of us were allowed to enter the brewery's gift shop. In the back, a small kitchen—complete with sink, dishwasher, and transparent shelves of floating glassware—also functioned as a tasting room. Armand Debelder sat on one side of a red kitchen table, light reflecting off the taut skin on the top of his head. He wore a crisp dress shirt, button-up sweater, and a large-faced watch with commanding hands, an ensemble that made him look distinguished, like a French CEO on holiday. A plate of cheese made with the brewery's gueuze appeared on the table alongside slices of dark, chewy bread.

Armand took over the business from his father, Gaston, who bought the brewery in the 1950s. His purchase was ill-timed: the fifties marked the beginning of the demise of lambic brewing. The elder Debelder was a *steker,* the Flemish word for someone who blends the lambics aged in barrels then sells the beer as gueuze. In 1953 Beersel was home to fourteen lambic blenders, most of whom bought lambic wort from nearby breweries. Drie Fonteinen blended exclusively until 1999, when Armand used new equipment to brew lambic on-site for the first time ever. According to Jef Van den Steen, the De Glazen Toren brewer I'd met on my first afternoon in Belgium, by 1990 there were only six blenders in Belgium. In subsequent decades, their blending operations closed, creating a wake of tanks and coolships as the ship of modern, mass-produced lagers forged ahead, as it had been doing for decades. Today, along with Jean Van Roy, Armand is one of just a handful of brewer blenders in Belgium.

"I'm not a brewer, I'm a brewer blender," Armand told us defiantly.

As a child, Armand worked with his father, moving bottles of beer and developing his palate. "Armand, you have to smell this, he said, and then I'd take a sip," he remembered. The elder blender was always tasting something. When Armand was eight years old, the family decided he was old enough to serve gueuze. But he wasn't tall enough to reach over the counter in the café his father had added to the brewery. So Armand stood on a wooden crate filled with bottles of gueuze and waited for an adult to remove the corks from the beers, so he could pour the drink into glasses. At a young age, Armand was allowed to drink a common beverage for Belgian children: two fingers of beer mixed with three fingers of water.

"I hate those people who take alcohol out of a child's life," he told us. "That's not an education."

Maybe because we hadn't yet proved we were worthy of even a child's education, I had become acutely aware that there was no beer at the table, aside from what was in the cheese. But I wasn't about to ask for a drink; my mother had taught me manners. Besides, I didn't want to interrupt Armand, who was recounting stories from his childhood, the kind of tales I knew would forever alter the taste of Drie Fonteinen beers for me.

When Gaston recognized lambic was in decline, he told his son, "You're crazy, it's over." But Armand wasn't about to abandon tradition. In 1997 Armand helped found the High Council for Artisanal Lambic Beers (HORAL), a group of brewers and blenders who sought to protect and preserve the dying beer style. In 2004 the future of lambic making was called into question when the European Commission, a subset of the newly formed European Union, began a campaign to end production of the beer, claiming the use of barrels is unhygienic and therefore a health hazard. Armand fought the mandate, but he credits the beer for presenting the most compelling argument for its existence. Because the finished beer has a pH of less than four, dangerous bacteria, including salmonella, will not form in the liquid, a fact that convinced EU officials to keep the beer alive.

"That's why the beer is so exciting," he told us. "It protects itself. Don't ask me why. You don't have to explain everything."

I'd perceived a tension among Belgians, who, despite sharing what in many ways appeared to be a harmoniously blended linguistic and cultural heritage, constantly self-identify according to their primary language and familial and geographic origin. "I'm a Flemish guy, and in Belgium, that's important," Armand said. "Being Flemish means drinking lambic." The beer style had given him a sense of purpose. "You can be a top sportsman and have the best bicycle," he continued. "When your chain is broken, she's broken. I've tried to be that small part of the chain. Not the best bicycle, just a part. The history's not broken." He paused. "That's my life."

Until then, I hadn't thought much about the demise of beer styles. But listening to Armand made me think about dying languages, which illustrate the grind toward a more homogenous world. How are beer styles any different? Beer drinkers' palates are sure to change, as will brewing technologies and beer ingredients, but the permanent loss of any beer style, and the knowledge it took to make it, marks a moment of no return.

=====

A woman with short gray hair and a dusky-blue velvet blazer burst into the room: Lydie Hulpiau, Armand's wife. Before she arrived, Armand had told me he fell in love with her the first time they met. Then, while he was talking to Sarah and Dimi, Lydie told me she fell in love with Armand the first time they met. Before she came into his life, he said, he lived "like an artist," with total freedom and an ignorance about the business side of Drie Fonteinen. "Lydie changed my life," he said matter-of-factly, before he caught her eye and smiled radiantly. I imagined a fluttering inside his chest was rippling through the gift shop and into all the beer in the brewery.

Before they met, Lydie said, she was a beer drinker. "I would drink a lot of beers with crazy names, and I would think I was drinking the best," she said. "Lambics, I got acquainted with very quickly, but gueuze took me a bit longer. But once you get into gueuze . . . "

With a background in marketing, Lydie took charge of the brewery's marketing, finances, and sales. She began to raise the prices of the beer and started to think about which importers were best suited to sell the beer outside of Belgium. She said that, even though they could easily export all of Drie Fonteinen's beers—international demand is strong—they were committed to keeping 50 percent of the brewery's beers in Belgium, reversing an exporting trend. For example, Belgians have a difficult time finding Orval, a famous abbey ale made with *Brettanomyces,* while I can walk from my house to a bottle shop and find a bottle of Orval on most days. "It's easier to export than be a good brewer in Belgium," Lydie said. "We have the reputation of being a good brewer in Belgium. We want to keep that tradition."

Armand's phone beeped. When he answered, I wasn't sure if he was speaking Flemish, Dutch, French, or a hybrid, but his fluid singsong made my mind feel as brittle as a dried stalk of barley. After he ended the call, Armand said, "That's my next generation. You might call him my protégé." Five years earlier, on one of the first sunny days of April, Armand had been eating a few slices of bread for lunch, waiting to interview three people for a job at the brewery. The first person was a no-show, and so was the second. But the third, Michael Blancquaert, arrived right on time. When he walked through the door, Lydie said to Armand, "That's him." Earlier she'd had a feeling he'd be the one. Ever since he started working for Drie Fonteinen, Michael has given Armand and Lydie hope, like the first grandbaby in an aging family. Armand doesn't have children, so he'd assumed the brewery would end with him. As a protégé, Michael bought 50 percent of the shares of the brewery in 2012, and he will inherit the title of blender when Armand retires.

"Sometimes I ask if he's from this planet," Armand said. "It's unbelievable what happens to me."

Lydie looked at the table and made an important observation. "They're not drinking beer!" she exclaimed. "This is a problem."

"They are coming for the beer, not for me," Armand said, with a wry smile.

Armand pulled a bottle of the angel piss we'd tasted with Dimi the night before from a small fridge in the tasting area. I was eager to see if the beer would taste the same as it did last night by the fire. How would being at the brewery with Armand and Lydie alter my sensory experience? I'd never find out, because when Armand dislodged the cork from the 2008 gueuze, the room was silent. There had been no celebratory pop, which meant the beer contained little carbonation. "That happens," Armand said. He sounded nonplussed. "It doesn't mean it's not drinkable. You will not die from it." Most likely, the bottle had been stored upright, so the cork had dried and failed to adequately protect the beer.

We tried the spoiled gueuze anyway. Dimi put his nose inside the glass and inhaled. "The perfume," he said, "it's . . . " As his sentence trailed, we were each left with a blank space for inserting the right adjective for our subjective experiences. For an instant, I resisted the call to define the beer with words, the antithesis of what I was training myself to do. In Belgium even more than at home, I'd been feeling the urge to simply experience many beers instead of approaching them like teaching tools in need of dissection. While analyzing any beer increased my appreciation and understating of the beer itself, the action also seemed to pull me out of the moment. With my nose in the glass and my mind racing through the properties of certain beer styles, I could easily miss a sideward glance, the quality of light in a room, or the texture of a wooden plank in a barrel. Since my moments in Belgium were limited, I wanted to be present in every way possible. When Armand loosened the cork on the next bottle of gueuze, a festive pop commanded my attention.

Gueuze is special, in part, because of the blending process, an art that requires a master blender to taste beer from individual barrels (each barrel holds its own microbial flora and, therefore, flavors) and predict how each lambic might taste years later, alone or blended. Armand said, when he's blending, he relies only on intuition. "You don't have to think," he said.

Inside the oak wine barrels, which Drie Fonteinen sources from wineries in Italy and France, a white film, or skin, called a pellicle develops on the surface of the beer as sediment falls to the bottom. During this phase, it's essential not to knock, move, or otherwise disrupt a barrel of lambic. "The sediment is the mother, and the beer is lying on the mother," Armand explained. "When you separate the mother and child, the child cannot live anymore." Part of the art of blending is placing a valve in the barrel to retrieve a taste of the beer without disturbing the beer inside. The first taste from the barrel is never a good representation of the beer, Armand explained. In the second taste, he discovers the true essence of the beer, a moment that brings him great joy.

"Does the beer ever surprise you?" I asked. "Is your intuition ever off?"

"I'm always surprised and sometimes disappointed," he said. "That's why I have a nice job. I've never made the same beer twice."

The gueuze with the happy cork pop was a lambic aged for one year in a sherry barrel, a type of barrel Armand was using for the first time. The beer had a name, but since it wouldn't be released until fall, Armand wouldn't reveal what it was.

"This is very special," Sarah said, swirling the beer in her glass. "It's crazy." Her eyelids looked heavy, as though the beer had just transported her to someplace peaceful and serene.

"*Formidable,*" Dimi added, with a heavy sigh. "Some bottles you open for something special, like yesterday when you came." He nodded at Sarah and me. "But this, it's different. *Magnifique.*"

"It's perfectly balanced," Sarah continued. Her voice sounded rich and warm. "All the complexities are melding together. It's not too acidic. The texture's just right."

Despite the fact that I sensed greatness in this beer, I couldn't find the language to contribute to the conversation, which made me feel like a tourist, someone who came to gawk, not participate.

"To find that balance is the thing," said Armand. "Michael's tasting to learn."

Dimi nodded. "He is getting the experience of you."

—————

Like Cantillon, Drie Fonteinen brews only between October and April, when there is less of what Armand called "rotting bacteria." By the time summer arrives, "If you have meat or you're making your own mayonnaise, you will have conservation problems," he said. "Our grandparents knew that. *Les temps de cerise est les temps perdu.*" The time of the cherry harvest (that is, June and July) is the time lost. Dimi muttered something about *amoureux,* and the two men chuckled. Not only is the cherry harvest a time of rotting and decomposition—too much wildness for spontaneously fermented beer—it is the time for lovers.

Eventually Armand led the three of us outside, then into the building that housed the brewery, where the floors and tanks gleamed in stark opposition to the scene at Cantillon. Large laminated labels identified each piece of equipment, which made giving tours easier. Small fans mounted above the coolship helped bring the wort down to temperature while circulating yeast and bacteria, the equivalent of the window louvres at Cantillon. A dingy, plastic saint-like figure stood atop a temperature-control box, the patron saint of precision.

Things looked more like Cantillon when we walked downstairs, into a dark, cave-like space filled with barrels of lambic in various stages of fermentation. Without thinking, I put my hand on one barrel, hoping to feel its life force, real or imagined. Armand shot me a look.

"Be careful not to disturb the beer," he said tersely.

I'd forgotten about the skin-film and the sediment, the mother and child. I whispered apologies to the beer and slowly backed away, hoping the micro-universe inside the barrel was tougher than my touch.

At the far end of the barrel room, a hidden stairway led to the Drie Fonteinen restaurant, a white-tablecloth bistro that felt like a place my grandparents would have visited somewhere in Europe in the 1950s. Armand, Lydie, Lydie's French cousin and her twelve-year-old son, an aspiring American brewer named Luke, a videographer from Antwerp, Sarah, and me sat down together at a long table like an extended family forced together at a holiday meal. The menu listed an array of rustic Belgian dishes and French classics, including *sole meuniere* and *chateaubriand*. Many of the dishes were made with beer, including a kriek vinaigrette and the *vlaamse stoofkarbonaden,* aka *carbonnades à la flamande,* which was braised in oude gueuze and would be my dinner. *Frites* arrived in silver serving containers with serving spoons, the only vegetable on the table. Armand and Lydie ordered a grainy Beersel Blond with plenty of bubbles—a bright aperitif—and I followed suit.

In the tasting room, Armand had described a pivotal moment in his career. On a weekend morning in 2009, he had walked into the brewery and found bottles of gueuze exploding, creating a dangerous spray of glass chards and beer. The heating system had malfunctioned, and as the room warmed, the bottles couldn't withstand the pressure building within.

"The glass jumped," Armand said. "God protected me at that point."

In a panic, he tried to shut off the temperature control system, but he couldn't figure out how to do it. Then he realized turning off the electricity would stop the heat. By the time the room cooled and the explosions stopped, 126,000 bottles of gueuze had been destroyed or ruined. He called Lydie to tell her the news. Within minutes she was there, jumping out of her car in her pajamas. He told her his life's work was over. He was bankrupt.

"She took me like this and started shaking me," he said, placing his hands on imaginary shoulders. "She said, 'Armand, stop it! Armand, stop it! You don't have a bad disease. You can work again tomorrow.' That helped me cool down a bit."

The bottles exploded on a Saturday. Armand had asked Lydie to marry him that Wednesday.

At the dinner table, Lydie's eyes filled with tears as she remembered arriving at the brewery that Saturday morning. "I'm sorry," she said, "but this makes me a little emotional." As news of the explosion reverberated through the beer community, people started to help. Dogfish Head brewed a Belgian white beer called Namaste, and sent some of its proceeds to Armand. A distiller in Brussels offered to transform the ruined gueuze remaining in 63,000 bottles into a distilled spirit. To transfer the ruined gueuze to the distillery, every bottle needed to be opened. For three Saturdays, local volunteers opened every bottle of ruined beer at Drie Fonteinen. The finished liquor became Armand's Spirit, a high-end eau de vie. The story of cross-cultural compassion—a Flemish brewery saved by a French Wallonian distillery—became a local media sensation.

When we'd finished dinner, Armand quietly picked up the tab for the entire table and beamed when we thanked him. Then he handed Sarah and me each a bottle of 2004 gueuze. I cradled the beer in my arms as he rattled off a list of instructions. Store on its side in a cool but not cold environment. Let the beer sit upright at room temperature forty-five minutes before serving. Gently remove the cork. Gently! Pour the beer with the bottle tilted at a slight angle. Not too fast. Not too slow. Most important, "Drink this beer with someone who will appreciate it," he admonished. "It's special. It's not a beer for someone who doesn't like beer." As I tucked the beer into Klara's backseat and thought about securing it with a seatbelt, I wondered how the beer would survive the trip to Portland. Because the person I wanted to drink the beer with lived five thousand miles away and had probably just packed a small lunch that included a starch, protein, vegetable, and fruit. Armand hadn't given any instructions for that part of the journey.

———

The evening before Sarah caught her plane to D.C., we drove through a blue fog on the way back to our hotel in Brussels. It had been an exciting day: we'd visited a small brewery called Alvinne, where two Spanish brewers were brewing a collaboration beer. Then we'd toured Rodenbach, a brewery founded in 1836. The brewery produces the country's most famous Flemish red ales, which are fermented in giant wooden *foeders,* barrels capable of holding a whopping 553 barrels of beer. (The foeders are so important to the production of the beer, they're crafted at the brewery in an on-site cooperage.) During our tour, Sarah kept fidgeting and sighing loudly. Rudi Ghequire, brewmaster and brewery manager, who boasted a thirty-three-year tenure at the brewery, gave us a tour that included very basic facts about brewing and fermentation, an obvious regurgitation of a tour he'd give anyone off the street. For a moment, I felt briefly annoyed with Sarah for not appreciating that, unlike her, I might appreciate hearing rudimentary summaries of the brewing process. But in reality, I was also bored during much of the tour. As I was starting to think about saying good-bye to Sarah, I realized how much I'd miss the way her perceptions brought mine into sharper focus. I had learned so much from her, not only about brewing, beer distribution, and the culinary world, but about the joy of exploring foreign beer landscapes with a friend.

"I'm really glad you were with me at Alvinne," I said. "I don't know what it was, but I would have felt uncomfortable being there by myself."

Every so often, at beer events or in breweries, being a beer woman outnumbered by men bothered me. I tried to make a conscious effort not to notice, but more often, I counted the number of women in the room and then figured out gender percentages. Five percent.

Eleven percent. Twenty percent. For some reason, the numbers had mattered to me at Alvinne. There had been five men: two Belgian brewers, two Spanish brewers, and an English brewer. That made me and Sarah 29 percent of the people in the room, a fairly high percentage of women in the grand scheme of the beer scene. The mood had been festive—*jamon Iberico* and a strong Basque sheep's milk cheese for snacking, which paired well with the jubilant anticipation of a beer festival that weekend. There was no logical reason why I would have felt uncomfortable, and yet, while I was taking pictures of barrels filled with beer for a summer wedding, I was comforted by the fact that Sarah was upstairs.

"My husband put it to me this way," she said as her hands gripped the wheel. "You'll always be the anomaly. You'll walk into the room at any beer event, and you'll be the anomaly because you're a woman."

"So, you're okay with that?" I asked.

She paused. "Yeah, I am."

I thought about her answer. Even though I was always prepared to be in the minority, I never liked it. A sleek BMW zoomed past us in the left lane. We hung back behind a boxy truck.

"I get really tired of being one of the only women in the room," I finally said.

"I know," she replied.

"It's not fair."

"Eh," she said, "it is what it is. This isn't the only industry where women are under-represented. It's not the first, and it won't be the last."

"Maybe someday that will change," I said.

"Maybe," she said.

Sarah held her line, keeping her eyes on the road.

She turned down the volume on the robotic female GPS voice, flicked the turn signal, pressed on the gas, and steered us into the left lane. We glided past the truck that had been holding us back for so many miles.

The next morning, before the sun rose, I drove Sarah to the airport, then returned to Saint-Gilles and ate a soft-boiled egg at our favorite neighborhood café, Le Dillens. I watched people drinking coffee before they went to work, and I felt a pang of loneliness. I wished I could tell Sarah how the toast soldiers were perfect (she'd appreciate the way the butter nearly soaked through the toothsome whole wheat, even though a glimpse of the unctuous egg would have made her ill), but she was somewhere over the Atlantic. I buckled in for the drive to the Hainaut province of Belgium, near the border of France, where I would meet Olivier Dedeycker, brewmaster at Brasserie Dupont. For the rest of the trip, just Klara and me would be shifting ratios.

PERFECT PAIRINGS

It is impossible to have bad taste, but many people have none at all.
—GEORG CHRISTOPH LICHTENBERG

AS THE SUN SET on the sleepy town of Watou, population about 1,900, I pedaled a bicycle down a road flanked by fields of dirt clods. I could see a distant hill, which I knew sat just over the border in France. The smell of earth and farm animals was thick, as though summer's sun had been baking the fields all day, but it was only early March. I felt like I was riding through the fumes of a funky sour ale, but really, spring was just standing at the door, getting ready to knock. When I arrived in the town center, an eerie quiet wrapped the historic buildings and laminated the cobblestone streets. It was Thursday night, and every car that passed me seemed to be filled with someone heading home for dinner. I was the only one on a bicycle, which didn't bother me one bit. After more than a week navigating Belgium's roads inside Klara, I was delighted to discover the bed and breakfast where I was staying had bicycles for guests.

I rode from restaurant to restaurant—I'd already mapped out their locations—only to find that, for some reason, Thursday night was like a holiday in Watou. Everything was closed.

Eventually I saw a light glowing in one restaurant, and the door was cracked open. Inside, a woman paused from shuffling through a pile of receipts to glare at me over the top of her bifocals.

"We're usually open," she said, "but tonight we're going to a meeting."

She could have been going to any type of meeting, but I imagined a town meeting filled with people arguing about things like restoring the church steeple and creating a speed limit on the cobblestones. Maybe I could crash the meeting, I thought. There was a chance they'd have snacks and, most likely, beer. Instead, I continued riding, stopping to admire the cemetery around the base of the town's church. Across the street, in the front yard of a stately two-story home, some chickens were pecking at food. They looked delicious.

Then I saw it: a glow of neon, a beacon that said, *Come and eat*. It was a fast-food *friterie*. Inside, I waited as a couple in front of me ordered. After ringing them up, the man behind the counter dunked a metal basket of fries into bubbling oil then pressed some buttons on a microwave, which I realized was how he was cooking their dinner. When it was my turn to order, I felt uninspired.

"What are *stoofvlees*?" I asked. The man looked slightly panicked and motioned for a woman to come help. She said something to him in Dutch.

"From the cow!" he told me, brightly.

I ordered *stoofvlees* and *frites*, with dipping mayo, of course, along with a Rodenbach, a blend of old and new Flanders red ales from the brewery Sarah and I had visited a few days earlier. My meal arrived on a plastic tray: a steaming plastic rectangle of reddish-brown *carbonnades* (a far cry from the version I'd had at Drie Fonteinen), a pick-up-sticks pile of fries, and a chilled bottle of beer served alongside an empty Rodenbach glass. The tray held what I now understood to be typical Belgium fare: meat, *frites,* and a drink, which was never water.

As I ate, families came and went, saying their hellos to the man behind the counter in friendly, small-town style, before they stepped out into the chilly evening with plastic bags of hot takeout. The woman, who was married to the cashier, was in the back of the restaurant, at a table with their six-year-old son. She told me it was his first year of school.

"He has a hard time reading," she confided, glancing back at him. With his head bowed over a workbook, he looked studious.

I thought about Tony and Oscar, about what they'd eat for dinner and the books they'd read at bedtime. I thought about how someday, years from now, I'd be helping Oscar learn to read. If I was there. I knew I was being too hard on myself, but I still felt a pang of guilt tinged with sadness, the bittersweet feeling of being somewhere justified by the mind but abandoned by the heart. Right then, I wanted nothing more than to be at home participating in the sweet daily grind, proper glassware and Cicerone study be damned. I finished my beer in a quick slug, taking note that the red ale tasted unspectacular, like a rip off of a red table wine. I pulled on my hat and gloves and rode under the moon toward my bed for the night.

=====

The following evening at dusk, I stood outside the same *friterie* again with my bicycle. The church was illuminated a ghastly neon green.

This time, I had a reservation—not for anything from the microwave—but for a table at 't Hommelhof, a restaurant known internationally for its focus on beer. Inside, a few early birds sat at tables draped in white. Candles were nestled inside glasses filled with malt, and dried hop bines loaded with an arresting amount of flowers hung above the bar. The chef, Stefaan Couttenye, described the scene in his book, *Cooking with Belgian Beers:*

> Hop vines hanging from the beams, worn out floor boards, antique furniture and vintage ornaments take you back to a bygone era when the living was easy and the word "stress" had not yet been invented. Whether you like it or not, you automatically switch down a gear, which only benefits the enjoyment.

Nothing was lost in translation. After spending much of the day getting lost on poorly marked country roads on my bike, I was ready to unwind, even if it meant also taking notes and photos. I'd first heard about 't Hommelhof from a brewer who described an indulgent beer-focused meal in the middle of nowhere, then again from my friend Evan who runs bike tours in Belgium.

"Do you think it would be a weird place for me to have dinner by myself?" I asked him over beers at a Belgian beer bar in Portland. It had been many years since I'd eaten a luxurious meal in a restaurant alone, but I remembered enjoying the last one.

"Sitting down for four hours and eating good food and drinking great beer?" he said. "Why not? Just go. You'll enjoy it."

I decided a meal at the restaurant would be a way to study food and beer pairings. The Cicerone exam would test my knowledge of generally accepted pairing principles, the kinds of concepts that were quantified by words like "intensity," "resonance," and "contrast." Those concepts translate into tangible things like the way hop bitterness intensifies spicy heat and how tartness contrasts with fat, umami, and salt.

I'd been e-mailing the restaurant for weeks trying to get a reservation, with no response, so I was starting to panic. One of the reasons I was in Watou was to eat at 't Hommelhof. That morning, out of desperation, I asked the woman who ran the bed and breakfast where I was staying if she knew the chef. Within seconds, she had him on the phone. I gave him my spiel about being a journalist studying for a beer test. He kindly agreed to chat with me if I came in early, before the kitchen was humming. After all, it was Friday night.

Chef Stefaan Couttenye wore a day or two of gray stubble and the glasses of an architect. He'd opened the restaurant thirty-one years earlier, the year the first American brewpub of the craft beer era opened on the East Coast. While that brewpub stayed open for just two years, Stefaan continues to cook beer-centric food in the same building, a structure from the seventeenth century that once housed a beer tavern and a court of law, at the same time.

After apologizing profusely for the quality of his English, Stefaan told me he was first drawn to cooking with beer, not pairing food with beer. The cooking part, he said, is "not so easy," thanks to beer's inherent bitterness. "It takes over the taste in your mouth," he said, "and you can't taste anymore what's on your plate."

I knew what he meant. One time, setting out to make a beer-braised pork stew, I sautéed some onions, browned some cubes of pork shoulder, then braised them in twelve ounces of a hoppy pale ale. After three hours of simmering, the meat was falling apart but it tasted as bitter as a poisonous plant. That's because as water in beer cooks off, the flavors in the beer intensify, the classic formula for a good reduction, except for the bitterness piece. Stefaan had two solutions: First, not to cook with really bitter beers, which had been my first mistake. And, if it's too late and the dish tastes horrible, tone down the bitterness with lots of butter. That was a strategy I could endorse.

't Hommelhof, which means "the hop garden," serves the beers of the region—the very immediate region. All the beers at the restaurant come from the two breweries of Watou, a strategy Stefaan said caters to tourists, who crave a connection to all things local. "People from Antwerp don't come here to drink De Koninck," he said.

Stefaan pointed out that tourists from abroad seemed to appreciate Belgian beers more than Belgians themselves. After all, 62 percent of Belgian beer is exported. "Belgian people are not, how do you say it in English, chauvinists. We are not proud of our products," he said. "I always say, if France had been a beer country, we'd all be drinking beer." On that note, he opened a bottle of Cuvée 't Hommelhof, a blend of white beer and Kapittel Abt, a strong, fruity Belgian tripel, brewed just for the restaurant, a palate cleanser for the meal that was about to unfold.

———

Every night 't Hommelhof offers a *het land van amen*, or "land of amen" menu. Tonight, all four worshipful courses were devoted to hop shoots. During the month of March, hop shoots begin appearing in restaurants all over Belgium. Like fresh bamboo shoots in Japan, the ingredient is a way to celebrate the new growth of the impending spring season, a mark of the return to bounty. In *Natural History* (book 21, chapter 50), Pliny the Elder, the Roman naturalist and author, wrote that the Romans ate hop shoots like asparagus. (Pliny has become famous for his beer writing, which includes such resonant passages as, "The perverted ingenuity of man has given to water the power of intoxicating where wine is not procured. Western nations intoxicate themselves by moistened grain.") I had to have the hop shoot meal. After all, I was smack in the middle of a region of Flanders where hops have been farmed for almost eight centuries.

Belgian hops don't have the same reputation as hops from Germany, which some years grows more hops than any other country in the world, and which boasts the Hallertau region, a center of hop growing and research. Belgian hops don't have the cache of the storied English hops, such as Golding and Fuggle. But the crop is culturally significant, something I had explored earlier in the day at a hop museum in the town of Poperinge, which was, theoretically, a thirty-minute bike ride from Watou. The four-story museum occupies a former warehouse where hops were once weighed and inspected. Poperinge was once an important cloth-making town but was conquered by the French then the English, events that destabilized its economy. When the locals began farming hops, a new economic boon began, and even though World War II created a setback for hop farmers, the town was behind Allied lines, so it wasn't destroyed like many of its neighbors. The postwar decades included prosperous hop farming.

Outside the museum, there was an abstract sculpture of a woman shaped like a ball, weighted by a belly of soil and with a wire extending from her oversized hands. A hop bine would climb the wire come spring. Inside, one room buzzed with the sound of wasps and flies, the predator insects that eat one of the hop plant's worst enemies—

aphids, *bladluizen*. In one exhibit, I had learned that a member of the Order of Saint Benedict, a woman named Hildegard von Bingen, aka Saint Hildegard, had written extensively during the twelfth century about the evils of the hop plant. "Makes men melancholy and depressed," she wrote. "Bad for the testicles."

Hops were also considered aphrodisiacs, antiseptics, and soporifics. In 1409 the Duke of Burgundy, known as John the Fearless—and possibly the inspiration for Gambrinus, a mythical figure in Medieval poems and songs who made a deal with the devil to become the King of Beer—created the Order of the Hops. The group honored brewers who made hopped beer, and had a Flemish motto, *Ich zuighe,* which means, "I savor." In one room, I had stood face-to-face with a mustached straw man, a replica of what hop workers once burned as part of their end-of-harvest celebrations (and what I guessed was the possible inspiration for the Burning Man gathering). In another area, shelves were packed with products made with hops that had nothing to do with beer, from breast enhancements to sleep aids.

Until I sat down for dinner, I hadn't tasted hops since I popped a hop caramel into my mouth at the museum, an unsatisfying mixture of sweetness and bitterness. Even though I was ready to taste hops, I knew the hop shoot dishes wouldn't satisfy that craving. Earlier in the week, at Jan's house, I'd eaten hop shoots in preface to the spectacular cheese board dinner. One of his friends, Eric, had bought the hop shoots from a local farmer. "They're the first of the season," he said. He opened the top of a small, brown paper bag, and when I peeked inside I didn't see a tangle of green asparagus-like sprigs, the kind of early hop plant growth that pops up during spring in my yard, but something that looked more like two-inch-long bean sprouts, blushing pink. At Jan's we sat down to eat at a dining table designed to host large dinner parties, with Sarah and me, the honored guests, sitting at each end. When the plates were served, atop the nest of blanched hop shoots spiked in a cayenne broth, I saw a single, stark-white poached egg; we were told this was a traditional Flemish way to serve hop shoots. I caught Sarah's eye across the long, blond table before she quickly looked away.

I was tempted to say something that would excuse her from having to eat the egg, but the only thing I could think to say was that she was allergic to them, and while I would have fully gone along with her lie, I didn't feel comfortable creating that one on her behalf. With the slow deliberateness of someone dissecting a rare animal, Sarah proceeded to eat her entire portion of poached egg and hop shoots. Later that night, when we drove back to Brussels, I said I was proud of her.

"I was proud of myself," she said.

I had liked the dish. As though I had been searching for the saffron in paella, the hop shoots were so delicate, I had to focus to find their flavor. The crunchy, earthy sweetness of the shoots contrasted nicely with the creamy, orange egg yolk.

At 't Hommelhof, Stefaan explained that the hop shoots were pale because they hadn't been exposed to sunlight, and therefore haven't been triggered to produce chlorophyll, the same deviation that creates white asparagus. To harvest the shoots, farmers kneel near the base of the hop plant and dig up its rootball before cutting the new, white shoots from the woody part of the rhizome. Stefaan told me if the shoots are pink or purple, they've "gone too far." He preferred pure white shoots. Some farmers near Watou grow hop plants in greenhouses just so they can harvest and sell the shoots as early as December. But greenhouse hop shoots are expensive,

Stefaan explained, something he'd serve only for Valentine's Day. That made me think Belgian hop shoots could be the country's truffles, if they actually did have aphrodisiac qualities.

=====

My meal started in traditional Belgian form, with the server pouring a beer into a goblet then carefully placing the bottle on the table so the label faced me. The beer was a Framboise Boon, a lambic from 2013 that had been fermented with whole raspberries. Light shone through the brilliant pink beer, which was blanketed with two inches of frothy pink head. Then the food arrived: slices of beef that had been marinated in the Framboise Boon then grilled. The beef was drizzled with hop shoots cream, raw hop shoots, and salty chunks of what the menu described as "mature cheese." The fruity beer united the rich smokiness of the beef with the aged cheese and sweet hop shoots.

For me, a good pairing simultaneously elevates the beer and the food, a simple idea that's surprisingly difficult to execute. Most chefs create pairings based on their inherent knowledge of flavors and textures. They don't actually cook a dish then try it with multiple beers, but let their imaginations predict the outcome. I discovered one exception: at Luksus, a small prix-fixe restaurant in Brooklyn that serves just one alcoholic beverage—beer—Chef Daniel Burns prepares modernist dishes designed to pair with specific beers. To nail the parings, he holds regular tastings with the restaurant's staff.

Stefaan said, when he thinks about pairings, he abandons a sense of rules. "In the beginning, it was always fish with white beer, meat with a stronger beer, and game with a very strong beer," he said. For years, I'd heard the same thing about wine. Pinot noir *can* go with halibut, and a Riesling *can* pair well with a steak. While I liked the idea of total freedom when creating good parings, I knew better. There are some rules. Just ask the Cicerone test makers.

When it comes to food pairings, comparisons to wine are inevitable. During a trip to New York City the previous summer, I stopped by Brooklyn Brewery to see Garrett Oliver, brewmaster and author of *The Brewmaster's Table*. Even though the book is more than a decade old, it's still considered the preeminent tome on beer and food. Garrett told me, when he cooks multicourse meals for friends at home, he doesn't create a competition between beer and wine. He serves both beverages throughout the meal, depending on which pairing is best. But he seemed to be rooting for the beer: "Beer can bring fruit, acidity, plus caramelized and roasty flavors wine doesn't have," he explained. And since beer usually has less residual sugars than wine, it shines alongside foods like asparagus and artichokes, which can make wine taste metallic. With those foods, beer with a light, crackery malt and a burst of citrus can open new dimensions. Wine can come off as extra acidic next to acidic foods, including vinegar, citrus, and tomatoes, but a beer with high levels of acidity, such as a Berliner weisse or *oud bruin,* a cousin of the Flanders red, can diminish the perception of overall acidity in food.

Garrett told me the term "wino" originated from a time when wine was looked down upon as the cheap drink of immigrants. "In Rome, you go into a trattoria and you ask for 'red' or 'white,'" he said. "It's not fussy. British have plonk, a cheap wine. In France, they fill their containers from a spigot in the village. We're the ones who are fussy." We have to demystify wine and demystify beer, he continued. "There are some drinks for everyday and some for having a special experience," he said. "The restaurant is a place to put those things together, a place to have a good time."

But how often did most people think of a restaurant as a place to enjoy a fine beer with food? Even though 't Hommelhof has been known as a beer restaurant for decades, Stefaan said he still feels like he's bucking tradition. "People are not used to it, so it stays difficult. Look," he said under his breath as he glanced at a nearby table. "They're drinking wine." We sat quietly and watched how, at another table of two, the man ordered a beer but his female dining companion ordered iced tea. At yet another table, a few women had glasses of sparkling wine, while the men had beers adorned with orange slices. Nearly an hour into my time at 't Hommelhof, I had yet to see another woman drinking beer.

A new friend arrived at my table: a tangerine-hued beer with a white head that reminded me of a pencil-thin mustache. The server announced the beer as though he were a herald announcing a guest to meet the queen. "Watou's Wit, from Brouwerij Van Eecke," the same brewery as the first beer Stefaan and I had shared. In keeping with the traditional witbier ingredients, the beer was brewed with wheat, Curaçao orange peel, and lemon peel, which created an earthy, yeasty, and lemony effect. A delicate white fish called plaice was served with butter turnips, burnt leek, a hop-shoot-infused cream, and tiny North Sea shrimp. Every ingredient was bathed in a buttery, frothy yellow sauce made with Watou's Wit.

I noticed a pattern. The first dish was prepared with the same beer with which it was served. So was the second. Stefaan had left me with a copy of his cookbook, an engaging dining companion with zero conversational skills. I started flipping through the pages. Sure enough, every recipe was paired with the same beer that was listed as an ingredient. I wondered if he was going for a no-fail practice that would inevitably lead to harmonious pairings, which seemed like cheating.

"Taste is very personal," Stefaan had said before he left the table and went back to work in the kitchen.

I knew the jolly bald man who marked the beginning of course three: a defrocked monk, he was the smiling Medieval man on the label of every St. Bernardus beer. Earlier that morning, I'd walked from my bed-and-breakfast next door, to the St. Bernardus brewery, a place with a unique significance in the canon of Belgian beer.

During the Middle Ages, when beer was first being brewed in this place now called Belgium, the area was already experiencing what would develop into a long tradition of being conquered. Counts of Flanders claimed towns, and began fortifying their borders to protect them from Norsemen. Then German kings made claims. In 977 Charles, Duke of Lorraine, built a fortress on the Senne River, the skeleton of what would become the city of Brussels. Then a more peaceful tribe entered the region. Inspired by the Benedictine abbey Molesme, a monastery that focused on the teachings of Saint Benedict, who taught devotion to God through labor and self-sufficiency, a tradition began. As part of the Order of Cistercians, the monks farmed their own land and cultivated vineyards. The Order began to decline in 1342, but the teachings inspired La Trappe Abbey in Normandy, which began to institute reforms based on the Saint Benedict traditions. By 1664 the monks who adopted these practices, which included silence, prayer, and living by the work of their hands, were called Trappists, men who brewed beer, made wine and cheese, and baked bread. The Rules of Saint Benedict don't mention beer but do address wine consumption, stating that monks can have a "hemina," or just under half a liter, of wine per day: "we do not drink to satiety, but sparingly, because 'Wine maketh even the wise to fall away.'"

In Belgium, Trappist monks developed a reputation for brewing high-quality beer, especially ones with higher amounts of alcohol and more flavor. When hard liquor was banned from cafés in Belgium in 1919—a law designed to spare the working class from the damages of alcohol, not repealed until 1983—the high-alcohol Trappist beers became even more sought after. Monks brewed to financially sustain their monasteries, supply themselves with beer, and create money to donate to charity. In 1962 the Trappists claimed their brand by insisting that only products made inside certified Trappist monasteries be labeled as Trappist. Other provisions stipulated that monks oversee brewing and that the brewery be secondary to the functioning of the monastery. These days, there are twenty Trappist monasteries, eleven of which make some of the world's most well-regarded beers: Westvleteren, Chimay, Orval, Rochefort, and Westmalle. The most recent addition to the fold happens to be in the United States: the monks of Saint Joseph's Abbey in Massachusetts brew under the label Spencer Trappist Ale.

In 1946 the monks at the Saint-Sixtus Abbey in Westvleteren licensed their brewing operations to a nearby dairy and cheesemaker in Watou, where the beer was brewed under the name St. Sixtus (the monks continued to brew beer for themselves at the monastery nearby). In 1992, all brewing operations were returned to the monastery—the end of the St. Sixtus label—but the brewery at the dairy kept making beer under the name St. Bernardus. As part of the secularization of the brewing operations, St. Bernardus changed the monk on the label to a Medieval man wearing a jacket instead of a religious habit. St. Bernardus continued brewing using similar recipes, and possibly the same yeast, but Westvleteren became famous. Today, the monks there brew some of the most highly sought-after beers in the world. Westvleteren produces just four thousand barrels a year, which makes every bottle of their beer somewhat of a rarity. To get your hands on the Westvleteren 12, a quadrupel of 10 percent ABV, you must call the "beer phone" at the brewery, which Reuter's reported receives as many as 85,000 calls an hour, sixty days in advance of the date on which you plan to drive at the brewery to pick up your one case of beer per car. St. Bernardus beers, on the other hand, are available at my local Fred Meyer. While I suspect the St. Bernardus Abt 12, also a quadrupel, may be just as good as the Westvleteren 12, I've never tasted the Westvleteren. Someday I'll do my dream tasting of the two beers side by side and come up with the definitive answer.

The St. Bernardus third-course beer was a tripel, a classic Belgian-style beer invented in 1932 at the De Drie Linden brewery. Two years after that, Westmalle Abbey released its own version, which has become the iconic representation of the style ("the mother of all tripels," according to the brewery's website). The name of the style refers to the amount of malt and the original gravity of the wort before it begins to ferment. That triple strength translates to notoriously high alcohol, between 8 and 10 percent ABV. The beer in front of me looked golden and benign, but with one sip, I knew its appearance was a trick. The tripel was complicated and intense, with a soft texture that evolved into a bloom of intense cloves, fruit, and yeast that finished dry and neat. It came with the meal's pièce de résistance: fat pink slabs of duck breast braised in—what else—the tripel, and topped with a pretty pile of spring vegetables and hop shoots.

At this point in the meal, I made note of a few things. One, the hop shoots were starting to lose their poignancy. In fact, I was pretty sure I didn't want to see any more of them until next spring. Two, the more food I ate, the more I could drink. It was so simple! And so hilarious! For the grand finale, the server delivered a bottle of St. Bernardus Abt 12, a beer I knew from the night before. We'd shared a bed. It isn't every day I drink beer in bed, but as you might expect from a bed-and-breakfast that shares a door with the St. Bernardus brewery, the B&B's honor bar was filled with St. Bernardus beers. I'd dropped some euros in a jar and helped myself to an Abt 12. A couple from Brazil, who was touring Belgian breweries and also staying at the B&B, had either left the building or scurried off to their room to drink something from the honor bar. Instead of sitting in the common room by myself, where, sadly, the large fireplace was just a cold, dark hole, I poured the Abt 12 into a goblet and went to my room, where I sat in bed and savored the decadence of drinking the beer all by myself, without having to utter a single word or take any notes.

At the restaurant, even though I wished I could have a sip of the Abt 12 and call it a night, I felt obligated to eat the "hop shoots phantasy," a complex arrangement of cakes, creams, cute yellow dots, and a puff of white meringue that was sliding off the top like a beret. Stefaan returned to my table after I'd eaten the mélange, and helped me dissect the dessert with autopsy-like precision. There had been a hop shoot meringue, hop shoot ice cream, brownie, white chocolate mousse, and a sponge cake.

"What about the foam?" I asked.

"Ah, right," he said. "Espuma, a mousse of hop shoots." The mousse tasted warmly of nutmeg, a flavor that came alive with the beer, the final note of a meal I would remember as decadent but slightly disappointing, a feeling that started when I discovered the predictable pairings. Under a waning moon, a sliver slight of full, I slowly pedaled back to the bed-and-breakfast, past the dark, open fields. I wished I could spend another day in the countryside, but tomorrow I would return to Brussels. I had to make an important meeting.

———

Meeting a stranger at a European train station felt like playing a role in a juicy spy novel. In this case, the stranger and I used the coded language of text messaging to make plans. We would come together to exchange goods then travel to a secret location. There, we would brew some beer. When I found the stranger in the Gare du Midi in Brussels, he didn't seem all that strange. Emilien Hommé had a kind smile and ruddy cheeks; he seemed like a mash-up of old friends. We had some important things in common: we love beer, and we love bikes. The previous summer, Emilien and his girlfriend, Hélène, had gone on a five-month bike tour through the United States. When they were in Portland, they'd stayed with my friend Diana, who'd put us in touch. "You must meet my friends!" she said. "They'll even brew beer with you."

Emilien and I took the Metro to a stop he told me was near the Atomium, a building shaped like the basic structure of an iron crystal magnified 165 billion times, constructed for the World's Fair in 1958. Emilien knocked on the door of a house in what felt like a typical Brussels neighborhood: old residential buildings tightly packed together, row-house style, on a narrow street lined with parked cars. A man with a long brown ponytail and a wide smile, who looked like he was in his early thirties, opened the door. Ronoy De Smedt was a member of La Foire Aux Savoir-Faire, a DIY group in Brussels that organizes projects like making elderberry syrup and teaching children to create weavings on a bicycle wheel. The homebrewing subgroup included Ronoy and Emilien, who got together a few times a year to make beer.

We followed Ronoy to the back of his house, where there was a narrow kitchen with cabinets painted in primary colors that felt bohemian. Sliding glass doors revealed a compact courtyard with a budding tree waving against a stark blue sky. Even though the room was small and a bit cluttered, I immediately felt comfortable; it was obviously a communal house populated by eclectic people, where an American student of beer could relax. Before Emilien and I arrived, the day's brewing session had begun. Lionel Etienne, who was brewing for the first time today, was wearing a thin scarf wrapped tightly around his neck. He stood next to the glass doors, stirring a steaming porridge of mash with a wooden paddle that looked like it belonged with a canoe, the kind of tool used to make beer before humans discovered yeast and bacteria. The kettle was sitting on the floor on a burner linked to a tank of propane. One time someone's pant leg had caught on fire due to the setup, the three guys told me. Not to worry, they said. The pants had had very wide legs.

When Emilien invited me to brew, he told me the process would take ten hours, a vast extension of the three or four hours it took Tony and me to brew. I assumed the Belgian brewers would be doing a batch of all-grain, which they were, but I wasn't sure what else would take so long. As Lionel stirred, Ronoy showed me pictures of their handcrafted milling contraption, something the group used at the start of every brew day to mill the malt. At that moment, I started to understand their dedication to the DIY ethos, time be damned. I'd never spend ten hours brewing on any day in Portland. But, here, I was free. I had nothing to clean, mend, consign, or return. I didn't have a child who needed to be fed, dressed, or assisted in making Lego creations.

The guys told me they were brewing a stout, which would become a maple stout if they decided to add a can of syrup gifted from some Canadians. The malt bill was a mixture of Cara munich, CaraRed, Munich, and Pilsner malts, a mix that was designed to create "900 EBC," Ronoy reported. Not only I was struggling to keep up with the rapid-fire French between the three men, but I realized I'd also need to translate their language of brewing. Thanks to Google, we figured out EBC is the same as SRM, Standard Reference Method, the way many brewers quantify beer color. I could only imagine what other conversions were headed my way.

The recipe reminded me of high school algebra:

$$M = (B \times D) / 26$$

M = quantité de malt en kilo [how much malt]
B = quantité de bière désirée [end amount of beer]
D = degré de bière désirée [alcohol by volume]

They hoped to end up with 48 liters of beer, or 12.6 gallons. (Tony and I usually brewed 5 gallons at a time.) Ronoy told me that once he'd calculated their homebrew cost at 1.40 euros per liter, or 70 cents a pint. He insisted they weren't in it for the cost savings.

On the recipe, hops were categorized as *houblon amere* or *houblon aromatique*, bittering or aroma hops. There was space to record *épices*, spices, and I guessed that *levure* must mean yeast. The French words made me feel the strong presence of the nation to the south, the wine country with a surprisingly strong beer tradition. Brewed in small batches in rural villages, table beer has long graced French glasses. The country's most well-known style, *bière de garde*, is an earthy, funky ale that was originally brewed in farmhouses in Northern France. It tastes like a cousin of Belgian saisons.

Despite the language differences and conversions, I felt a warm familiarity. After all, beer is just beer, something I hadn't yet contemplated on this trip. There was something about being in a small kitchen with a wooden paddle that humanized the drink I'd been analyzing for nearly a week in a foreign place. When I took my turn stirring with the paddle, I scraped the bottom of the kettle vigorously, to prevent the malt from sticking, remembering the kettle burn that created my snow-globe beer last summer. When I'd visited Dupont a few days earlier, I learned that brewers there intentionally caramelized some of the sugars in the mash using a direct gas burner under the boiling kettle. This traditional technique gave extra body to the beer, but also created a daunting cleaning project. I tried to stay focused on stirring, knowing at least one of us would need to clean the kettle later that day, but everything seemed distracting, from the French to the strange assortment of objects in the room, including a bubble machine and turntable.

Eventually, the man they called master brewer arrived. Bertrand Backeland was a good-looking Frenchman and artist in his thirties who was wearing an oversized Norwegian sweater. ("He doesn't have trouble getting girlfriends," Hélène would later tell me.) He shook my hand and mumbled that he was sorry he had a cold and didn't know English very well, which was not what I was hoping to hear from the person who knew the recipe best. Bertrand said he wanted to raise the temperature of the mash four times, which reminded me of Ben Edmunds's lesson in step brewing. By piecing together sentences between Ronoy and Emilien about the *emptage*, or mash, I gathered that the first steps required holding the mash at 50 degrees Celsius for five minutes, before raising it to 63 degrees for thirty minutes. The flame seemed small and imprecise. I guessed that keeping the temperature steady for any amount of time would require someone to adjust the flame by centimeters every few minutes. That's when the group's driving philosophy emerged.

"We like to talk about *plus ou moins*," Emilien said. "In English it means *more or less*."

"It can be the answer to every question," said Ronoy.

Plus ou moins—which Bertrand told me can be written as + / −, like on a battery—was the name of their first beer. "It means beer is not an exact science," Bertrand would tell me later in an e-mail. He said the temperature on the top of the mash might be 63 degrees while the back of the mash was 65 degrees. "It's more or less," he wrote. "What's important is to take the temperature in the same manner."

Immediately, I had a clearer understanding of the ten-hour brew session.

Between the French and the metric system, my mind was tired, and I started slipping from active participant to cultural observer, which may have had something to do with the fact that we had started drinking beer. Ronoy poured me a splash of a previous homebrew.

"What kind of beer is it?" I asked.

"We don't know, and we don't care," he replied with a flourish. "Does it taste good?"

In fact, it tasted great. The beer was reddish and highly carbonated with a dry finish, which I guessed masked a high amount of alcohol. It tasted Belgian, through and through.

For lunch, Emilien went for takeout and returned with *frites* and gyro-like chicken wraps that were sloppy and perfect with our rotation of mystery homebrews. Emilien ate a giant spectacle of a sandwich called a *mitraillette* (which translates to "submachine gun"), a wide baguette filled with slices of fried meat, fries, and a goopy sauce. Eventually we opened a bottle of St. Bernardus Pater 6 that I'd brought from Watou. The fresh, fruity dubbel reminded me that, even though I was in an unknown location with a bunch of guys I didn't know, I was still in the same country as yesterday, the place of abbey ales and hop farms.

The guys kept talking about *drêche,* spent grains. Ronoy said he liked to dump the drêche in his neighbor's empty lot. (The neighbor had given permission.) But to get the spent grains, we needed to separate off the wort. Bertrand had crafted a metal filter for the inside of the kettle and a tap that attached to the bottom. That's where the wort drizzled out into various small plastic containers sitting on top of an adjustable stool. When the small plastic containers were full, we took turns dumping them back into the kettle, so the wort could seep down through the grain bed again, which extracted more sugars. The containers needed to be monitored and switched so they didn't overflow. "Recirculating is the step of a very artisanal gesture with this homemade material," Bertrand would write. He hoped to recirculate the wort at least three times, which filters and clarifies the wort, but without knowing how much of the wort had circulated, it was just another *plus ou moins* activity. The stool collected overflow wort in a small, brown puddle.

"I want to sit on it," Emilien said.

He reminded me of something I read about the late Middle Ages. In Alsace-Lorraine and Bavaria, regulators would pour beer on a wooden bench and sit on the wet bench for an hour. When they tried to stand, if the bench stuck to their pants, the beer met their regulatory standards. If their pants easily separated from the bench, the beer was too light and would need to be sold for cheaper prices.

The recirculation process was so slow and tedious, I felt like I was watching Buddhist monks creating a mandala. Finally, all the wort went back into the kettle, which Emilien had kindly cleaned while the rest of us did nonessential tasks. After the wort came to a boil, Bertrand carefully added sacks filled with Northern Brewer and fuggle hops. I remembered that I'd bought two packages of Oregon-grown aroma hops to give to these homebrewers, but the hops were still in my freezer in Portland. Oh well. At least I had showed up with beer.

Ronoy poured a portion of the wort into a smaller kettle, which he placed on the kitchen stove. He'd take that portion, his personal portion, to an outdoor role-playing fair in July, where he'd play a monk who sells beer. He showed me pictures of previous role-playing beers, which had hand-drawn labels of a head in profile that looked like Ronoy, with a long braid of hair that circled the name of each beer. One was called Du Viking; the other, Otik Qui Troll.

Whether it was because I was a guest or an aspiring beer expert, Ronoy started asking me to make decisions.

"Lucy, should I add all of the hops in this packet or just a portion?"

"All."

"Lucy, should we add the maple syrup?"

"Let's taste it first."

We each dipped a finger in the can. The syrup was lighter and less sweet than I thought it would be.

"Add it all," I said.

Finally, we were done. Only we weren't. A hydrometer revealed an original gravity of 1.040, which would probably produce a beer with less than 6 percent ABV. Ronoy frowned dramatically. He'd been hoping for 8 percent ABV. Bertrand mumbled something in French.

"He says the wort might be too hot and it's affecting the reading of the hydrometer," Ronoy translated.

Suddenly, I noticed the darkness through the doors to the back patio, which made sense when I looked at a clock. Ronoy and Lionel had started brewing at ten in the morning, before Emilien and I had arrived, which meant things were right on schedule. It was 7:30 P.M. Instead of pouring the wort into a sterilized carboy, Ronoy and Bertrand secured the kettle's lid with rubber bands, a risky move that made the wort susceptible to bacterial infection because it wasn't enclosed in a sterilized environment. But it was late, and everyone was tired. *Plus ou moins.*

When I said good-bye to the DIY brewers, I felt nostalgic for all my friends who brewed in their homes in Portland. I'd never brewed with any of them, yet here I was five thousand miles away, brewing with strangers. In the future, I vowed, I'd find the time to brew with friends, old and new.

———

A few days later, Lionel sent those of us who brewed an e-mail. *"Je me suis bien amusé samedi à brasser, apprendre plein de trucs et voir Ronoy et Bert se chamailler . . ."* ("I had fun brewing Saturday, learning stuff and seeing Ronoy and Bert bickering"). So that's what all the French had been about.

In the following months, I would receive a few updates from the brew crew. "Bertrand is confident about a sweet, not so light beer," Emilien wrote. "That sounds good!"

After they sampled the beer we had brewed, Bertrand told me, "The beer is pretty good, sincerely we can have something with homebrewing near like the best commercial beer!" He compared it to a Westvleteren 8, a classic dubbel of 8 percent ABV, which he and Ronoy had shared three days earlier: "Verdict is that it's near it, with same color (CaraRed malt + 900 EBC malt), a fortuity mix! The Westvleteren 8 is very oriented with malt taste. Our dry-hopping has oriented on hop, but it's a good balance between malt and hop, and finally near Westvleteren 8." He would enter the beer in a homebrew contest in September. "I think we have chance to go far with it!" he said.

What the guys told me would be a maple stout turned out to be a Belgian dubbel, an amusing reminder that Belgians do not like conforming to beer styles. I was also thrilled to discover that *plus ou moins* is a methodology that produces great beer. I longed to transport myself to Ronoy's kitchen for a side-by-side tasting of the Westvleteren 8 and the homebrew. Instead, from my living room in Portland, I would congratulate myself on playing a small but supportive role in brewing a Westvleteren simulacrum, aka a "Westy clone."

A LITTLE ROCK 'N' ROLL

It takes beer to make thirst worthwhile.
—GERMAN PROVERB

WHEN I LEFT my rolling suitcase full of bottles of beer in Brussels, I felt like I should attach a note about proper care, as though I were leaving a house sitter with a puppy or a bonsai tree. But I trusted Emilien and Hélène, who had not only let me stay with them in their high-ceilinged one-bedroom apartment, but had taken me out for an Italian dinner and cooked me pancakes in the morning. I was touched that people I'd just met were so generous, and, on the ninth day of my trip, it felt great to have someone taking care of me. "It's a lot of pressure to cook pancakes for an American," Emilien said, as he carefully flipped them with a spatula.

The couple lent me a small backpack, which I filled with two days of clothes, then Emilien walked me to the proper bus stop for getting to the train station. Later that day, I entered Germany without a passport (I had accidentally left it with my beer), without changing any money—a step I still expected—and without feeling the train slow at the border. I wasn't accustomed to Europe as the European Union, a place that was more streamlined than I'd imagined. But I knew economic unification wouldn't have destroyed the beer border built up between Germany and Belgium, differences embedded over the course of centuries.

When I'd first dreamed about doing beer research in Europe, I'd wanted to divide my time between Belgium and Germany. But once I started looking into the logistics of traveling in Germany, which was hulking in size compared to Belgium, I didn't know how I'd make it work. So I came up with a compromise. Because Germany shares a border with Belgium, at least I could cross briefly into Deutschland and learn something, anything, about Germanic beer culture.

Aside from airport layovers, the last time I'd been in Germany was during college. I was twenty years old and a student in an art history program that took me to Munich, Rottenburg am Neckar, and Nuremberg, before we moved on to other European countries. In Germany, I drank legally, with gravel crunching under my feet, in romantically lit beer gardens where hours slipped away. The beers were a revelation: smooth, frothy, and golden in a way that made me feel like I was discovering the drink for the first time. Two decades later, I was headed to Germany with a focus that would have surprised my college-aged self. I wanted to understand what made German beers German, something that would help me place all beers, especially Belgian beers, in a broader context. So many styles were invented in Germany, from the wheat beers of Bavaria to dark lagers and bocks.

Before I left on my trip, I had decided to track down an expert on German beers. Alan Taylor is a brewmaster who owns two breweries in Portland and one in Albuquerque. He has a master's degree in

Germanic studies, and he studied brewing science in Germany after doing a brewing internship at Luisen-Bräu in Berlin. He's also married to a German woman. He told me the key to understanding the country's brewing is *Weisswurstlinie,* the "veal–sausage line" that serves as a cultural delineation between northern and southern Germany. Northern pilsners have a drier malt profile and bracing hop bitterness, while southern German beers include Czech and Bohemian lagers, which are more about malt, with their round sweetness and touch of spicy hops. As one might expect, beers of central Germany mediate the two extremes, with more balanced expressions of malt and hops.

Alan had said that, while beer styles tend to develop from the availability of ingredients, they also represent the tastes of the people who live in the region, preferences influenced by local food. In far-northern Germany, people have a preference for tea, Scandinavian herbal liquors, and anise-flavored drinks, beverages with bracing, astringent notes, he said. Then there's southern Germany. "Combine a soft baked pretzel with sweet mustard and a weissbier (the German category of wheat beers), and it's just heaven," Alan said. He was talking about weisswurst, a traditional Bavarian breakfast. "That same weissbier up north with freshly caught eel isn't going to be quite the same." Instead of a beer with a sweet, round malty flavor, he said, the oiliness of the fish would pair well with a dry, bracing pilsner.

Alan suggested I stop thinking about "German" beers and start thinking instead about "Germanic" beers. Since the country of Germany was formed in 1871, talking about German beers excludes many influential beer styles of the region—namely pilsner—which originated in the Kingdom of Bohemia and the modern-day Czech Republic. Pilsner spawned many styles, including Munich helles,

Dortmunder export, pilsners brewed by German immigrants in the United States before Prohibition, and all manner of lagers brewed around the world.

Traditionally, German states and towns claimed a single style of beer, the one locals drank without question. That idea made me think of my namesake, my great-grandmother Lucy, the daughter of German immigrants to the United States. Lucy worked as a seamstress, and ever since I was a little girl, my mom told me that my great-grandmother drank half a beer a day, during evening card games, up until the day she died in her nineties. I liked to think about my great-grandmother popping open a can of some East Coast beer—she drank local, like her German parents did before they crossed the Atlantic—pouring half into a glass and the other half down the sink, especially because I'd become proficient at pouring beer I didn't want down sinks and into dump buckets. There were simply more beers I needed to taste than to drink.

I wondered what kind of beer my great-grandmother would have liked. My mom guessed some kind of bock, a family of strong German lagers that originated in Einbeck, a central German city, during the fourteenth century. Einbeck brewers were some of the first to replace the spices of *gruit*—the herbs that preceded hops in beer—with hops, which made sense, because the city was located in an early hop-growing region. It's said that brewers in Munich adopted the style during the nineteenth century, but my beer professor Bill Schneller theorized that the bocks of Munich used different malts and had much lower alcohol contents than the bocks of Einbeck, and were therefore less related than beer historians like to think. In fact, Einbeck beers were probably ales and lighter in color, while the Munich versions are dark lagers.

The link between the two cities can be traced to one man, Einbeck brewmaster Elias Pichler. During the late Middle Ages, Einbeck became known as a brewing capital unlike any other. Many burghers liked to brew beer at home, but none of them were allowed to own a brewery. Instead, the city-owned brewing equipment was transported through wide city gates to the houses of homebrewers, where the malting and brewing process was overseen by a city-hired brewmaster, who ensured consistency and quality. As a member of the Hanseatic League, a powerful merchant trading empire, Einbeck exported its beers through member port cities as far as Scandinavia and even Jerusalem. But the beer really caught hold in Munich, and when exports from Einbeck stopped arriving in the city thanks to the Thirty Years' War, the beer drinkers of the city had a problem. Under Bavarian Duke Maximilian I, Elias Pichler came to Munich's Hofbräuhaus in 1617 to recreate Einbeck bocks. What he created was a maibock, or helles bock, a beer that was traditionally served during the month of May. Maybe my great-grandmother had been drinking an American version.

Or maybe she preferred one of my favorites: the complex and rich *doppelbock,* a term that refers to the strength of the beer. Doppelbocks were originally brewed in Munich by the monks of Saint Francis of Paola to sustain themselves during fasts, most notably during Lent, when no solid food could enter their bodies. During the fast they became "purified" by liquids, especially the sweet, malty, rich beer, which contained not only enough nutrients to keep them alive during the forty-day fast but also, one can imagine, just enough alcohol for a pleasant beer buzz. The Paulaner monks named their liquid bread "Salvator," for the Savior, and in 1780 their version became a secular brew, which we now know as doppelbock. Three hundred and seventy-five years later, Paulaner Salvator doppelbock is still a dark and chocolately bottom-fermented, unfiltered beer, something I look forward to drinking every holiday season.

———

Until the past three or four years, German brewing was "traditional, nonexperimental, and rigid," Alan had said. Those attributes are embodied by the Reinheitsgebot, the famous Germany Purity Law that states that brewers can only make beer using four ingredients: water, malt, hops, and yeast. (The law still remains in effect, despite the shift in attitude Alan mentioned.) Nearly every beer brewed in Germany and sold commercially meets these requirements. That means brewers can't make beers with pumpkins, apples, passionfruit, cinnamon, habanero peppers, thyme, donuts, oysters, rice, corn, or jasmine flowers. But there's one ingredient I was surprised to learn they can use: sugar. It can be pure cane, beet, invert sugars, or, as Ben Edmunds probably knows, dextrose. These sugars can be used only in top-fermented beers, which mean the beers are ales, not lagers, but Germans prefer to use the term "top-fermented." Under the Purity Law, in top-fermented beers brewers can use any type of grain that can be "caused to germinate," which makes rye and wheat fair game. It turns out the current law has stricter rules for lagers and more lenient rules for ales.

The Purity Law originated in the southeast region of Bavaria in 1516. Michelangelo had recently painted the ceiling of the Sistine Chapel, and Martin Luther was launching the Protestant Reformation. Created under the Bavarian duke Wilhelm IV, the law was designed both to put a stop to brewers making beers (mostly lagers) with wheat, which was needed to make bread, and to set pricing for beer. "In all cities, markets, and in the country, the only ingredients used for the brewing of beer must be Barley, Hops and Water. Whosoever knowingly disregards or transgresses upon this ordinance, shall be punished by the Court authorities' confiscating such barrels of beer, without fail." (Centuries later, yeast was added as an acceptable ingredient, after scientists discovered its role in fermentation, as were the distinctions about top-fermented beers.)

In 1777 Frederick the Great, king of Prussia, which made up much of today's northern Germany, who was dismayed by the amount of money being spent on his subjects' emerging coffee habit, declared: "It is disgusting to note the increase in the quantity of coffee used by my subjects and the amount of money that goes out of the country in consequence. Everybody is using coffee. If possible this must be prevented. My people must drink beer. His Majesty was brought up on beer, and so were his officers. Many battles have been fought and won by soldiers nourished on beer; and the King does not believe the coffee-drinking soldiers can be depended upon to endure hardship or to beat his enemies in case of the occurrence of another war."

Germany adopted the law in 1906, and in 1918, Bavaria joined the German Weimar Republic under the condition that the country uphold the Purity Law, which was named Reinheitsgebot. The law was enforced countrywide until 1987, when the European Court ruled that non-German brewers could sell beers in Germany that did not adhere to the law, while German brewers still had to conform to the strictures for beers sold domestically. The Reinheitsgebot represents more than a German tendency for order, but also for purity. While Americans tend to view the law as limiting, most Germans see it as necessary protection of quality, tradition, and ingenuity. In effect, the law became one of the first pieces of consumer protection. It shielded German beer drinkers from subpar beer.

I was heading to the city of Köln, known as Cologne to the English-speaking world, to attempt to understand the rigor and tradition of Germanic beers. Köln is the home of Kölsch, the name of both the dialect spoken in the city and a blonde-colored, effervescent style of beer that was invented to compete with pilsners. Even though by most standards kölsch seems like a pilsner, it's fermented at warmer temperatures, which makes it a top-fermenting beer and, therefore, a rarity in German brewing. Kölsch is an ale. The beer has a low alcohol content and a soft roundness, something you might want to drink on a summer day. The style isn't for everyone. My travel-writer friend Ryan, who'd recently been in Köln researching a Lonely Planet guidebook, told me the city's famous beer tasted "like water." American craft brewers have made many iterations of the style. A Portland-brewed kölsch was one of two beers Tony and I served at our wedding, because we wanted a lighter beer that would appeal to anyone who didn't like the IPA.

In 1986 the twenty-four breweries in the city signed the Kölsch Konvention, which mandated that, within Germany, anything called a kölsch must be brewed in Köln; have a pale color; be top-fermented, brewed with hops, and filtered; and qualify as a "vollbier," one of four German beer tax categories that states a "full beer" must have an original gravity of 11 to 14 percent. That decree followed earlier mandates, like one in 1603 that stated all beers brewed in Köln must be top-fermented, and then the one that created the Kölsch Konvention, a group formed to protect the style. Today, a majority of the breweries in Köln brews kölsch. Even though a city with a signature beer style seems like a rarity, Köln isn't the only one.

Upriver on the Rhine, Dusseldorf is the city of *altbier,* or "old beer." Altbier is also a top-fermenting beer, one made with darker Munich malts instead of the light pilsner malt in kölsch. Dusseldorf and Köln are notoriously competitive about their respective beers.

To get my first glass of kölsch on the ground, I decided to skirt Köln's most famous attraction, the Kölner Dom, or Cologne Cathedral, which was built starting in 1248 and was finished 632 years later. Today, six million people a year visit the hulking mass of Gothic architecture, which is hard to squeeze into the boundaries of a single photo. On the far edge of the cathedral's plaza is Früh, one of the city's largest breweries, which was founded in 1904 by Peter Josef Früh. When he died eleven years after hanging his shingle, his widow and two daughters took over the company, a rare gender reversal. Früh brews just three kinds of drinks—kölsch, radler, and Früh Sport, a nonalcoholic sport drink—all of which are made at a large facility on the outskirts of the city. I had an appointment to visit the brewery the following day, and I wanted to arrive having already tasted a Früh Kölsch.

In the outdoor beer garden, red-cheeked soccer fans wearing scarves were boisterously preparing to march to the FC Köln (the Köln Football Club) match. Indoors, shards of jewel-toned stained glass, dark wood-paneled walls, old clocks, and dim lighting made me feel like I had entered a church, a place where Sunday afternoon meant worshiping an ale that was considered obscure anywhere but here. In Köln tradition, the servers in the pubs are usually men who wear a very specific uniform: crisp white button-up shirts and long, navy blue aprons. The men are called Köbes, and from the moment I stepped inside, I was trying to get out of their way. The servers moved with a striking efficiency and brusqueness, spinning, twirling, and showboating round metal trays with central handles and holes for holding tall, straight-sided, six-ounce *stangen* glasses, which translates to "stick" or "rod." The glasses, which are used only for kölsch, are intentionally small, so imbibers will drink the beer before it warms. Near the front door, men wearing vests over their white shirts poured beer from a barrel into glasses. They moved like efficient machines. On closer inspection, I noticed the barrel's tap was actually protruding from a metal keg underneath, which made me feel like I'd just tried to pull a handle on a faux drawer. While the brewpub felt weighted with tradition, I also detected performance, as though the pub was just a portrayal of authenticity.

I was seated at a communal table, and I was alone until two older women sat a few seats down. They were so engrossed in conversation with each other, they seemed oblivious to the room, Köbes, and football fans. But eventually the three of us started chatting. They told me they met as young nurses in Switzerland. One of them went on to marry a German man she met in Israel, and the other married a Frenchman she met in Morocco. Even though the friends parted ways and led separate lives, they made a point to meet and travel together on a regular basis.

"We never forgot each other," said the one wearing a bright pink scarf. They both giggled.

"You remind me of myself forty-five years ago," she told me. "Sitting alone in a restaurant, writing. I remember it so well."

Sitting alone in restaurants and scribbling in a notebook was one of my favorite things to do. I felt a warm connection to these kindred spirits. I asked the friends what I should order.

"You want to have something from here, something typical?" the woman with glasses and a dark bob asked. "You must get kölsch. You can drink the other beers here, but it is sacrilege."

"We had that Paulaner in Bavaria," the pink-scarfed woman added wistfully. "But when you're here, you drink kölsch."

A spectacled server breezed up to our table and seemed immediately impatient. I ordered a Früh Kölsch, which the menu said was "direkt vom fass," or on draft. A minute later, the server returned, tossed a paper coaster next to my notebook, plucked a beer from his tray, and offered me my first taste of the city. The beer had shades of that elusive, golden German beer taste I remembered from college. Only now, as an aspiring Cicerone, I couldn't just enjoy that nostalgic observation. I pushed for more precise words to describe the malt, and I guessed the beer's International Bitterness Units. Twenty. "Crackery malt, herby, smack of lemon," I wrote in my notebook. It was one of those moments when I felt not only how my perception of beer had changed, but how I'd changed. In nearly two decades, I'd gone from American girl drinking to get drunk to American woman drinking in the pursuit of knowledge, a different type of pleasure.

The women had also recommended trying what the English menu called "smoked minced meat sausage made of roughly meat." The plate of food arrived in a glorious display of everything I dreamed of when I thought about eating in Deutschland: a fat sausage arching off the edges of the plate, a smooth smear of mashed potatoes, and a meat-flecked tangle of tangy kraut. This was the German stamp in my passport.

Kölsch etiquette goes like this: when you finish a beer, the server automatically brings another one and makes a tick on your coaster. When you're ready for the check, the ticks are tallied. To signal you don't want another beer, place the coaster on top of your empty glass like a lid. But be warned. If you forget to give the signal, or even hesitate for longer than thirty seconds, you will find yourself presented with another small, low-alcohol beer that costs less than two euros. At that point, you may think, *It's just a little beer and it's already here. I might as well drink it.* Next thing you know, you've been in Köln for two weeks and have become a top supporter of the FC Köln, otherwise known as the Billy Goats. Kölsch service is an engrained tradition. One Früh advertisement showed an empty glass with a coaster on top. *Du sollst nicht lügen*, it read. Don't lie. The next night, I'd visit Gaffel, another of the city's large kölsch brewers. There, my server would chug a glass of kölsch while standing next to my table, before wiping his mouth with his sleeve and showing the American man at my table his tongue piercing. Then, he balanced a full beer on top of the coaster I'd placed on my empty glass. So much for tradition.

After my meal at Früh, I decided to climb one of the cathedral's towers to reach a viewing area three hundred feet above the ground, which promised views of the city and the murky Rhine. To get there, I had to walk up 533 well-worn stone steps, an impressive corkscrew pointed toward God. Hundreds of tourists packed the stairwell, so I took deep breaths and consciously avoided thinking about the height I was gaining and the smallness of the space we all occupied. On the way up, I ran my right hand along a cold, rounded stone wall. On the way down, I appreciated an actual railing.

Later, I descended into the cathedral's vaults. Between ominous stone walls, which were the building's foundation, glass cases separated visitors from antiquities bathed in dazzling light. I took in elaborate tapestries, glittering robes, staffs adorned with chunks of jewels, and slivers of saints' bones wrapped in gauze. The whole time, I was searching for one thing: evidence of beer. My world had become a place where beer was not just a drink delivered in stangen glasses but something interwoven with religion, architecture, and mythology. In Europe I'd started to view beer as a thread through human history. Instead of creating access to new territory, like a ribbon of fresh asphalt, beer was a cobblestone street worn smooth by generations of feet and bicycle tires. It wasn't that European brewers were so bound to tradition they weren't expressing themselves through their recipes—the brewers I met weren't above creating new beers, equipment, or brewing techniques—but they brewed as though they didn't have anything to prove. They had history on their side. Even if, in these hallowed halls, the fat-fingered, bejeweled, gold-threaded Catholic power players chose to fill their chalices and goblets with fermented grapes, I knew beer had been here. Beer had been everywhere.

======

On my final evening in Köln, I lingered in my hotel room for as long as I could stand, hoping to catch Tony and Oscar on Skype. Our attempts at daily Skype calls were falling through with an increasing frequency during the past few days. When the two of them were getting ready for the day, eating dinner, or doing bedtime rituals, I was in places without WiFi. I was starting to feel disconnected from my little family in North America. The Skype app bleeped and bleeped. No answer. So I made a video of the train station, which I could see from the hotel window, then looked into my phone and told Oscar I'd be coming home soon. I sent the video to Tony, then I bundled up and headed back out into the city.

After drinking nothing but kölsch since I arrived, I longed for some variety. That's how I ended up sitting on a bar stool next to Peter Esser, a Köln brewer known for treating Reinheitsgebot as a suggestion—for other people. Peter is the owner and brewmaster of one of the city's smallest breweries, Braustelle, a brewpub in an emerging artists' quarter. Brandon Evans, the brewing intern at Cantillon, said he always heads straight to Braustelle when visiting Köln, which is how I heard of the place. With a chalkboard beer menu, brew kettles in the corner, and a lack of any blue-smocked servers, the brewpub felt more Portland than Köln. In fact, the brewery might be better known in Portland. American craft beer lovers might not recognize the name Braustelle, but many of them will know Freigeist Bierkultur, a gypsy brewing label created by Peter and a young brewer named Sebastian Sauer. Freigeist beers, some of which are brewed on-site, have a distinctive white ghost on the label, and the name translates to "freethinker" or "free spirit."

Peter told me he started out as a homebrewer before he enrolled in a brewing school. After he graduated, he brewed at a handful of German breweries before opening Braustelle in 2010, when he decided to push the boundaries of tradition by reviving old beer styles using interesting, modern ingredients. Not much of what he wanted to brew conformed to the Germany Purity Law, so Peter decided to label his beers "beverages with alcohol." Without calling his beers "beer," Peter wasn't breaking any laws.

Braustelle represents a small but growing craft beer movement in Germany. The country hasn't escaped the influence of U.S. brewers, an effect that's evident everywhere from Italy to Japan. But in Germany, a place of longstanding beer traditions, the craft scene presents some interesting possibilities. For one, craft beer can excite younger generations of drinkers, who seem to have slowly abandoned beer, the drink of their grandparents, for cocktails and sport drinks. In 1991 the average German drank about thirty-seven gallons of beer a year. In 2014 that number fell to twenty-six gallons a year, about the same as the American average.

Some rule breakers from Freigeist and Braustelle include a gose made with oysters, a lambic-style beer fermented with cherry blossoms, and a lichtenhainer, a traditional eastern German tart, smoked-wheat beer. As Peter and I talked, I drank the Pink Panther, a vibrantly pink ale brewed with hibiscus flowers. Even though the beer seemed a bit watery, it was a refreshing dose of punk rock in a city of smooth jazz.

"I don't care about styles," Peter told me, which made him sound more Belgian than German. For example, he said in choppy English, once he wanted to create a strong black beer with smoky characteristics. He didn't care how it would be categorized. He liked to begin with a single ingredient and build a recipe around it. "The idea is in the head, the taste, and ingredients," he explained. "You do it for your own."

Next, we shared a bottle of Raqui, a beer Peter told me was made with what he thought were "sour apples" in English. He wrote the German word *quitte* in my notebook, which I later found out means "quince."

"I think I like this beer," Peter said, smiling. I liked it, too. Its bracing tartness showed off whispers of hay and dried grass.

I was amused to discover Braustelle brews the only altbier in Köln, as well as its own version of kölsch. Of course, Peter's interpretation doesn't conform to the rules of the Kölsch Konvention; it is unfiltered, a pre-Konvention practice, which actually makes the beer more traditional. In the glass, Peter's kölsch was cloudy and dried-ginkgo-leaf yellow, which reminded me of something Alan Taylor told me about the evolution of pilsners, the foundation of modern German brewing traditions (outside of Köln). He said pilsners could have only come about in the industrial revolution, when people could see their beer for the first time; affordable glassware had just become available.

"You could see dark, chunky stuff floating around in your beer that you'd really never thought about," Alan said. "Or you could look at a brilliant golden beer with a beautiful white frothy head." People began to demand beautiful beer. "These days, people take all these pictures of their food," Alan continued. "This was the first picture of beer. It was eye candy."

Peter showed me around the brewery, some of which was directly underneath the pub, in a cramped basement. One room had metal doors that made me feel like I was on the set of *Das Boot*. ACHTUNG UV-STRAHLUNG! a sign read. It was a warning about UV light, which helped kill bacteria and flies in the fermentation room. A handful of barrels made up the "sour room," which I imagined was an attraction during the on-site brewing seminars Peter offered to the public. After he shows tour attendees how he brews and then offers them samples of beer, inevitably, the discussion turns to the Reinheitsgebot.

"Most people think it's a good thing," he said. "It's different to say something against it."

As if to offset his nonconformist beers, Peter recommended that, before I catch my train back to Brussels, I stop at Päffgen, a Köln brewery founded in 1883. There, he said, the kölsch had low carbonation, good foam, and more malt. It was "not like water." The next morning, I smelled the malty sweetness of beer brewing long before I saw the door to Päffgen, which was tucked into a street of high-end shops that hadn't yet opened for the day. Uwe Wisskirchen, brewmaster at Päffgen had a strong handshake and spoke very little English, but he kindly showed me around the brewery. "More work and more time," he said, "but the beer tastes better." Most of the time, I didn't know what he was saying, and the language barrier was so thick, at one point, he drew a diagram of something that looked like a rainbow spilling into a tube. *Weigel-Schnellabläuterung*, he wrote. In the fermentation room, pillows of foam in tall, open-topped fermenters bubbled and burped, which caused foam to splat onto the floor every few seconds. The spillage would have seemed wild and un-German were it not for Uwe's calm demeanor and fact that we were surrounded by gleaming equipment.

Even though they brewed every batch using the same 130-year-old recipe, he said, each brew was slightly different. "There's change, variation," he said. "This is a small house brewery. We make hand-crafted beer."

I asked him what he thought of Peter.

"Peter and I are good friends," he said.

"You can still be friends even though he's breaking the law?" I hoped he'd detect my sarcasm. He laughed.

"Yes, it's OK," he said. "A little rock 'n' roll."

In less than forty-eight hours, I would step off a plane and see Tony and Oscar, a moment I was imagining more frequently, especially when I sat down to eat a meal by myself. I couldn't wait to be home. I longed to feel Oscar's silky round cheek against mine when we hugged, and I couldn't wait to kiss Tony and feel his stubble on my face, a gentle rub of masculinity that seemed very far away. I was still taking pictures of Oscar's little car, everywhere from bakeries to brewpubs, but the photos felt lifeless. The car was just a metal hull; it had been too long since Oscar touched it. But what was more difficult to admit, because it felt like a betrayal, was that part of me didn't want to go home. I regretted I had to leave a beer-rich country I'd only just begun to explore. I wouldn't have the chance to taste a fresh doppelbock in Munich or a yeasty hefeweizen brewed by Benedictine monks in Andechs. Not this time, anyway.

JUDGMENT DAY

In the beginner's mind there are many possibilities, in the expert's mind there are a few.

—SHUNRYU SUZUKI

I PRESSED THROUGH the revolving door and stepped into the lush, clean air of Portland in March. In the pickup lane at the airport, I saw a familiar set of bike racks approaching, the top rails of a familiar car. Behind a harsh white glare on the front windshield, Tony grinned, revealing the charming gap between his front teeth. In the back seat, Oscar looked like a giant, his long legs spilling out of his car seat, which pinned him down like Gulliver on Lilliput. Tony hopped out, kissed me, and threw my bag in the back.

"He's asleep," he said. "I tried to keep him awake, but we had to keep circling while we waited for you to land."

When I got into the front seat, I turned and squeezed Oscar's knee. "Sunshine, I'm home!"

He emitted a tiny snore. I sighed.

At home, we had our full reunion, which included chicken soup Tony made, the perfect antidote to a long day of travel that had begun with rolling my bag from Hélène and Emilien's apartment to a bus station before the sun rose. I was too tired to drink a beer, so instead I carefully unrolled the sweaters and pants padding more than a dozen bottles of Belgian beer. (Sarah taught me the packing technique the night before she flew home.) None of the bottles had broken or leaked. One at a time, I handed them to Tony.

"Thank you," I said, after he carefully set the beers on the kitchen table in a bowling pin formation. Oscar was in another room making vroom-vroom sounds.

"No, thank *you*," he replied and hugged me from behind. "I'm so glad you're home."

"Was it hard?" I asked. "Taking care of Oscar all those days by yourself?"

"Not really," Tony said stoically, "but I never want to do another bedtime." I couldn't imagine getting Oscar into bed—a drawn out process that often included tears—thirteen times in a row. I promised to take more than my share of bedtimes in the coming weeks.

For the next few days, I felt disoriented and exhausted. One night at the dinner table, I noticed Tony and Oscar were staring at me, waiting for me to respond to something I hadn't heard them say. I'd been thinking about which flashcards I would make while Tony cleaned up the dinner dishes. That night, I woke up at two o'clock and stared at the light coming in through the blinds in the bedroom. Heat emanated from Tony, who was sleeping soundly next to me. The Cicerone exam was just four weeks away, and I knew I wasn't ready. I desperately wanted more time. If only I could have another six months, I thought. Instead of riding my bike to work, which made me feel invigorated and relaxed, I started taking the train so I could review flashcards—the ones I'd barely touched during my trip. Tony drove Oscar to and from school so I'd have extra time to study.

When friends and co-workers asked me if I felt ready to take the test, I tried not to snap at them. Of course I wasn't ready. Megan Flynn, who'd taken the Cicerone exam a few months earlier, sent me encouraging text messages. "Study the beer styles," she admonished. "Beer styles, beer styles, beer styles." But I hadn't even made flashcards yet for at least a dozen styles; I'd been studying other things.

One evening, I was mumbling something about IBUs as I flipped through a few flashcards before dinner, and Oscar said, "Mama, are you going to burn your flashcards after you take the test?" I was taken aback. I knew I'd been complaining about the test, mostly to Tony and my close friends, but I hadn't wanted my test anxiety to infiltrate Oscar's world. A naive hope—of course the test was affecting him. The way he was watching me, and taking note of my experiences, made me want to try even harder to become a Cicerone. I wanted him, and Tony, to be part of something victorious.

———

In February, two weeks before I left for Belgium, I'd started going to a weekly Beer Judge Certification Program course, which prepared people to take a beer exam that would certify them to judge homebrew competitions. While I didn't have any aspirations to become a BJCP judge, the Cicerone exam would test me on the BJCP style guide, so I knew the class would be good prep. (When Tony suggested I also take the BJCP exam, I stared at him blankly. For me, there would be only one beer exam.) During each BJCP class, we learned about one or two beer styles and an off-flavor by listening to a lecture from an instructor. More important, we got to taste a bunch of beers. One night, we tried beers that were so skunky and light-struck, they reminded one of my classmates of the aroma at a Willie Nelson concert. Another night, we sloshed through the sherry, soy sauce, and wet-paper-towel flavors of oxidation.

During one of the final BJCP classes before my test, we learned about strong ales. As we did every class, we ended the night by blindly tasting beers and judging them by filling out official BJCP scoring sheets. I sniffed, sipped, and dutifully wrote my impressions of a barley wine. I liked this beer, I thought, before shelving the idea so I could objectively evaluate what I was tasting. After all the students had finished scoring the beer, one of the instructors said, "So, what did everyone think of this beer?"

"Brett!" replied a chorus.

Brett? I thought. As in *Brettanomyces,* the yeast that produces the barnyard notes I loved so much? I smelled the sample again and noticed a woodiness that reminded me of a wet barrel. The beer did have a hint of sourness, something that shouldn't have been present in a barley wine. I'd given the beer a high score for being an awesome English barley wine, a style I knew was supposed to be rich, nutty, caramely, and slightly hot with alcohol—everything this beer wasn't. Since the beer wasn't true to style, it deserved a low score, the methodology for most beer judging. It turned out the beer was an English ale made with *Brettanomyces,* an oddball designed to trick the students who were thinking, not perceiving. I was tricked.

———

I was down to the last days before the exam. One night, I promised myself if I studied for forty-five minutes, I could watch an episode of

Gilmore Girls, my current favorite form of escapism. A few minutes later, I was in a panic. Every beer style seemed like a new invention. What were the color variations between a dry stout, sweet stout, oatmeal stout, foreign extra stout, American stout, and Russian imperial stout? And wait, why didn't I have a flashcard for Irish stout? I started flipping between random entries in *The Oxford Companion to Beer.* I read about Ringwood Brewery, an English brewery with a now-ubiquitous signature yeast. My rational self knew that reading any type of encyclopedia was a sure a way to feel ignorant, but I couldn't stop. Every time I read something new, I realized how much I didn't know. The vastness of my ignorance was like seeing the Milky Way for the first time.

Earlier in the day, I felt I'd made progress: I'd learned so much about beer since last June. But what constituted my new knowledge, exactly? I would rely on the test to answer that question. I thought about less stressful ways I could have uncovered this truth: by organizing a beer dinner for friends, making a batch of homebrew blindfolded, and waltzing into the Widmer taste panel only to dazzle them with my insights. But I'd chosen to take a test.

Forty-five minutes turned into two hours; Rory and Lorelai Gilmore never appeared. Instead, I watched a YouTube video about how to deal with test anxiety, which made me think of Ray Daniels laughing about the guy who had to see a therapist. By the time I heard the clink of a key in the shop door outside, which meant Tony was home from his nighttime bike ride, the living room was a mess of flashcards, open books, empty bottles of sparkling water (I couldn't remember the last time I had drunk a beer just because), and one disassembled faucet, all of which had migrated to the floor from the dining room table, a surface that had been covered with study materials since I got home from my trip. When Tony walked into the room, I was sitting cross-legged on the floor, surrounded by detritus, with my finger on an entry in the encyclopedia.

"Did you know linalool is a chemical in hops?" I said without looking up. "It's probably too obscure to be on the test, but it's good to know it creates flowery and fruity aromas. I could throw that into an essay question and probably score an extra point."

"I can't wait for this test to be over," he said, his voice vibrating at a higher pitch than normal.

"What?" I replied, making sure my finger was fixed to the entry before I raised my eyes from the page. He was standing in the doorway of the living room in his baggy bike shorts and red wool bike jersey, the rise and fall of his breath visible in his chest, as though he'd just sprinted up a steep grade. "Did you even hear what I said?" I replied. "I've learned some really interesting things about hops since you left."

"Are you serious?" he said, his voice rising with each syllable. "Did you even hear what I said? I'm so tired of this damn test. I can't wait for it to be over."

"How come you never help me study?" I blurted out. From the kitchen, a soothing NPR voice emanated from the stereo.

"It makes me wonder," Tony continued, as he took a step toward me. "Why are you even doing this?"

"How can you even ask me that?" I said, tears welling up in my eyes.

"I'm sorry, babe, but this is crazy." Before I could say anything else, he turned and walked out of the room. I heard him close the bathroom door gently, before water hissed from the showerhead.

I knew I'd been distracted lately, to say the least, which wasn't a great reward for the person who'd been doing extra cooking, cleaning, and child shuttling. At the same time, I was slightly annoyed by Tony's question. Why should I have to justify the way I was approaching one of my passions? I was pursuing something difficult—a deeper relationship with something I loved—and yes, that might be inconvenient. But for years, I felt like I'd supported Tony in his quest for bike accomplishments. I thought of all the Sundays I'd spent standing in the rain so I could watch him race bikes, or the evenings I'd spent by myself so he could finish welding a bike frame in the shop.

I looked at the mess on the floor. Somehow, my pointer finger was still anchored to "linalool." I felt frozen. If I closed the book and put everything away, the thought I'd been avoiding all night might have the space to surface. I didn't want to think about not passing the test. Not only would I have failed to accomplish what I set out to do, I would be letting down the two people who meant the most to me. I unfolded my legs then sat back down on my knees and leaned forward so I could get closer to the encyclopedia's small print.

———

The morning of the test, I tried to focus on Oscar, who was doing funny things with Snoozy Blacknose, his favorite stuffed animal. He seemed extra cheery, as though he knew I needed a distraction. Since the test would take four or five hours to complete, and the instructions said we weren't allowed to bring food in to the exam, I waited a few hours to eat a huge breakfast. While I was getting ready, I remembered to not wear any lotion or perfume; scents were banned from the exam space. And even though my hand lingered over some lip balm in the bathroom drawer, I wasn't about to risk ruining a beer with something that would kill its aroma and head.

Since I had started studying for the test, my lips were almost always naked.

At a beer distributor's headquarters in an industrial area of North Portland, I entered a conference room with rectangular tables pushed together in rows. A few sheets of paper and plastic cups of water marked where test takers were supposed to sit. The empty chairs between spots would make it impossible for test takers to see each other's tests. Giant flat-screens hung from the perimeter of the ceiling. Some showed charts, which appeared to be sales numbers for beer brands, while one played something that looked like a TED talk. A guy talking on a stage was interspliced with beautiful people in clubs and on beaches drinking various Anheuser-Busch beers. The video reminded me of the corporate reality of the drink I'd spent so much time examining from other angles. I started mentally preparing to block out the screen once the test began.

I chose a spot in the middle of a row, between two men. The guy to my left had a giant, bushy beard and a serene look on his face. When I walked past his chair, I noticed he was reading a dense and technical-looking book. (We were allowed to review study materials until the test began.) Fifteen of us were taking the Certified Cicerone exam that day, and I counted three other women in the room, one of whom was reading *Tasting Beer*. I felt my throat tighten. The YouTube video recommended not cramming right before the test, but maybe the other test takers knew something I didn't. I remembered I'd stashed a notebook in my bag, which happened to have some BJCP class notes inside. I flipped to a page on English ales and stared at my own handwriting. Nothing made sense. My heart pounded. If I couldn't focus now, how could I possibly concentrate during the test? I'd traveled to Europe, made hundreds of flashcards, attended beer classes, brewed batches of beer, and missed many irre-placeable moments with Tony and Oscar. What if, after all my hard work, the test revealed I didn't know much about beer?

A bearded guy wearing glasses and an unbuttoned sports coat paced across the front of the room. Chris Pisney, a Certified Cicerone, was the test proctor for the day. He had a bevy of assis-tants, employees of the Cicerone program who were in town for the Craft Brewers Conference. One of them was Nicole Erny, the Master Cicerone who'd taught my off-flavor class last summer.

"It's nice to see you," she'd said when I walked into the room. "I'm glad you're finally going for it."

I realized at least two years had passed since I first interviewed Nicole for a story, a conversation during which I told her I wanted to become a Certified Cicerone someday. Then I remembered why I was in that room feeling scared. I was tired of merely thinking about doing something big.

"We're waiting for one person," Chris announced. "We'll give him five minutes, and then we'll start the test."

"If I was this late," the guy to my right muttered, "I wouldn't expect them to wait for me." His face was a pasty color that made him look like I felt: slightly ill. He'd been shuffling papers and flip-ping through books with the speed of someone with a photographic memory. "I was ready at ten," he huffed. Even though the test started at eleven, I too had been ready at ten. I'd puttered around my kitchen, knowing that being in the testing room too early would only fuel my nerves.

Once the final test taker arrived, and we reviewed a seemingly endless litany of housekeeping items, which included signing a waiver that said explicit disclosure of exam content was grounds for revocation of certification, Chris placed a packet of paper, held to-gether by a single staple, facedown in front of each of us. We had three hours to finish the written portion of the test, which seemed like a generous amount of time that would give me space to thor-oughly review all my answers.

"You may begin," he said, with authority.

I turned the test over. At the top of each sheet, I wrote my test taker code, a number we created so the judges would never see our names. Since I'd chosen my phone number, I easily wrote my digits dozens of times, which gave me the chance to quickly look at each page. I knew the answers to some of the fill-in-the-blank questions. I didn't know the answers to others. A few sections had diagrams and photos I needed to label, and the last pages had the three essay ques-tions. When I saw one of those questions, which asked for deeply specific information about a single style of beer, I swallowed hard. By the time I had written my phone number on the top of the last page, I felt exposed. Ray Daniels had been right. There was no place to hide.

Much like a state bar exam, you can retake the Certified Cicerone exam, either the written or tasting portion, or both, until you pass. I'd heard stories of retakes that resulted in getting 78 or 79 percent, a brutal nearness to the 80 percent needed to pass. Right then, I wasn't thinking about retakes, points, or percentages. I moved through the test as though I was hacking a path through a jungle with a machete while being chased by wild pigs. When I didn't know an answer, I left it blank and kept going.

There were questions about hops and hop farming that made me think about standing next to hills of dried hops at Bale Breaker with Meghann Quinn. The section about draft systems, which I immedi-ately knew was not my forte, made me think about running across the freshly mopped floor at Hair of the Dog with Adrienne So, who was now a new mother. I'd told Denver Bon I was taking the test today, so I knew he was out there somewhere in Portland rooting for me. Questions about brewing technique made me think of Ben Edmunds and his clipboard. Then I remembered stirring mash with a wooden paddle in Ronoy's colorful kitchen in Brussels. A question about the properties of one Belgian beer reminded me of Sarah Jane Curran, and the way she looked peaceful and far away after she'd tasted a beer in the tasting room of De Dolle Brouwers. When Chris announced we had fifteen minutes to finish the written portion, I couldn't believe it. I barely had time to go back and guess on the questions I'd left blank.

After everyone had turned in their written tests, Chris told us it was time for the tasting portion of the exam, a moment I'd been dreading. I was an English major, so I knew how to write. But did I know how to taste? This would be new territory for me. Chris instructed us to bring thirteen beer samples from a table at the back of the room to our seats. Two-ounce pours in clear plastic glasses were labeled with single letters, and I made at least three trips, holding the cups gently in both hands while trying not to warm them with the heat from my palms. Once everyone had their beers, Chris said we could begin. I sniffed through the first set of beers, which were spiked with off-flavors, just like Nicole had taught me. "Trust your training," my friend Natalie once told me, days before I ran a marathon for the first time. The motions felt familiar, and immediately, I knew which one was the control beer. The next section asked us to identify which style of beer we were tasting, out of two listed choices. I grinned when I saw that one beer was either a kölsch or a Belgian blonde; I'd learned the difference between those two by taking a train to Köln.

The last part of the tasting test was the most difficult. We had to taste beers, each of which was identified by brewery and style, and explain if the beer was good enough to serve, with justification of our decision. Some, but not all, of the beers were spiked with various combinations of off-flavors. Instead of just perceiving each beer's aromas and flavors, I started thinking. Since I was pretty sure there hadn't been any diacetyl on the test yet, I guessed I'd taste the compound in one of these beers. From somewhere far away, I heard Rob Widmer say, "Fail," a reminder of the last time I'd chosen to ignore the chemical compound.

Chris had told us to keep our samples after we finished writing down our answers, because we'd review the tasting section together, as a group. It wasn't that the Cicerone organization wanted us to have an idea of how we scored, he explained, but that they'd calibrate scoring based on the group's responses. If all the test takers missed one spike, for example, they'd give less weight to the scoring of that sample. "Don't try to figure out your scores based on what we tell you right now," he warned. "I know you're going to try, but don't." But I couldn't help myself. After we reviewed each answer in the tasting section, I was pretty sure I got ten out of twelve correct, but the two I missed were on the more heavily weighted last section. There had been no diacetyl.

Finally, we were instructed to enter a room, one at a time, and sit in front of a video camera, where we'd demonstrate how to use parts of a draft system. When it was my turn, I walked into the windowless room and sat down in front of a tiny point-and-shoot camera on a tripod. Chris went behind the camera and looked at me.

"Are you ready?" he said. He had a kind smile. "Just follow the instructions on your paper."

In my right hand, I held a thin strip of paper, the size of a week-long grocery list. He pressed a button on the camera then left the room. The door wheezed shut behind him.

I took a deep breath, looked into the camera, and stated my name. I started to do the demonstration described on the paper, while adding a rambling commentary about my actions. Before I could take another big breath, I was done. I had nothing left to say. When I walked outside, a warm spring breeze caressed my face and the sunlight hurt my eyes, as though I'd just escaped from being trapped in a mine. My test-taking neighbor, the guy with the beard, was standing nearby looking at his phone.

"I feel good about the written test," he said with a calm confidence.

"Really?" I said. When I looked at him, I felt like I was looking at a Certified Cicerone. What did he see when he looked at me? "I'm not sure how I did."

"It's the tasting part I'm worried about," he said. "I made some mistakes."

I hadn't aced the tasting portion either, but I'd done better than I thought I might. Still, I wasn't sure I passed the test, which felt disappointing. I'd done some guessing. I'd done some bullshitting. I'd even gone back and changed a few answers, which felt like a misstep. I wanted to walk out of the testing room feeling the relief that would only come with knowing I'd become a Cicerone. Instead, I faced six weeks of worry while I waited for my score. Not only had I wanted to leave knowing I'd passed, I wanted to feel different, which would have proved I had stepped across the line that separated aficionado from expert. Instead, I just felt like myself.

When I got home, I wasn't sure if I needed a drink or a nap. Tony had the answer. He opened the fridge and produced a slightly chilled Drie Fonteinen gueuze, the beer Armand Debelder had handed me after our dinner in Beersel. As Tony and I stood in the kitchen, I tried to describe the test, but I didn't feel like talking much. Instead, I wanted to focus on this beer.

"2004," Tony said, as he looked at the label. Then he set the bottle back on the counter. "It was made the year before we moved to Portland."

"The year before I got into beer," I said, straightening my spine so I stood a little taller.

The beer was older than my fascination, a reminder I was a dust particle in the vast universe of beer making. Tony and I clinked glasses, and right then, I felt victorious. I had successfully given beer the kind of gravitational pull it deserved by giving in to my gnawing, genuine curiosity. Along the way, I'd walked under cobwebs in Cantillon, stood next to the gnashing machines in a hops-processing plant, and poured heavy bags of sugar into a steaming kettle of wort. I'd spent time with many passionate people—the ones who judged beer, made beer, and saved beer. I'd made new friends while waiting in beer lines, driving across Belgium in a rental car, and disassembling sticky faucets. Each moment helped me move toward a place that had seemed unimaginable when I started. Finally, I'd arrived.

Later in the week, a friend would take me out for a celebratory lunch, and another would bring me flowers. These were people who'd never heard of Cicerone certification, and had little interest in its significance in the world of beer. They just knew I'd finished something that mattered to me.

I turned to look into the eyes of someone who never stopped telling me I could do it.

"To you," Tony said, and I smiled. We clinked glasses.

The gueuze in our glasses seemed equally alive and dormant, the same quality I sensed in the farmlands I had ridden my bike past near Watou. Inside the beer, things were still happening. Microbes were inciting chemical changes, a continuation of what they'd been doing for more than a decade. Even though the action was invisible, I could detect the changes below the surface. All I had to do was pay attention.

———

One afternoon in May, five weeks post-test, I stood in my kitchen, scrolling through e-mails on my phone. It was the end of my workweek and almost Memorial Day weekend. Tony, Oscar, and I were getting ready to go on a road trip to Montana for a wedding. When I saw the subject line, "Certified Cicerone Exam Results—Lucy Burningham," my heart pounded. I read the e-mail once, twice, then three times, before I started pacing around the house. A minute later, Tony walked inside. He had a smudge of dirt on his cheek from working in the shop.

"OK, OK, OK," I said rapidly. "I'm not sure if I passed the test. Read this e-mail and tell me what it says."

"Well," Tony said slowly, squinting at the screen. I jumped up and down impatiently. "It begins, 'On behalf of Cicerone Program Director Ray Daniels and the Cicerone Exam Management Team, I'd like to congratulate you on passing the Certified Cicerone exam.' I'm pretty sure that means you passed the test."

I ran into the living room, flopped down on the rug, and put my hands over my face.

"I can't believe I did it," I murmured.

"I can," Tony said. "You worked really hard. Congrats, sweetie. You did it. You're a Cicerone."

EPILOGUE

The larger the island of knowledge,
the longer the shoreline of wonder.
—RALPH W. SOCKMAN

AN ARMY OF SMALL, clear plastic cups filled with beer multiplied on the table in front of me as rain pelted the single window in the room. Eight months after learning I had passed the exam, I was back at Breakside Brewery, this time not as a student of beer but as a judge. One of the city's alt weekly newspapers, the *Willamette Week*, had assembled a group of judges—people they called "industry insiders"—to choose the winners for the Oregon Beer Awards. We would blindly taste beers by style, like other professional beer competitions, including the Great American Beer Festival. Today were the preliminary rounds, which meant I would spend the day tasting and discussing beers with rotating panels of judges.

In many ways, the Cicerone title hadn't changed my life. I didn't open a brewery, go to school to become a hop breeder, or launch a beer-and-bike-tour company in Belgium (although that option remains tempting). I still loved beer, but in a different way: my preferences about what I liked and didn't like felt clearer and more pronounced. I noticed I had little patience for beer that seemed average or missed the mark. I knew what good beer was—and how it was made—and that's what I wanted to drink. In subtle ways, the moment I became a Certified Cicerone marked the beginning of a new chapter, one in which people paused to hear my opinion after I took a sip of beer and expected me to bring exceptional beers, accompanied by juicy side stories, to dinner parties. Those moments felt validating.

When I arrived at my judging table, which was wedged into a small room in Breakside's offices, I found Bill Schneller, my beer professor, sitting alone and looking expectant.

"Bill!" I exclaimed. "Are you judging at table six?"

"Indeed I am," he replied with a smile.

The other judges arrived at the table: a growler-fill shop owner, a head brewer, and a sales manager for a brewing-ingredients distributor (he was also a GABF judge). An experienced beer judge had been preassigned to be the captain at each table, and I was right when I guessed our captain would be Bill. I felt nervous—not Cicerone-exam-day nervous, but the kind of low-level nervous that reminded me I hadn't done this before. Not only was Bill there, and I wanted to show him I knew my stuff, but I wasn't evaluating homebrew in some obscure competition. Instead, I was judging some of Oregon's finest commercially brewed beers in a competition with medals that would be widely publicized. The task felt important.

Ben Edmunds, who was in charge of the competition, popped into the room with the list of thirteen beers we'd judge in the first round—

part of a catch-all category called "Classic Styles," which the judging manual said could range from Irish ales to English barley wine. The actual beers we'd judge included a dark lager and a golden lager.

"This is the perfect category for you," I said to Bill, remembering his impassioned monologues about British bitters and German lagers. He nodded.

I set my trusty copy of the 2008 BJCP style guide on the table. The 2008 version had finally been updated in 2015, but since we weren't judging precisely to style—we had been instructed to reward standout, "harmonious" beers, even if they deviated from classic style parameters—I thought it wouldn't matter much. I needed a safety net, something that could gently nudge me to remember the precise properties of, say, steam beer. After all the beer samples were delivered to our table, I started vigorously swirling, sniffing, and sipping. For each beer, I jotted down notes about the aromas and flavors, familiar actions that, even though I was doing them for the first time as a judge, felt routine. One beer, the Märzen lager, exuded butterscotch. "NO," I wrote next to its number. "Diacetyl." While I'd like to think that a year ago I'd have been able to identify the compound, I had doubted my pre-Cicerone self. Today, no problem.

We only had an hour to choose three beers that would advance to the next round, which didn't seem like enough time. Each beer was a universe in a glass, one that deserved my full consideration. When I tried to work faster, I sloshed some beer on my pants.

"I already spilled beer on myself," I announced. The four men were silently squinting, smelling, and furrowing their brows as they wrote notes. They chuckled.

"It's bound to happen," said the brewer sitting to my left.

Finally, I circled the three beers I thought should advance and put my pen down. Bill proceeded to announce the number of each beer, then we talked about its attributes.

"Ooh, that Märzen," Bill said. "What a shame." The other judges shook their heads in disappointment because, as I expected, diacetyl was not an acceptable attribute of a competition beer. We took turns pouring that beer into the dump bucket.

When it was time to talk about beer 9091, I jumped in.

"I think this is a great beer," I said, "but I might like it because it's the crispest, most refreshing beer in the group." This is where judging the catch-all category seemed especially tricky.

"I agree," the brewer said. "It passes the would-you-order-another test."

"Just think about having this beer on a hot summer day," Bill said dreamily. "Man oh man, I would happily drink it all day long."

For a brief moment, I felt like I was back in Bill's beer literacy class. Then I snapped back to the task at hand.

"Let's hold on to this one," I said.

———

When I got home, it was almost seven in the evening, and I was exhausted. Never had I spent that many hours so intensely focused on beer. By the last round, which included one beer made with cinnamon sticks soaked in bourbon and another made with cocoa nibs from Ghana, the conversations between the judges seemed to have deteriorated into inane conversations about personal preferences. To me, one beer tasted like rancid peanuts, while another judge said it tasted like Nutter Butter cookies. He liked Nutter Butter cookies, while I considered peanut butter a last-resort food, something that belonged in emergency kits.

A pan of warm chicken enchiladas and a pot of rice were on the stove. Oscar's portion, which was cut into neat squares, was still on the kitchen table, a tableau of a child who'd probably snacked too much that afternoon. In the living room, Tony and Oscar were putting together a jigsaw puzzle of a Porsche to a soundtrack of Black Sabbath. I pulled a bottle of beer out of my bag and handed it to Tony.

"Beer!" he said, grinning. "You always know what I want."

"I had a hard time deciding between this and the straight-up IPA," I said, "but I thought you might like to mix it up a bit." We'd had the Breakside IPA earlier in the week, so I'd chosen the brewery's Wanderlust IPA, a close cousin with a hint of tropical fruit that came from Mosaic hops.

"Do you want me to pour you some?" Tony asked, as he headed to the kitchen.

I laughed. "It may be hard to believe, but after tasting fifty beers today, I'm just going to eat enchiladas and drink a gallon of water."

As I lifted a slab of enchiladas onto my plate with a spatula, I realized I did actually want a beer, but not one I would find in my fridge. I was thinking about 9091, the beer I'd liked so much during the first round. Our table agreed not to advance the beer, which felt slightly heartbreaking, but like the right thing to do. It was too much of an outlier in the category, like a plum in a group of tomatoes. The only thing I knew about the beer was that the brewer listed it as a Dortmunder export, a pale German lager invented in the 1880s to compete with pilsners, a style the GABF manual said was "on the decline" in Germany in recent years. I thought about sipping the Oregon-made version one more time, so I could smell its sublimely subtle perfume. Drinking it had made me feel like I was waltzing into spring wearing a crisp cotton sundress.

When I was cramming for the Cicerone exam, Oscar once said, "Mama, did you know a pilsner is a lager?" I'd been proud, of course. He was paying attention. Maybe one day Tony, Oscar, and I could ride our bikes through Germany together. Before we arrived in Dortmund, the industrial city where the Dortmunder export was invented, we'd ride past fields of barley, tour the maltster where the grains were roasted to pale, and see the river that fed water to the city and its breweries. When I finally tasted a Dortmunder in the place it was invented, and I'd understand the beer with new dimension. And inevitably, that sip would lead to my next question.

ACKNOWLEDGMENTS

I am grateful to my editor, Jennifer Urban-Brown, who took a chance on this book, and to the talented team at Roost. Thank you to my agent, Michelle Tessler, who believed in the project from the beginning.

I'm humbled by the kind and generous people of the beer community, from brewers and beer writers to hop farmers and homebrewers. This book exists not only because of the beer they make but also because of their willingness to let me in. Thank you, John Harris, Phil Roche, Ben Edmunds, Denver Bon, Sarah Pederson, Bill Schneller, Jeff Alworth, Alan Taylor, Stan Hieronymus, Rik Hall, Garrett Oliver, Mitch Steele, Nicole Erny, Cam O'Connor, Gayle Goschie, Adrienne So, the Widmer crew, and Lady Brew PDX.

Thank you to Sarah Jane Curran for being an intrepid adventurer, Klara driver, and friend. I couldn't have done Belgium without Evan Coen, Diana Rempe, Emilien and Hélène, the +/– brewers, Kris and Jan Schamp, and Dimi. Prost and santé to all the German and Belgian brewers who let me drink their beers.

I had some wonderful readers along the way, especially my writing group, Helmet and Boots, which supplied me with plenty of encouragement and smart critiques. Members past and present include Deborah Reeves, Ian Reeves, Marnie Hanel, Fiona McCann, David Shafer, Bethany Gumper, Greg Tudor, Sam Davenport, and Lola Oyibo. Thanks to Christina Cooke, Megan Flynn, and Katie Vaughan. Gratitude to the professors and students in my master's program all those years ago, in particular Paul Collins, who still finds the time to offer me good advice.

To all the dear friends who told me to be brave—and there are too many to name here—you are my scaffolding. I owe everything to my parents, who taught me the value of education, and supported me when I applied that philosophy to beer. All the love to Tony, my partner in this sweet life. Oscar, you are my sunshine. Don't ever stop showing me how curiosity and discovery lead to joy.

BEER TASTING SHEET

Try completing this form for any beer you're drinking. Attributes for each category are listed in progressive order. Use the Points Scoring Key on page 265 to help you score each category.

Beer Name_____

State / Country of Origin_____

Style_____

Brewery_____

ABV%_____

APPEARANCE

Color: Pale Straw, Gold, Copper, Amber, Red, Honey, Caramel, Brown, Root Beer, Black

Clarity: Clear, Hazy, Cloudy

Head: None, Diminishing, Lasting | Fizzy, Rocky, Creamy | No lacing, lacing

APPEARANCE SCORE (5):_____

AROMA

Malts: Sweet, Biscuity, Caramelly, Chocolaty, Nutty, Toasty, Roasty, Smoky

Hops: Floral, Citrusy, Leafy, Grassy, Piney, Herbal, Earthy, Spicy

Yeast: Clean, Estery (Fuits, Spices), Floral, Barnyard, Sour/Tart

Other: Alcohol, Metallic, Oxidized, Skunked, "Off"

AROMA SCORE (15): _____

TASTE

Malts: Sweet, Dark Fruit, Biscuity, Grainy, Caramelly, Chocolaty, Nutty, Toasty, Roasty, Smoky

Hops: Floral, Citrusy, Leafy, Grassy, Piney, Herbal, Earthy, Spicy, Bitter, Resinous

Yeast: Clean, Estery (Fruits, Spices), Floral, Barnyard, Sour/Tart

Other: Alcohol, Metallic, Oxidized, Skunked, "Off"

TASTE SCORE (25): _____

MOUTHFEEL

Consistency: Crisp, Smooth, Silky, Velvety, Creamy, Viscous

Carbonation: Delicate, Light, Creamy, Champagne-like, Prickly

Body: Light, Light-Medium, Medium, Medium-Full, Full

Finish: None, Fades Quickly, Average, Long, Everlasting | Dry, Wet | Warming

MOUTHFEEL SCORE (5): _____

NOTES / ASSESSMENT

TOTAL SCORE (+50 POINTS):_____

OVERALL DESCRIPTION OF THIS BEER

(circle one): Crisp Balanced Fruity Malty Hoppy Complex

POINTS SCORING KEY

APPEARANCE	AROMA	TASTE	MOUTHFEEL
1 = Dull or Lackluster	1-3 = None or Totally Off	1-10 = Light or Unappealing	1 = Dull or Lackluster
2 = Below Average	4-6 = Noticeable/Light	11-15 = Ample or Satisfactory	2 = Below Average
3 = Average	7-9 = Nice/Appealing	16-18 = Lots of or Appealing	3 = Average
4 = Appealing	10-12 = Strong/Inviting	19-20 = Abundant or Very Appealing	4 = Appealing
5 = Alive or Inviting	13-15 = Powerful/Alluring	21-23 = Bountiful or Love It	5 = Alive or Inviting
		24-25 = Powerful or Want Another	

CRAFT BREW ALLIANCE
SENSORY VALIDATION BALLOT

This is a reproduction of the Widmer taste panel mentioned on page 31. See if you can detect any of these flavors or compounds in beers.

FLAVOR	DESCRIPTION
Acetaldehyde	green apple, solvent, painty, pumpkin
Acetic	vinegar aroma, sour, "sharp" sourness
Caprylic	goaty, waxy, crayons, roller rink
Caryophyllene	carrots, spicy hop, floral, noble hops
Clove	spicy, phenolic, cloves, Belgian
Diacetyl	buttery, buttered popcorn
DMS	creamed corn, canned olives
DMTS	garlic, onion, rubbery

Ethyl Acetate	nail polish, solvent, fruity
Ethyl Butyrate	Juicy Fruit gum, tropical fruit, pineapple
Ethyl Hexanoate	red apple, anise (black licorice)
Fusel	whiskey, alcoholic, hot, solvent
Indole	jasmine, floral, fecal, barnyard, mothballs
Isoamyl Acetate	banana, circus peanuts
Isovaleric	cheesy, sweatsocks
Lactic	sour, no aroma, "smooth" sourness
Mercaptan	natural gas/propane, hot garbage
Metallic	blood or coins in the mouth
Myrcene	green hop, Cascade hops
Papery	wet paper, cardboard, oxidized

FURTHER READING:
A BEER MASTER'S BOOKSHELF

These titles deeply informed my studies, and I can't recommend them enough to anyone who wants to expand their beer knowledge.

Ambitious Brew: The Story of American Beer by Maureen Ogle. Orlando, Fla.: Harcourt, 2006.

The Beer Bible by Jeff Alworth. New York: Workman, 2015.

Brew Like a Monk: Trappist, Abbey, and Strong Belgian Ales and How to Brew Them by Stan Hieronymus. Boulder, Colo.: Brewers Publications, 2005.

The Brewmaster's Table: Discovering the Pleasures of Real Beer with Real Food by Garrett Oliver. New York: HarperCollins, 2005.

For the Love of Hops: The Practical Guide to Aroma, Bitterness and the Culture of Hops by Stan Hieronymus. Boulder, Colo.: Brewers Publications, 2012.

Good Beer Guide Belgium by Tim Webb and Joe Stange. St. Albans: Campaign for Real Ale, 2014.

How to Brew: Everything You Need to Know to Brew Beer Right the First Time by John J. Palmer. Boulder, Colo.: Brewers Publications, 2006.

IPA: Brewing Techniques, Recipes, and the Evolution of India Pale Ale by Mitch Steele. Boulder, Colo.: Brewers Publications, 2012.

Michael Jackson's Beer Companion: The World's Great Beer Styles, Gastronomy, and Traditions by Michael Jackson. Philadelphia: Running Press, 1997.

Michael Jackson's Great Beers of Belgium by Michael Jackson. Boulder, Colo.: Brewers Publications, 2008.

The Oxford Companion to Beer by Garrett Oliver. New York: Oxford University Press, 2012.

Tasting Beer: An Insider's Guide to the World's Greatest Drink by Randy Mosher. North Adams, Mass.: Storey, 2009.

Vintage Beer: A Taster's Guide to Brews That Improve over Time by Patrick Dawson. North Adams, Mass.: Storey, 2014.

RESOURCES

American Homebrewers Association, www.homebrewersassociation
.org

Beer Judge Certification Program (BJCP), www.bjcp.org

Brewers Association, www.brewersassociation.org

Campaign for Real Ale (CAMRA), www.camra.org.uk

Cicerone Certification Program, cicerone.org

Great American Beer Festival, www.greatamericanbeerfestival.com

High Council for Artisanal Lambic Beers (HORAL), www.horal.be

CREDITS

The following articles were adapted in this book. These stories, which I wrote and researched, informed some sections of *My Beer Year*.

"Another Place at the Table," *BeerAdvocate*, May 2015

"Beer Lovers Make Room for Brews Worth a Wait," *New York Times*, June 25, 2008

"Beer Pairings Menu," *Mix*, November 2009

"Bottle Shares Spread the Beer," *Wall Street Journal*, November 1, 2013

"Brewer David Logsdon Makes Flavorful Beers Using New Yeast Combinations," *Mix*, March 2013

"Brooklyn Beer," *Beer Northwest*, Winter 2010

"Ciao, Vino," *Beer West*, Fall 2011

"A Feminist's Guide to Beer Drinking," *Travel Oregon*, December 2015

"Flower Power: Fresh Hop Beers," *Saveur*, November 2011

"Hop Crop," *Imbibe*, September/October 2014

"A Hop and a Sip to Fresh Ales," *New York Times*, October 20, 2009

"The Lake Effect," *Beer West*, Winter 2012

"A Portland Beer Expert Shares Lessons from Belgium," *Portland Monthly,* June 2015

"Portland Beer Makers Collaborate to Make Special One-Off Brews," *Mix,* September 2013

"Reign of Terroir," *Wall Street Journal,* January 25, 2013

"Sour Beer Is Risky Business, Starting with the Name," *New York Times,* June 1, 2010

"Tapped In: Kegged Beer Goes beyond the Frat Party," *Saveur,* January 31, 2011

"Warren Steenson," *Beer Northwest,* Fall 2007

"Welcome to the World of Black Market Beers," *Bon Appétit,* December 18, 2012

"Why Brewers and Coffee Roasters in Portland, OR, Don't Want Fluoridated Water," *Bon Appétit,* April 17, 2013

INDEX

ABOUT THE AUTHOR

 LUCY BURNINGHAM is a writer whose work has appeared in dozens of publications, including the *New York Times*, the *Wall Street Journal*, *Saveur*, *BonAppetit.com*, *Imbibe*, *Bicycling*, *Men's Journal*, *BBC.com*, and Lonely Planet guidebooks. She coauthored *Hop in the Saddle: A Guide to Portland's Craft Beer Scene*, *by Bike* and earned a master's degree in creative nonfiction writing from Portland State University. She lives in Portland, Oregon, with her husband and son.